San Francisco Chronicle: "Under all the jokes there is an amazing amount of good, solid information, and answers to those gnawing questions that plague the prospective buyer. Entertaining as always, eminently readable."

Gene Roddenberry: "I'm jealous. I wish I could write as simply and understandably and humorously."

All Things Considered: "Pleasant and reassuring."

Harvard Business Review: "An unusual blend of information supplied in a highly readable style on how the equipment works and what it will do for the user."

New York Times: "As a general introduction to the world of personal computers, Mr. McWilliams offers a carefree tour, ranging from microprocessors and central processing units, to computer use in the home and office, computer-induced back and neck pains, radiation worries and California's Silicon Valley."

Detroit Free Press: "Thorough, lucid, helpful, and a lot of fun."

Philadelphia Daily News: "The Mr. Wizard of computer talk."

Houston Post: "Peter McWilliams' book provides far and away the best coverage in simple, non-technical and outrageously funny prose. McWilliams is the prototype of the computer term 'user friendly.'"

Library Journal: "McWilliams' opinions are always thoughtful and amusingly presented."

Detroit News: "Perfect for the beginner, especially someone who is a little paranoid about the new machines."

Cleveland Plain Dealer: "McWilliams combines a breezy, entertaining style with brief, understandable explanations of how computers and software work."

Changing Times: "A fun and painless way to explore the worlds of bits and bytes."

Chicago Sun-Times: "Peter McWilliams is the leading writer of introductory computer books. The most knowledgeable and certainly the most entertaining popularizer of the personal computer."

Philadelphia Daily News: "A refreshing change from the ponderous, heavy and fear-inspiring tomes that dominate the field."

San Francisco Examiner: "Our favorite author on computer topics."

William Safire: "Happily helpful."

Hugh Prather: "The mood of Peter McWilliams' fine text on word processing embodies what computers will not replace: warmth and humor. However, since you can't buy Peter, do buy a computer, and let his book direct your purchase."

Ben Fong-Torres: "Peter McWilliams is an authoritative yet easy-going guide. Simply put, he has written the best computer books around."

Nashville Tennessean: "If you know all about computers, or if you have lost interest in finding out about them after trying to muddle through the works of lesser wordsmiths, McWilliams' books are worth the investment."

Newsday: "Unique in the computer writing establishment in that he writes well. The book is the best on the market."

Los Angeles Herald-Examiner: "Lucid, straight-forward, non-threatening, humorous. McWilliams communicates brilliantly with computers and with his fellow humans alike."

Nashville Tennessean: "Reading McWilliams, in contrast with most computer authors, is such a pleasure that his books ought to carry a warning label."

New York Times Book Review: "Irreverent, informative handbooks."

Philadelphia Inquirer: "By far the best seller in the field, with cause. McWilliams is truly witty on a bewildering subject."

San Diego Union: "The witty writer and poet has helped erase much of the fear and pomp surrounding computers."

Seattle Times: "It is the humor which has made the books the industry leaders. Helpful, refreshing and delightful in their irreverence."

Washingtonian: "For an entertaining and informative introduction to personal computing, the best sellers by Peter McWilliams are hard to beat."

Dayton Daily News: "Ingenious, and thoroughly readable, because this guy has talent not only with a word processor, but with the word."

Atlanta Journal-Constitution: "A very funny, up-to-date and easy to understand description of the phenomenon of computers. McWilliams is careful not to take himself or his subject too seriously."

The
Personal
Computer
Book

by
Peter McWilliams

Senior Editor: Christopher Meeks

Cover Design: Paul LeBus

Desktop Publishing: Victoria Marine

First Edition, March, 1990

Published by
Prelude Press
8165 Mannix Drive
Los Angeles, California 90046
213-650-9571

For additional copies of this book , please send $19.95, or call
1-800-LIFE-101.
Special Case Price: 20 books ($399 value) for $275.
All above prices include postage and handling.

This book is for

John-Roger
William F. Buckley, Jr.
&
Fran Howell

Thank you.

Table of Contents

PART I
The Personal Computer

PART II
The Personal Computer
in Business

PART III
Word Processing

Table of Contents

Table of Contents

PART VIII
Utter Nonsense

The New York Times.

NEW YORK, FRIDAY, APRIL 8, 1927.

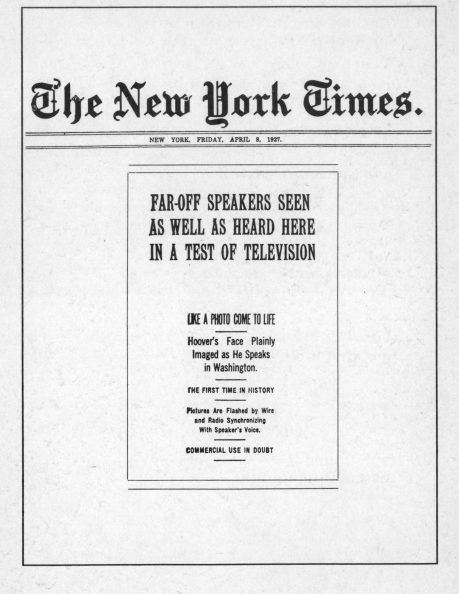

FAR-OFF SPEAKERS SEEN AS WELL AS HEARD HERE IN A TEST OF TELEVISION

LIKE A PHOTO COME TO LIFE

Hoover's Face Plainly
Imaged as He Speaks
in Washington.

THE FIRST TIME IN HISTORY

Pictures Are Flashed by Wire
and Radio Synchronizing
With Speaker's Voice.

COMMERCIAL USE IN DOUBT

Preface

If you have a *burning need* to know all about personal computers *right away,* don't start here, go directly to Chapter 2. Bye!

Hold on. They're not all gone yet. Okay. There. Now that we've gotten rid of those in a hurry, we can relax and enjoy ourselves.

Welcome to *The Personal Computer Book.*

This is a book for people who know little or nothing about computers, personal or otherwise. It's a book for those who wonder what personal computers are and what they have to offer. It's for people who don't know the difference between a microprocessor and a micro-organism.

If you think Pac-Man might be a member of The Sierra Club (or think that Pac-Man *should* be a member of The Sierra Club), this book is for you.

I will assume you have some familiarity with a typewriter and a television. If not, might I suggest you read "The Wonder of the Age: A Machine that Writes Like a Book" *(Scientific American,* June, 1867) and "Far-Off Speakers Seen as Well as Heard Here in a Test of Television—Like a Photo Come to Life" *(New York Times,* page one, April 8, 1927).

As you read along, you will discover this is a book for people who aren't all that serious about computers. I am reminded of the late Alan Watts, who said that he was not *serious* about his work, but that he was *sincere.* I am sincere in my admiration of personal computers as powerful tools, and I am sincerely amused by those who take these tools too seriously.

In researching this book, it was necessary to attempt reading some other introductory books on per-

sonal computers. One claimed that computers were the most important invention since fire, or perhaps the wheel. I only got through three or four more pages of that book. Another said computers were the most important step, evolutionarily, since our ancestors jumped from the trees. I stopped reading that book right there.

Having, in my own haphazard way, studied computers for the past decade or so, I find it difficult to accept as a guide anyone that *serious* about computers.

If I were asked to look at the time line of history and locate an evolutionary turning point that most closely resembles the advent of personal computers, I wouldn't have to go back more than forty years: the popular acceptance of television. Television was successfully demonstrated in 1927. It was made commercially available in 1939, but it wasn't until the late 1940's and early 1950's that television became truly popular. (In 1946, there were 10,000 TV's in the United States. By 1951, there were 12,000,000. In 1958—50,000,000.)

Few will deny the impact television has made on the United States and most of the industrialized world. Observing us coolly from north of the border, the late Canadian philosopher, Marshall McLuhan, noted that the world had become a global village.

I do not think, however, that television rates the same niche in the evolution of the species as fire or learning to walk on two legs. Nor do personal computers.

As with all technological advances of the last hundred years—TV, radio, movies, phonographs, telephones, electric lights—personal computers have and will change our lives, and our lives have and will change them.

In some areas, personal computers have proven invaluable. Many people consider them a necessity—professional writers, for example, or small businesses. Word processing, accounting, cost projections, inventory control, and similar functions are handled so swiftly and effortlessly by personal computers that the small businessperson has become as addicted to small computers as the big businessperson is addicted to the big.

In most areas, true to its name, the value of a personal computer will depend upon the personal interests of the person using it. Personal computers play games—from chess to Missile Command—better than anything around. But you must fancy games. They will chart your biorhythms with great accuracy. But you must care to know your biorhythms. Connect a personal computer to a larger computer over telephone lines and you can research any subject imaginable. But first, you must have something to research.

For the most part, personal computers will prove their worth to the degree that they fit into your daily life, not to the degree that you adapt your life to The Computer Age.

In this book, we'll explore the things that personal computers do well, and the things they don't do well. You can decide if any of these accomplishments warrant inviting this latest prodigy of the industrial revolution into your home or office.

TYPEWRITERS.

24575 A perfect typewriting machine for less than $1.00. It does practical work and is so simple a child can operate it. With ordinary care it cannot get out of order. Is light and portable, weighing only 1 pound complete. Writes with practice 10 to 20 words a minute, Our price, each.................................... $0 80
Postage .... .20

Odell Typewriter.

24578 This typewriter prints directly from metal type, no ribbon being used, and gives a much cleaner impression than can possibly be obtained from an ink ribbon. The Odell machine has perfect alignment and is a very good typewriter for manifold; the double case machine writes 78 characters, representing capitals, small letters, all of the punctuation marks, together with percentage marks and fractional figures. Weight, 7½ pounds.
Price, Double Case Machine.. . . . . $13.00

Edison Mimeograph.

24579 The Edison Mimeograph Type writer. A practical working machine, that does perfect mimeograph work. It has steel type, keeps good alignment, prints from a ribbon, is a heavy manifolder, and is strong and durable, at same time being light and portable. Writes 78 characters, caps and small letters.....$22.00

Merritt.

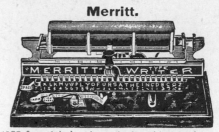

24577 One of the best low-priced machines on the market. It writes 78 characters, and does work equal to any $100 machine made. It is a double case machine, having interchangeable METAL type, from which it prints direct; no ribbon being used. It is portable, durable, has perfect alignment, and is very cheap. The writing is done by pressing the handle into the niche indicated. Price, complete, with case..$11.00

The American.

24576 The American Typewriter is complete, simple, durable and rapid. A serviceable machine at a price far below other makes, for same value. Weight, less than five pounds, as put up in sliding cover wood box. Iron base and metal parts. Writes 71 characters, capitals, small letters, figures and marks. Work always before you. An instrument for private or commercial use. Price, each........................$5.70

Typewriter Supplies.

24 90 Typewriter Oil, per bottle................$0.15
24591 Type Cleaning Brushes, each.............. .20
24592 Typewriter Ink, red, purple and green, 1 oz. bottle. Each.............................. .25
24595 Typewriter Ribbons for Caligraph, Remington, Smith-Premier, etc., machines,in purple, blue and green copy and black record. Each, .60
24596 Typewriter Carbon Paper for manifold work, in sizes, 8x10½; 8x12; 8x13 inches; and in colors: Purple, blue and black.
Price, per box of 100 sheets....................2.50
24597 Typewriter Paper, "State Bond" (No. 10), superfine; medium weight. Price, per ream (500 sheets).

Legal size, 8x13 inches................$1.70
Ruled with marginal lines 1.80
Letter size, 8x10½ inches............. 1.50

Introduction

It all began with a mechanical rabbit. Computers didn't begin with a mechanical rabbit—my series of computer books did.

In 1971, I used a word processor for the first time. It was at *The Detroit News*. I was being interviewed, and while the reporter was busy on a phone call, I used the newly installed word processing system. I was hooked.

I'm a poor speller and a worse typist. Any machine that could correct my spelling and never make me retype anything was for me. I investigated the cost of a 1971 word processor. $100,000. That's 100,000 1971 dollars. (I could, however, publish a small newspaper with it.) I decided to continue paying typists.

In 1979, I met Durk Pearson. When Durk heard I was a writer and that I had not heard about word processing on what were then called microcomputers, he told me about them. Forty-five minutes later, I was again hooked. He gave me a list of what to buy. It added up to $7,500—the precise total of my life savings.

After nine months of investigating microcomputers, I came to the same what-to-purchase conclusions as Durk. I was still, however, having trouble plunking down my hard-saved $7,500. I asked my friend John-Roger for advice.

He suggested I make two lists. The first, a list of all the reasons I should not get a computer; the second, all the reasons why I should. The Thou Shalt Not list began, "Too expensive." The Thou Shalt list began, "The ideal tool for writers." The lists went on and on—pro, con, pro, con, yes, no, yes, no—until my hand tightened in a familiar spasm. The last entry on the Thou Shalt list was, "No more cramped fingers!"

That decided it. I ordered my microcomputer the next day.

The next several months was a honeymoon of Hollywood proportions. No matter what my daily activities were, I couldn't wait to get back to my computer. I told every writer I knew. They responded as all bachelors do when confronted by a newlywed's tales of matrimonial bliss: with hostility, disillusionment, derision. They were not interested in hearing about my joy, and were not restrained in expressing their indifference.

"Their loss," I thought as I returned home to my newly discovered lifemate.

At the time, there was a program called The Word. It was a relatively unknown $75 spell-check program that was much better than the currently popular $295 spell-check program. I began spreading the word on The Word. I submitted a review to a popular microcomputing magazine. They had already reviewed The Word, but were starting a new computer magazine for novices. Would I be interested in writing an article about word processing for beginners?

"Sure," I said. "How many words would you like?"

"About 750," I was told.

I went to work. Finally: an outlet for the pent-up love of a devoted groom—and a *paying* outlet at that. The adoration flowed. If this article were for novices, I figured, I should begin at the beginning and explain what a microcomputer was. After what seemed an hour, but was probably two or three days, I did a word count. (The computer did it—one of The Word's many wonderful features.) I had amassed 2,200 words—and I hadn't yet gotten to word processing!

A quick call to my editor got the article expanded into a three-part piece—more money!—and a spark glowed in my mind: "There's a book in here."

Introduction

The words continued to stream, gush, rush, ooze, run, spring, emanate, come from, issue, pour, spill, stream, surge, and swell forth. (I didn't have a computerized thesaurus then, but, as you can see, I have gotten one since.) Soon I had a manuscript. I called it *The Word Processing Book: A Short Course in Computer Literacy.*

In those days, books about microcomputers were considered about as salable as books on, say, outboard motors or hang gliders would be today: a market, sure, but a small one; and how on earth do you reach it, anyway? And would it want to buy a book on the subject even if you could? This was certainly not a book for the general public, publishers said. I was relegated to the technical/science editor of whichever publishing company was willing to even listen.

Technical/science editors are not known for their sense of play. I remember showing the manuscript to one. He opened it to the first page and reviewed it somberly. He underlined a sentence with blue pencil.

"What's that?" he asked, passing the manuscript over to me.

"Humor," I answered sheepishly.

He continued reading. He underlined another sentence in blue. "What's this?" he asked.

"Humor," I answered.

I sat guiltily as he continued reading, his blue pencil active. After two or three pages he looked at me with only slightly concealed disgust.

"It's just *full* of it, isn't it?"

Nonetheless, that company offered me $7,500 to publish the book—providing I would do a thorough humorectomy. I was in agony. Here I could make back everything I had paid for the word processor and move on to that great American novel. Alas, the muse of

11

amusement would not hear of it, so, as no one else was interested, I undertook to publish the book myself.

I decided to put an etching or woodcut at the beginning of each chapter. The juxtaposition of the old and the new I thought might be good for a smile or two. This would show a dozen or so illustrations of an obviously noncomputer nature amongst photos of video screens and disks and such. While looking through a book of woodcuts for the appropriate chapter illustrations, it happened:

The mechanical rabbit.

There it was, a woodcut of a 19th century wind-up rabbit. It had a B, C, D, and E identifying the inner mechanism, obviously used to explain the workings of mechanical rabbits. I thought, "Wouldn't it be funny to put this etching in the book as an example of how computers work?" I laughed out loud, something I seldom do when alone.

That was it. The die was cast. The etchings, woodcuts and totally irrelevant illustrations streamed, gushed, rushed, oozed, ran, sprang, etc., etc. The book, it seemed, *was* going to be full of it.

I wanted a photograph of a microcomputer in a typical writer's working environment. As I was the only writer I knew who had a microcomputer, it meant cleaning off my desk. I procrastinated. Then I decided, what the hell? and took pictures of precisely the mess I lived and worked in.

The book was successful, as was its sequel (prequel?), *The Personal Computer Book: What Are Those Television-Typewriters Anyway?* One of the nicest things that happened was meeting William F. Buckley, Jr. He was kind enough to contribute unending encouragement to my self-publishing project, and also contributed the introduction for my next epic, *The Personal Computer in Business Book.*

To help us better understand how computers operate, consider the mechanical rabbit. Rubber band (B) turns wheel (C) which moves gear (D) and pulls rod (E). That should certainly clarify the operation of personal computers.

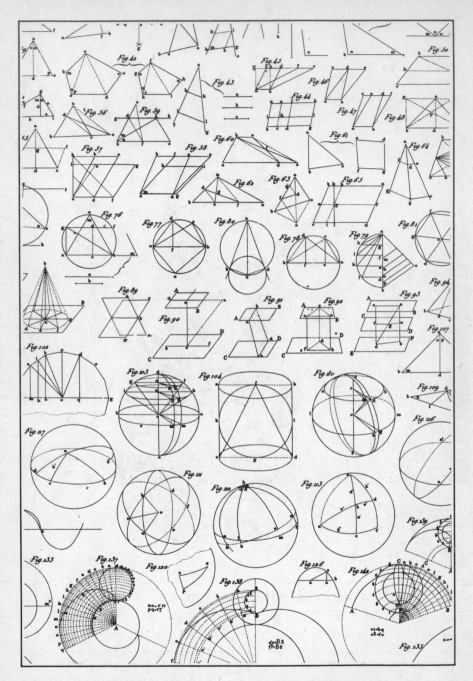

For those who find the "mechanical rabbit" explanation too elementary, here is a more detailed—although equally lucid—diagram

Here we have a typical writer's work space using a word processor. Can you find: (A) The Keyboard, (B) The Video Screen, (C) Quart of Haagen-Dazs Ice Cream (Maple Walnut), (D) The Computer (look for the black square indicating the disk drives), (E) Quart of Haagen-Dazs Ice Cream (Vanilla Chocolate Chip), (F) File to hold floppy disks, (G) Four months of neglected correspondence.

Here is another view of that same creative corner. Can you find: (A) The Keyboard, (B) Portrait of Gertrude Stein by Picasso, (C) Computer, (D) Portrait of Picasso by Picasso, (E) Printer, (F) Plastic knife holding light switch in place, (G) Comfortable chair.

People assumed I got rich from the computer books. I did not. I was, to use the politest word possible, cheated. I write this for the first time because, when I mention to people I'm doing a new edition of *The Personal Computer Book* incorporating all the other computer books, people who knew the books invariably ask, "What happened?" meaning, "Why were they off the market for so long?" It also answers those who say, "Boy, you really made a pile off those computer books, huh?"

The story is a sad but true one of Big Publishers and a Little Innocent (read: jerk), and if you've heard entirely too many of these stories, please count 14 paragraphs and continue reading.

While publishing the computer books, I invested all my profits back into the company, as the owner of any small company must. I decided I would cash in when I sold the business. When cashing-in time came, I had several million-dollar offers from big publishers.

By this time, large publishing houses were in one of three places concerning computer books. (A) They had (or were developing) a line of introductory computer books, (B) they desperately wanted a line of introductory computer books, or (C) they wanted nothing to do with computer books.

The folks in category A didn't need me, nor did the folks in category C. The B's, however, clustered 'round. The bidding got up to around a million dollars from several companies. I accepted the offer from a man named Richard Abrams at Esquire, Inc., a publisher of textbooks that wanted to start a line of computer books for bookstores. (No relation, by the way, to the magazine.) He asked me to trust him. I did.

I told my other suitors that I was bought, and they went off to acquire other affiliations in the introductory computer book field. (Not since Reverend Moon married 4,000 people in Madison Square Garden had so many brides and grooms been so frantically looking for an alliance.)

Within a matter of days of my accepting the offer, Esquire was purchased by Simon & Schuster (a division of Gulf+Western, a division of God). (Naturally, Abrams failed to inform me of this little detail that was being negotiated simultaneously with mine.) Simon & Schuster wanted Esquire's textbook division, but had no interest in its embryonic introductory computer book division. (Simon & Schuster already had one.)

One of those corporate decisions was made: It's cheaper to let McWilliams sue than to pay him even a portion of the million dollars now. They didn't even negotiate with me.

There's a funny provision in the copyright law. It reads that the transfer of copyrights must take place in writing, signed by both parties. It's funny because (A) its original intent was to protect writers from publishers, and (B) publishing, in practice, constantly relies on verbal agreements. If everything in publishing had to be put in writing and signed before publishers and authors went ahead with a deal, book publishing would grind to a halt.

But, in a court, written law *is* law, and the central part of our case—breach of oral contract—never even got before a jury. Five years later, I was left with fraud (difficult to prove) and emotional damages. I lost on fraud, but was awarded $250,000 in emotional damages.

Would I have been happy with $250,000? Absolutely. But then the attorneys representing me presented their bill: $295,000. Originally they said the case would cost, at most, $60,000. I took their word for it (again). Norman Oberstein, the attorney, hired another attorney to sue me. Do you have any idea what it's like to be sued by an attorney's attorney? I gave up. I broke even on the whole deal.

The books? They were all purchased (for far less than a million) by Doubleday for its new introductory computer book division, Quantum. Six weeks before the publication of my "big" book (a buying guide), Doubleday fired nineteen of the twenty Quantum staff. Doubleday was not pleased with the sales of another computer book (not mine) for which they had paid well over a million dollars. The books were put into Doubleday's backlist, where, abandoned, they barely floated and, one by one, sank.

By 1987, The Personal Computer Book had become a personal embarrassment. It was still being sold, and was written in 1984. It even had a brand buying guide, no less. I was ashamed to have my name attached, but it continued selling. I offered to do a new edition, for free. No, it wasn't selling *that* well. Then, please, let's declare it out of print. No, it's selling too well for that. A publishing Catch-22, and my personal apologies to anyone purchasing the book after 1985.

Doubleday's sense of fair play finally caught up, and the book was eventually declared out of print. This was the end of my computer book days, I sighed with relief.

But people kept writing. I would get letters from wonderful people asking for a new edition of the book. I told them that, alas, my computer book days were over. Some (who taught computers) wrote back and said they would continue using the old edition. (Ouch.) A computer book publisher approached me—but guess what he didn't want? Yep. He couldn't understand what "all those woodcuts" were doing in a computer book.

The last straw came when the computer book buyer for a major book chain asked for a new edition of the book. A *buyer* asking a *publisher* for a book? Book buyers say no to thousands of books a year. He told me there are no introductory computer books anymore—

The New Hardware Made Easy

A poet's pun-filled primer leads the list of bestselling guides

To a neophyte adrift in a computer store, it may seem a beacon of simplicity, sanity and humor. Amid all the intimidating machinery and densely technical literature, its plain white cover asks disarmingly, "What *are* those television-typewriters anyway?" Inside, it offers quaint woodcuts, turn-of-the-century ads and plenty of soothing printed words. No wonder that *The Personal Computer Book*, at $9.95, has become the fastest-selling computer guide on the market and has made its author, an erstwhile poet and promoter of Transcendental Meditation, something of an overnight celebrity. Peter McWilliams, 33, who wrote, printed and published the book, is currently negotiating with Universal Press Syndicate for a nationwide column on computers and preparing for a twelve-city publicity tour. Some 70,000 copies of his primer have been sold since its publication in November. The B. Dalton chain sold 1,623 copies in one week alone.

McWilliams' *TPCB*, now being distributed by Ballantine, is not the only computer book that is thriving. *Computers for Everybody* (dilithium Press; $6.95) has sold an estimated 47,000 copies since its release in October. *Apple II User's Guide* (Osborne/McGraw-Hill; $16.95) has sold some 200,000 copies since March 1981. In a year that is being described as the worst for the publishing industry since the Great Depression, computer books are one of the few bright spots, with approximately 2,500 titles accounting for more than 4 million sales. Nearly 3 million Americans bought computers last year, and as many as 6 million are expected to take the plunge this year. Since publishers estimate that new computer owners will buy up to ten books a year, it does not take a computer to recognize the scope of the market. Says Joyce Copland, director of marketing at Addison-Wesley Publishing Co.: "You could probably print napkins with the word computer on them and sell them like crazy."

The first computer books, like Adam Osborne's 1975 classic, *Introduction to Microcomputers* (Osborne/McGraw-Hill; $12.50), were aimed at computer hobby-ists, explaining the inner workings of the hardware down to the smallest transistor. These were quickly followed by books of software programs, like the popular *BASIC Computer Games* (Workman; $7.95), which provide page after page of prewritten computer codes that the reader can copy and run on his own machine. Now, as the domain of computer buyers expands, the bestsellers tend to be either step-by-step guides for new users, usually geared to specific machines, or introductory texts like McWilliams', which are intended for the computer illiterati who have not yet bought a machine. The author claims a special distinction for his efforts. "Mine," he says, "are the only books on the market that are funny."

McWilliams has been publishing his own writing for 16 years, starting with a book of love poems he wrote to avoid doing term papers at Allen Park (Mich.) High School ("This poem is a kiss for your mind"). At 19 he dropped out

Author McWilliams and explanatory diagram

of Eastern Michigan University to make his fortune as "the paperback Rod McKuen." In 1975, at 25, he hit the best-seller lists with *The TM Book*, a Q.-and-A. guide to Transcendental Meditation for the skeptical and the fearful ("No funny clothes? I can still eat Big Macs?").

After an unsuccessful venture in the greeting-card business, in which he used excerpts from his poems for the texts, McWilliams moved to Los Angeles and purchased his first computer, a North Star Horizon. *The Word Processing Book*, his first effort in the computer field, was researched in 18 months, written in four, and published last May under the Prelude Press imprint (named after his car, a Honda Prelude). Five printings and 100,000 copies later, he set off on *TPCB*. The tone for both works was set early. "I was looking for illustrations for what was a rather dry book on word processing," he recalls. He found an old woodcut of a mechanical rabbit and decided to run it over a deadpan caption describing its parts and concluding: "That should certainly clarify the operation of personal computers." Says McWilliams: "Once I decided to put that in, it was all downhill."

The heavily illustrated pages of *TPCB* are filled with puns and gags, like his remark that a computer's "yes/no circuits" are capable of saying no "faster than Debby Boone." A truncated section on the Apple II computer, which McWilliams does not admire, is padded with nine pages of anti-Apple cartoons and jokes. In his cavalier "Brand Name Buying Guide," the quirks and quips run so thick as to render the section practically useless. His characterization of the first Apple computer (priced at $666.66) applies to him: McWilliams was "born with a case of the cutes from which [he] has yet to recover." Yet he demystifies the RAMs and ROMs of microjargon and has found a painless and appealing way to advance the cause of computer literacy. So much so that his success has provided a subject for his next book: a guide to computers for the small businessman, based on his flourishing five-computer, three-computer operation. —*By Philip Faflick. Reported by Robert T. Grieves/New York*

The mechanical rabbit and I make Time *(January 24, 1983).*

everyone, it seems, bailed out during the Great Computer Book Glut of 1985.

So, here it is. The best (or at least what I still consider the most presentable) of all the computer books in one. Unlike previous editions, there is no name-brand buying guide. Books, I have found, are too permanent—and I've become far too ephemeral—for something that changes as rapidly as brand names, model numbers and prices. All the material, however, has been completely revised for 1990, and should remain relatively up-to-date for at least a few years.

Thank you, and enjoy.

"I'm back at the keyboard again,
Back where a disk is a friend.
Where you sit up every night,
Running programs till daylight.
Back at the keyboard again."

PART I

The Personal Computer

24

Chapter 1

An Incomplete and No Doubt Inaccurate History of Personal Computers Including Some Basic Information on How They Work

Boy, I sure wish I had Mr. Wizard to help me with this chapter. Somehow Mr. Wizard made "the magic and mystery of science" understandable. Even when it was incomprehensible, at least it was fun.

If this were television, there would be a shot of me leaning pensively on the edge of my keyboard, saying, "Boy, I sure wish I had Mr. Wizard to help me with this chapter," and suddenly Don Herbert would appear, maybe in a white lab coat, maybe in a suit, and I would become Everyperson and he would become Mr. Wizard and tell us all about how computers work.

Alas, this is not television; this is a book, and nothing appears suddenly during the writing of a book other than creditors. If this book ever becomes a TV show, perhaps the budget will permit Mr. Wizard to join us.

It would be nice to have Sir Kenneth Clark of *Civilization* stop by too. Sir Kenneth could show us, through the sketches of Michelangelo and the paintings of the Louvre, how computing has developed through the ages. *Computization* we'll call it. Besides, it's always good to have a "Sir" on the show.

Until that time we'll muddle through on our own, knowing that somewhere, somebody must know how to make all this stuff clear.

This is an optional chapter. You will never need to know *how* computers work. All you need to know is *that* they work. (They do.)

Somewhere along the line you may want to learn how to *operate* a computer, but that is very different from how a computer operates. Knowing how a computer operates is of no practical value whatsoever—unless you're a computer designer.

Most of the books and articles written about computers have been written by scientists—or worse, by people trying to *sound* like scientists—and what scientists find necessary to know they assume everyone will find necessary to know. We don't.

How many people know how their refrigerator works? Let's have a show of hands. Your cassette tape recorder? Your car? Your house plants? Your liver? Does it really matter if you don't? All that matters is that you know how to run it, play it, drive it, water it, or leave it blessedly alone so that it can operate as designed, unmolested.

At some point, even the most educated among us must say, "I don't know how it works," to some essential bit of machinery, and somehow that ignorance doesn't stop the machine from working. Somewhere there is an expert who knows how it works—or at least how to get it working again if it stops working—and that's all that is necessary.

And so it is with computers. That there are silicon chips sorting and re-sorting billions of binary bits per nanosecond is of no practical concern to the corporate attorney playing Pac-Man or the teenager using a computer to write his or her first love poem.

The much-used phrase "computer literacy" has little to do with knowing what goes on inside the machine. Computer literacy is getting what you want *into* the machine and getting what you want *out of* the machine, and feeling comfortable enough about this process of in and out to occasionally enjoy it.

"Turn the machine on, put the record on the turntable, put the needle on the record, and adjust the volume to your taste" is all one needs to know about a phonograph to enjoy everything from Bette Midler to Gustav Mahler.

The fact that sound is made up of vibrations, and that these vibrations are captured in the grooves of the record, and that the needle vibrates when going through the grooves, and that the vibrations when amplified recreate the original vibrations and, therefore, the sound of the original performance, is not necessary to know.

It can, however, be interesting. A *National Geographic Special* on the human body can be fascinating, even though we've been successfully operating our bodies for years without all those microscopic, time-lapsed, animation-enhanced "hows."

And so it is with the hows, as well as the history, of computers. (The hows and the history of most machinery are intimately connected.) What follows are some hows and some history of computing, presented in no particular order and selected because I found each of them, in some way, interesting. This is not a comprehensive overview of the history and functioning of computing machines. It's more a compilation of computer trivia.

If your eyes begin to glaze or your mind begins to drift during any of these points, don't bother to refocus and reread, just skip ahead to the next point. If you drift on several points, skip to the next chapter. This information is not in the least essential to selecting, purchasing, operating or enjoying a personal computer. Like all trivia, it can be interesting but it is, in essence, trivial.

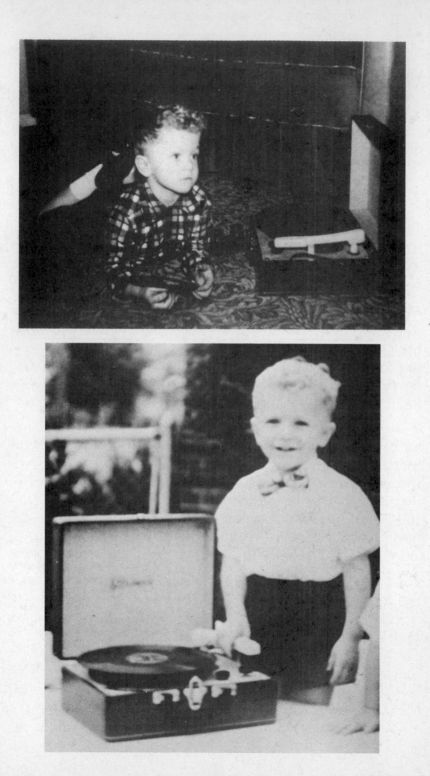

• The first computer was the abacus. The abacus is from the Orient, although its name comes from the Greek word, *abax,* meaning a calculating table covered with dust, which was named after the Hebrew word for dust. The abacus is more than 5,000 years old and is still the primary form of "number crunching" in many parts of the world. (Although the 1982 Chinese census was counted on modern computers, the census preceding it was computed on the abacus.)

The abacus is not only one of humankind's first complex machines, it's also the first mechanical device listed in most dictionaries.

• The next major breakthrough in computers came a scant 4,600 years later. In 1642, the French scientist Blaise Pascal invented an "arithmetic machine" to help in his father's business. (A father's necessity was the mother of this son's invention.)

The machine had eight wheels, each wheel having the numbers 0 through 9 painted on it. The wheels were attached to gears and the gears attached to each other in such a way that simple addition and subtraction took place by dialing the amounts to be added or subtracted. Its size made it the world's first non-portable computer.

Blaise Pascal was honored by having a high-level computer language—Pascal—named after him.

• In 1694, 52 years after Pascal's arithmetic machine, the German mathematician Gottfried Wilhelm Leibniz unveiled his 23-year pet project, the Stepped Reckoner. This machine was designed not only to add and subtract, but to multiply, divide and extract square roots. This was a major advance in features, and there was only one thing wrong with the machine—it didn't work.

It did, however, introduce a new concept to "reckoning," and that was "stepping." The concept was to break a mathematical problem into smaller steps, steps so small that the average human being would find following them tedious and time-consuming, but steps that a machine could do rather easily and without noticeable signs of boredom.

Whereas Pascal used ten symbols in each mathematical problem (0, 1, 2, 3, 4, 5, 6, 7, 8, and 9), Leibniz used only two (0 and 1). The former system is called the decimal system (*dec* meaning ten) and the latter, binary (*bi* meaning two).

It is far easier for a machine to keep track of only two variables than for it to keep track of ten. Two variables can be represented in concrete terms—on/off, yes/no, black/white, in/out, up/down, open/closed.

Absolute, concrete terms are something machines like. The gradation of information that humans enjoy, machines don't. It is not surprising that a Frenchman devised a gradation machine (0 through 9 in gradual increments) while a German introduced an absolute machine (0 and 1 and that's that). It would later take an Englishman, George Boole, to massage together the Gallic and the Teutonic approaches into the system of logic modern computers would eventually use.

• We all know how the decimal system of numbers works—it's the system of counting we use all the time. We have ten symbols (0, 1, 2, 3, 4, 5, 6, 7, 8, and 9). When we use up all the symbols, we must start combining symbols to indicate amounts larger than 9. We do this by columns. The right hand column represents the symbol itself. The column to the left of that represents ten times the value of that symbol. The column to the left of that represents ten times ten, or one hundred times the number. Each column to the left represents an additional ten-fold increase. (Remember, if you start to drift, move on to the next point. None of this is necessary.)

The first four columns of the decimal system are:

THOUSANDS   HUNDREDS   TENS   ONES

To write "eight", one would put an 8 in the ONES column. To write "eighty," or ten times eight, one would write an 8 in the TENS column and a 0 in the ONES column. The long way of reading that would be "Eight TENS and Zero ONES." (Is anyone besides me having flashbacks of second grade?)

The binary system works in the same way, except that there are only two symbols, 0 and 1. As in decimal, the 0 is used to represent nothing. Therefore, after indicating only *one* variable, the binary system needs a new column. The new column, to the left, indicates a number twice as large as the number in the first column. The next column to the left indicates a number twice as large as the preceding column, and so on.

The first four columns of the binary system would be:

EIGHTS   FOURS   TWOS   ONES

"Eight" in binary would have a 1 in the EIGHTS column, a 0 in the FOURS place, a 0 in the TWOS place and a 0 in the ONES place. The long way of reading that would be, "One EIGHT, zero FOURS, zero TWOS, and zero ONES." It would be written 1000. "8" in decimal equals "1000" in binary.

Before we attempt to represent "eighty" in binary, let's first count from zero to ten in binary.

Zero would be 0. One would be 1. So far so good, but already we've run out of symbols, so we must add a column to the left. Two would be 10 (one TWO and zero ONES). Three would be 11 (one TWO and one ONE). And again we've run out of symbols. We add an additional column and write 100 (one FOUR, zero TWOS and zero ONES). Five is 101 (one FOUR, zero TWOS, and one ONE). Six is 110 (one FOUR, one TWO, and zero ONES). Seven is 111 (one FOUR, one TWO, and one ONE). Again we've run out of symbols, so we add a column, and return to our old friend 1000 (one EIGHT, zero FOURS, zero TWOS, and zero ONES). Nine is 1001 (one EIGHT, zero FOURS, zero TWOS, and one ONE).

Ten is 1010 (one EIGHT, zero FOURS, one TWO, and zero ONES).

To get to "eighty" does not require as many columns as one might think, since each time we add a column to the left, it doubles the value of the column immediately to its right. The column to the left of EIGHTS would be SIXTEENS, the column to the left of that THIRTY-TWOS, and the column to the left of that SIXTY-FOURS. It seems that extending the columns this far to the left should give us "eighty."

It becomes sort of a puzzle (the sort of a puzzle which I, by the way, dislike)—"Using a maximum of one number from each column, arrive at the number 'eighty.'"

SIXTY-FOURS	THIRTY-TWOS	SIXTEENS	EIGHTS	FOURS	TWOS	ONES

Let's see, a SIXTY-FOUR and a THIRTY-TWO would give us ninety-six. Over the top already. A SIXTY-FOUR and a SIXTEEN equal—ta-da!—eighty. (Boy, did we luck out on that one.) So, we would write "eighty" in binary as 1010000 (one SIXTY-FOUR, zero THIRTY-TWOS, one SIXTEEN, zero EIGHTS, zero FOURS, zero TWOS, and zero ONES).

(Challenge: Write the number "twenty-seven" in binary numbers.)

It would seem as though one would require reams of paper to record large numbers in binary. Actually, this is not the case. Because the columns continue to double as they move to the left, the binary system becomes increasingly compact.

Whereas it takes seven binary columns to write the decimal number 64 (1000000), it takes only forty binary columns to write the decimal number 549,755,813,888 (1000000000000000000000000000000000000000).

Do you need to know any of this to operate a personal computer? No. None of it. Your computer will accept information in standard decimal form and return processed information in standard decimal form. All conversions to and from binary will take place within the computer.

(Answer to the challenge: "twenty-seven" in binary is 11011.)

• A computer is very simple-minded. It knows only two things: Yes and No. There are no Maybes. A circuit is either open or it's closed. There is no little-bit-open or almost-closed. It's black or white, no gray whatsoever. It's 0 or 1.

There are two reasons why computers can do all that they do knowing as little as they do.

1. SIZE. A great many yes/no circuits can fit into a very small space. As we saw above, it would take only 40 yes/no circuits to write all numbers from one to one trillion. Computer technology is such that you can hold *millions* of these yes/no circuits in the palm of your hand. This miniaturization allows the computing power of room-sized 1950 computers to fit into the pocket calculators of today. These yes/no circuits are so cheap that you can buy for $100 what would have cost you $1,000,000 forty years ago.

2. SPEED. One of these little yes/no circuits can say "no" faster than Debbie Boone. Properly induced, it can say "yes" just as fast. This is because each circuit is opened or closed electronically, not mechanically. (There are not millions of little fingers turning millions of little switches on and off.) This means that computers compute at speeds approaching one-fourth the speed of light. In fact, most of the time a computer takes to compute something is in interacting with a mechanical device, such as a disk drive or a keyboard.

The speed at which computers operate is so incomprehensible that someone devised this comparison: If you were interacting with a computer—you giving the computer data, the computer giving you data, back and forth—it would take you each time, in the computer's time frame, eight years to respond. Having to work as they do with binary numbers and human beings, it is fortunate that computers are not easily bored.

• It was the lack of these two elements, size and speed, that prevented Charles Babbage from constructing a fully functioning personal computer almost 150 years ago

By 1835 Babbage, an English inventor, had conceived an "Analytical Engine" that incorporated almost

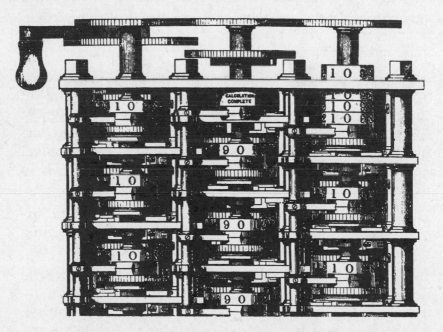

A small portion of Babbage's Analytical Engine.

every other element of computing, including programming, memory, printout, and the ever-popular punch cards.

But Babbage lacked the technology of size and speed, and his 1835 invention of the computer would go unnoticed and forgotten until his writings were rediscovered in 1937.

• Babbage used punch cards borrowed from the Jacquard loom, which Jacquard borrowed from the Vaucanson loom, which Vaucanson borrowed from the Bouchon loom, which Bouchon—the son of an organ maker—borrowed from the automated organ. (This organ to loom to computer connection is delightfully delineated in James Burke's *Connections,* both on the PBS television series and in the Little, Brown and Company book.)

Back in the days of the automated organ (the 16th Century, give or take a century), a peg was placed on a revolving cylinder for each "yes." As the cylinder turned, the peg would strike a note. This same principle is still used in music boxes today.

The automated weaving looms used paper with holes in it. If a rod could fit in the hole, a certain thread corresponding to that hole was included in the design. If there was no hole for the rod to slip into, the thread was not included. This allowed for intricate, inexpensive, and error-free weaving. It's the same concept seen in player piano rolls and computer punch cards.

Punch cards—which until a decade ago would arrive almost daily in the mail with the ominous warning not to fold, spindle, or mutilate them—work like this:

The card is designed with room to punch out little holes. These holes represent a basic yes/no binary circuit—if the hole is punched, that's yes; if the hole is not punched, that's no. These holes could be assigned to record any

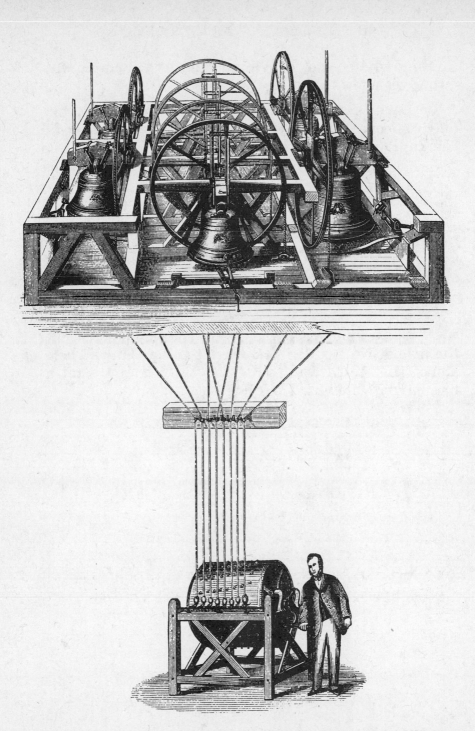

Each time a peg on the drum of this automated bell-ringer pulls a string, the bell attached to that string rings.

answer whatsoever, providing that the answer was either yes or no.

Let's take a very simple punch card that would offer someone the choice of a hot dog, a hamburger, or both. The card would look something like this—

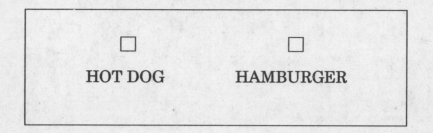

If one wanted a hot dog, he or she would punch out the hole above "hot dog" and leave the "hamburger" hole alone. The "Yes, I want a hot dog; no, I do not want a hamburger" card would look like this—

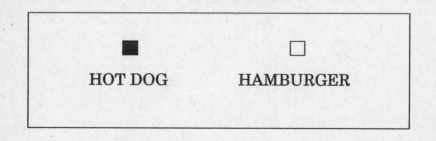

This card would communicate to a computerized kitchen, "I would like a hamburger but not a hot dog":

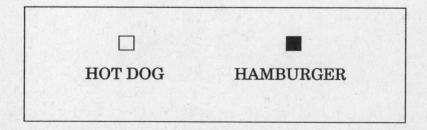

This card would say, "I am obviously hungry. I would like a hot dog *and* a hamburger."

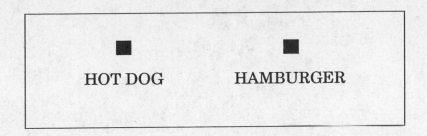

And an unpunched card might mean, "I am on a diet. Do you have any cottage cheese?"

In this way, a card with only two holes has given us four possible choices—hamburger only, hot dog only, hamburger and hot dog, neither hamburger nor hot dog. The choices given the card puncher could be geometrically increased by simply adding a few more holes.

	HOT DOG			HAMBURGER		
KETCHUP	MUSTARD	RELISH	PICKLE	ONION	TOMATO	CHILI

This would offer a range of choices from nothing, to a hamburger and a hot dog with everything.

• The 1880 census in the United States took eight years to count. What with the tired and the poor and the huddled masses streaming to America from the teeming shores of Europe, it was estimated that the 1890 census would be counted by 1902. At that rate we would know, by 1995, what the population was in 1940. A better way

Punch cards, once very popular, have been almost entirely replaced by magnetic disks and tapes. IBM is in the process of recycling billions of these cards. To get some cards for your bird, write IBM, Boca Raton, Florida.

of counting and sorting was needed and was duly discovered: The 1890 Census Machine.

John Shaw Billings, a medical doctor and lieutenant colonel in the U.S. Army, came up with the idea of using the punch-hole cards to speed people counting, and turned the project over to Herman Hollerith.

Hollerith designed cards that census takers could carry with them and punch in the field. The cards included information on sex, age, birth date, nationality— the standard census data. Then the cards were processed by a machine. Each time there was a hole in a card, a metal rod would pass through, complete an electrical circuit, and the data would be tabulated. However primitive, and although the rest of the computer was purely mechanical, this was the first use of an electric circuit in computing.

The 1890 census was completed, thanks to the computer, in less than three years. In 1911, Hollerith joined with the Computing Tabulating Recording Company, which later became IBM.

• The next two advances came from those two hotbeds of progress, war and universities.

By 1939, IBM had become a great American institution. It joined with another great American institution, Harvard, and together they made a computer, the Mark I. Partly electrical and partly mechanical, it was the world's largest adding machine. It was fifty feet long and eight feet high. It could add, subtract, multiply, divide, and—most importantly—make mathematical tables. The tables were used by the military in World War II. It told them, for example, where to aim a gun so that the shell and the enemy plane would reach the same place at the same time.

Until WWII, big guns were only asked to fire on stationary objects, such as buildings, or on slowly moving objects—ships, for example. Airplanes moved at

Here we have the 1890 Census Machine operated,
apparently, by men.

A few years later, when it became a Tabulating Machine, women were operators and men were supervising. Hmmmm.

several hundred miles an hour. The gunner on the ground needed to know *exactly* how far in front of the plane to aim. Hence a book of intricate tables was devised that almost required a computer to interpret.

Meanwhile, the University of Pennsylvania, not to be outdone, was working on the first fully electronic computer, the ENIAC (Electronic Numerical Integrator and Calculator). Was this, too, the birth of computer jargon?

The ENIAC took up 3,000 cubic feet (some computer *stores* today are smaller than that), weighed 30 tons, and used 18,000 vacuum tubes. On the average, one tube failed every seven minutes. (When they say that computers today are very reliable, they may be comparing them to the ENIAC.)

The ENIAC was a big hit. When it was first plugged in, in 1946 (the year my parents got married—ah, memories), it spent two hours doing nuclear-physics calculations that would have taken 100 engineers one year to compute. How many hours it took ENIAC to come up with *that* statistic we will never know.

• Remington Rand introduced the Univac in 1951. It was the first computer that could handle both numbers *and* letters. The computer was taught to read and write. The first customers in line for the Univac were the folks who started it all back in 1890—the United States Bureau of Census.

• I love full circles. Here are two more.

Magnetic tape—developed by the Germans during WWII while American computers used paper-punch input to devise gun charts—became the standard storage medium for computers during the 1950's. Those are reels of magnetic tape spinning in the science fiction movies of the period.

The Japanese, still happy with their abacuses (abaci?), took a neglected invention from the Bell

Laboratories—the transistor—and revolutionized the world with it. It began with the transistor radio in the late 1950's and moved to computers in the early 1960's.

Each small, cool, inexpensive, reliable transistor replaced a large, hot, expensive, volatile vacuum tube. Computers became smaller, cooler, less expensive, and more reliable.

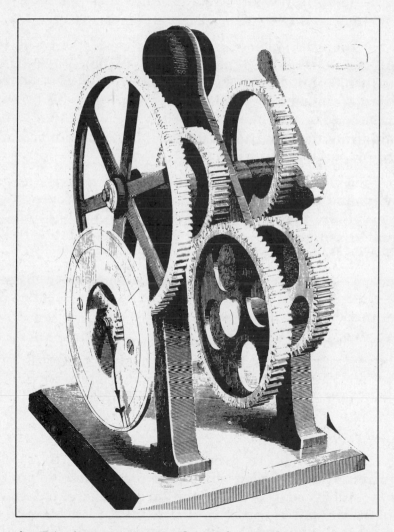

A transistor as seen through an electron microscope. (Scale: 1 inch = 5 miles.)

• The late 1960's saw the development of the silicon chip. Each chip, the size of a postage stamp, held the computing power of thousands of transistors, which had replaced thousands of tubes. The ENIAC's 18,000 vacuum tubes and the 30 tons of wiring necessary to connect all those tubes could now fit on a table top.

• The first personal computer was introduced in 1975. The Altair 8800 was a kit offered to hobbyists. It was remarkably—and surprisingly—successful.

Soon the Apple—named after one of its inventor's summer jobs in an apple orchard—made its debut. It cost $666.66. The Apple was born with a case of the cutes from which it has yet to recover. (And *Time* Magazine, in reviewing an earlier edition of this book, said the same thing about me. What goes around comes around, I suppose.)

Tandy Radio Shack, combining its hobbyist beginnings and its knowledge of marketing electronics to a mass audience, introduced the TRS (Tandy Radio Shack) 80 Model I. It was immediately dubbed the TRASH 80 by loving fans.

Commodore, maker of hand-held calculators, took the plunge and introduced the PET. (Users called it "commode door.")

Then the rest of the world jumped in. Entrepreneurs, corporations, shamans, geniuses, bankers, San Fernando Valley housewives, adding machine companies, photocopy giants, and, finally, IBM. They all introduced personal computers or peripherals or programs to a waiting but cautious world.

• After IBM's debut of its PC line, the world shrunk and expanded simultaneously. The companies that embraced the IBM standard and created computers compatible with the "IBM Standard" often did well—such firms as Compaq, Toshiba, Epson, NEC, and Zenith.

The companies that pushed systems with a non-IBM standard mostly withered. Stroll through one of my buying guides from the mid-1980's and you'll bump into companies that are no more: Morrow, Jonos, Tele-Video, Cromemco and others. You'll even see companies that made IBM clones and still vanished: Seequa, Otrona, Eagle, Columbia. This is because no-name clone makers sprung up and made machines cheaper than anyone else. In the early 1980's, an IBM PC or name-brand clone cost anywhere from $2,500 to $4,000. Five years later you could buy the same power in a plain box for under $1,000.

Today, the only players not up to the "standard" IBM standard are Apple (with its Macintosh), Commodore (with the Amiga), Atari, and, ironically, IBM. (The IBM line is now software compatible, but not hardware compatible, with the standard IBM itself created in 1983. More on this in the rather controversial chapter, *Why You Should Probably Buy Neither an Apple Nor an IBM*. The bottom line: If it's not IBM-compatible, it's probably not worth it.)

But these iconoclasts account for only a fraction of the personal computer market. This book will focus on the mainstream clone makers who offer power, value and compatibility in computing.

I'll have more to say on all this in the section on selecting and purchasing a personal computer. For now, what do I mean by "software," "hardware" and other bits of jargon dropped throughout this chapter? Ah, that's what the next chapter will make clear; or if not clear, at least a little less cloudy.

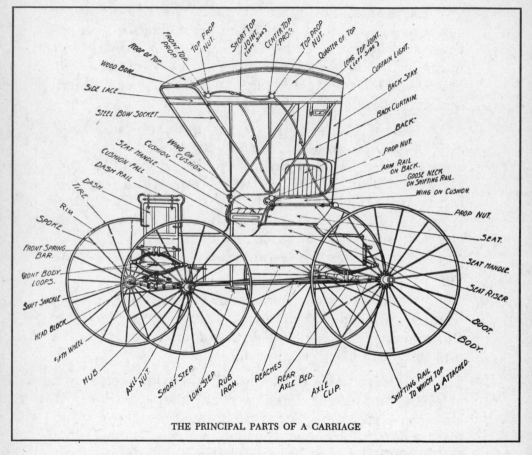

THE PRINCIPAL PARTS OF A CARRIAGE

An illustration from The Personal Carriage Book (1890).

Chapter 2

The Personal Computer

Before exploring what these ET's called PC's do, let's take a look at what they *are*.

Like most machines, personal computers are made up of metal, glass, paper, and plastic—with an occasional exotic-sounding substance such as phosphor thrown in for good measure.

If you feel intimidated by computers, there's no need to be. They are constructed of the same bits and pieces as televisions, tape recorders and typewriters. (Remember typewriters?)

This chapter will provide a general overview of a personal computer's component parts. We'll go into more detail, from a buyer's point of view, in a later chapter, *Selecting a Personal Computer.*

As we go along, I will also introduce you—as painlessly as possible—to that collection of jargon, technical terms, and buzz words known as Computerese. There's nothing to be intimidated about here, either. The people who created computerese are far less intelligent than you. How do I know they are far less intelligent than you? Because, considering the mishmash of acronyms, tortured conjunctions and fractured idioms they have jumbled together, it's obvious that they are far less intelligent than *anyone.*

And so, with intimidation on hold, heads held high, and a song in our hearts, let's take a look at personal computers and at the bits and pieces that make them up.

Personal computers come in many shapes and sizes. **Desktop PC's** are computers that fit nicely on a desktop. **Laptop PC's** are much smaller—10 pounds or less—intended for people on the go. **Portable PC's** are smaller than desktop ones, but are larger and heavier than laptops. They're for people who want all the power of a desktop PC, but still want to take (lug) their machines around.

The first piece of the personal computer we'll look at is the **microprocessor.** A processor in *any* computer does just that: it **processes** information. It sorts and re-sorts bits of information, something almost any human could do, but it sorts and re-sorts it at speeds no human can approach. It is this speed, not any innate ability, that gives computers the edge over humans at certain repetitive tasks.

In larger computers (known as **mainframes** because their frames are sometimes larger than the state of Maine), the processor can be any size at all. A big corporation can simply lease another floor to put it on. In a personal computer, a processor can be only so large or it stops being a personal computer and starts becoming a coffee table.

Once processors became small enough they were dubbed *micro*processors. (In the world of electronics, when something is made small it is prefaced with *mini*. When it is made smaller it is prefaced by *micro*. When it is made smaller still, by *mini-micro*. I am sure someday we'll have *micro-micros, mini-micro-micros, micro-micro-micros* and so on.)

Some microprocessors are primitive affairs, designed for a specific function within a specific product. A microprocessor inside a hand-held calculator, for example, may be constructed to simply add, subtract, tell the time, and play a heart-rending version of *Clair de Lune.* A microprocessor inside a microwave (yes, for "very small" waves, but that's another book) might be designed to display the time and tell you when the popcorn is ready.

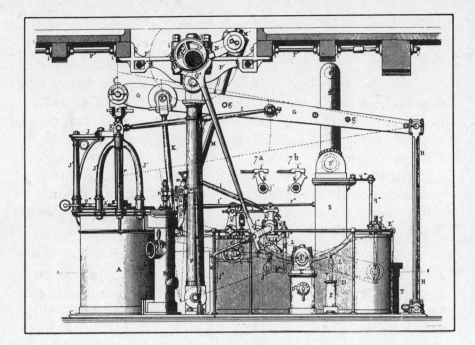

A processor.

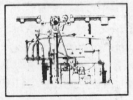

Microprocessor.

By the time they mature enough to be included in a personal computer, microprocessors assume the more sophisticated name of **Central Processing Unit,** which is usually shortened to the not-so-sophisticated **CPU.** These have numbers such as 8086, 80286, 80386, 80486 and so on, the longer ones shortened to 286, 386,

486, and so on. When people say, "I have a 286 machine," they mean, "I have a 80286 microprocessor in my personal computer."

What microprocessors process are **bits.** A bit is one of those on/off, yes/no, Debbie Boone units discussed in the first chapter. (If you skipped the first chapter, you missed the Debbie Boone joke. Sorry. Check the index.) Bits are small. It takes eight bits to make a single **character.** (A character in computing is any letter, number, punctuation mark or symbol that can fit on a single key on the keyboard.) These eight bits together form one **byte.**

Bytes are small, too. The word "word" takes up four bytes. The word "byte" takes up four bytes. Even the word "one" takes up three bytes. Most people talk, then, in **kilobytes.** There are approximately 1,000 bytes per kilobyte. (The actual figure is 1,024 bytes, for those of you who think there's going to be some kind of quiz at the end of the chapter.) Kilobyte is shortened to the letter K. (The letter K is made up of one byte.) A "360K disk" is a disk that holds 360 kilobytes of information. For easy reference, 2K is about the amount of information on a double-spaced typewritten letter.

When even kilobytes are too small a unit of measurement, we move to **megabytes.** A megabyte is approximately 1,000 kilobytes or 1,000,000 bytes. (For the precise: a megabyte is 1,024 kilobytes or 1,048,576 bytes.) You don't need to remember these numbers. Just remember that a kilobyte is a lot and a megabyte is a whole lot more.

Then there is a whole, *whole* lot more, and that's a **gigabyte,** which is 1,073,741,824 bytes—roughly a billion bytes, or a million kilobytes, or a thousand megabytes. Will you ever need to use the word gigabyte in personal computing? Hardly ever. I don't own a gigabyte of anything. It does make a nice song lyric, though: "Just a gigabyte/Morning, noon and night..."

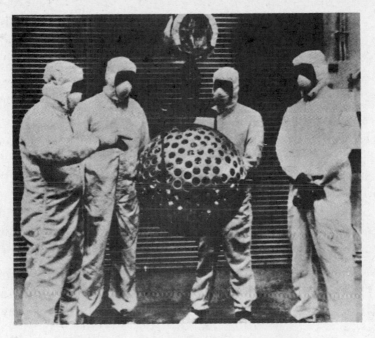

Bits must be handled <u>very</u> carefully.

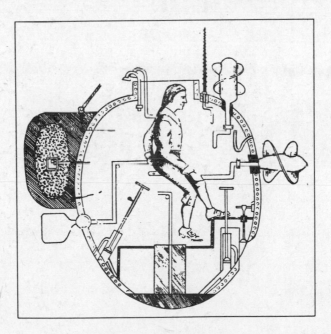

One bit, set to go.

Microprocessors are made of silicon. Silicon is a fancy word for glass. (Not to be confused with *silicone,* a fancy word for rubber.) It's called silicon because it is made from silica, a fancy word for sand.

It has been said that the meek shall inherit the earth. Remember those meek math students, running around high school with slide rules and pencils sticking out of their shirt pockets; the ones the jocks labeled nerds; the ones who never dated because (A) no one would date them and (B) they were always in the basement working on their science projects? Well, those meek have inherited the earth, the sand to be specific, silica to be more specific.

They have inherited, too, a chunk of actual earth in California called Silicon Valley (not to be confused with Silicone Valley, a section of Beverly Hills reserved

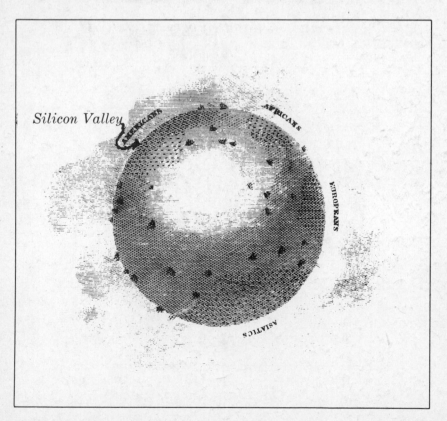

for plastic surgeons and their more affluent clients). In Silicon Valley the nerds have become rich with their science projects, and the former jocks are trying to save enough money to buy one of those mass-produced projects for their children.

A microprocessor is very smart but has little memory, rather like a genius with amnesia. To remedy this situation, two kinds of memory are combined with the Central Processing Unit in most computers.

The first is known as **Read Only Memory** or **ROM.** This memory can be "read" by the microprocessor, but the microprocessor cannot "write" anything into that memory. (*Reading,* meaning taking information from, and *writing,* meaning adding information to, are computerdom's token nods to a form of literacy other than computer literacy.) The microprocessor, then, is free to take information *from* ROM but it cannot add information *to* it.

The information in ROM is placed there—permanently—by the manufacturer. ROM is there as a helpful nurse, telling the amnesia-bound genius how to brush its teeth, get dressed, and otherwise prepare for the day. When electrical current first passes through the CPU, it will wake up and ask ROM, "What do I do now?" ROM will tell it, CPU will do it, and then ask, "What do I do now?" ROM will tell it, CPU will do it, and so on. ROM is, in other words, **programmed** to get CPU going in the morning and to help it with certain basic functions during the day.

At some point, however, CPU will have done everything ROM has been programmed to ask it to do. CPU is washed, dressed, and ready for the day—but what will that day consist of? CPU asks ROM, "What do I do now?" And ROM replies, "Ask RAM."

RAM is the second kind of memory in a personal computer. RAM stands for **Random Access Memory.** Not only can CPU read information from RAM, it can

THE PERSONAL COMPUTER BOOK

also write information into it. The CPU has random access to that memory; it can erase all—or any part of it—and write some more.

The CPU turns to RAM and asks, "What do I do now?" RAM has the daily schedule from the Big Boss (you) in hand. "During the morning, it's accounting," says RAM. "This afternoon word processing, and in the evening we have scheduled a series of intriguing electronic games." "Right," says CPU, and the three of them—RAM, ROM and CPU—set off for a productive day.

RAM can be thought of as an executive secretary who has not only the daily schedule, but also a steno pad. If CPU were to ask ROM to take a note, ROM would reply, "That's not my job. Ask RAM." RAM is more than happy to jot down anything from a telephone number to a telephone book, and to have that information ready for the CPU's use at a nanosecond's notice.

RAM is what people most often mean when they refer to the "memory" of a computer. "I have a 640K computer," means, "I have a computer with 640 kilobytes of Random Access Memory." In the computer store you'll ask, "How much memory does it have?" and they will answer with the amount of RAM.

RAM is obviously a more versatile servant to CPU than ROM, but RAM, alas, has a memory problem of its own. As long as electrical current flows through its little brain, RAM remembers everything. Once the current is withdrawn, RAM forgets it all. (ROM, on the other hand, remembers how to get CPU up and dressed, current or no current, indefinitely.) Every time a computer is turned off, it's *tabula rasa* for RAM.

56

RAM loses its memory when the power is turned off.

(There is a more expensive RAM, called **DRAM** [for Dynamic RAM—what's so dynamic about it is beyond me] that doesn't "lose its mind" when the power is turned off. The cost of DRAM has kept it from all but computers that *really* need it, such as laptops and high-end portables. As costs come down, the use of DRAM should grow.)

There must be a way, then, to (A) save the information in RAM before turning the power off, and (B) load the information back into RAM after turning the power back on. There is, and that way is **disks.**

Disks, naturally, come in two general types, **floppy** and **hard.** Floppy disks (or "floppies") are 3-1/2 or 5-1/4 inch circles of plastic covered with the same brown stuff that is found on music cassettes. (The brown stuff, by the way, is rust, ordinary garden-hoe-variety rust. Naturally, no one would want to pay money for a piece of plastic covered with rust, so the rust is known as "iron oxide.") These thin circles are permanently enclosed in a cardboard or stiff plastic envelope to protect them from dust, dirt, and sticky fingers. The small 3-1/2 inch disks, encased in stiff plastic, flop around about as much as the Rock of Gibraltar, but nonetheless are considered floppy disks.

Hard disks are often sealed inside the computer and hold 20 or more times the amount of information as do floppy disks. They also spin many times faster than floppies, and thus information is read more quickly from them. Whereas floppy disks are changeable, hard disks usually are not. Because of this fixedness of location, hard disks are sometimes referred to as **fixed disks.**

Disks require a special player known as a **disk drive.** A floppy disk goes into a disk drive while a hard disk is sealed away so fingers and dust cannot reach it.

(Hold your breath, because on the next few pages are the worst of our Stupid Disk Jokes)

How information is stored on disks: Here we have the disk for the video game, "A Weekend in the Country." As you can see, everything is made small so it can fit.

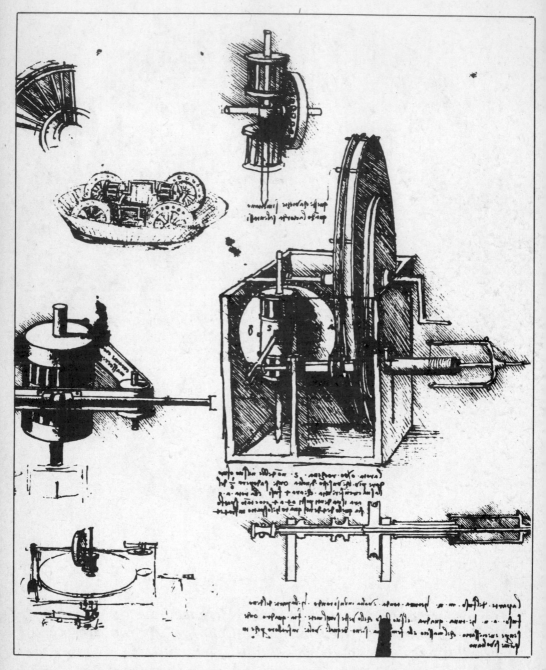

The idea for the disk drive is not new. Here are Leonardo da Vinci's sketches for a manually operated disk drive, circa 1490.

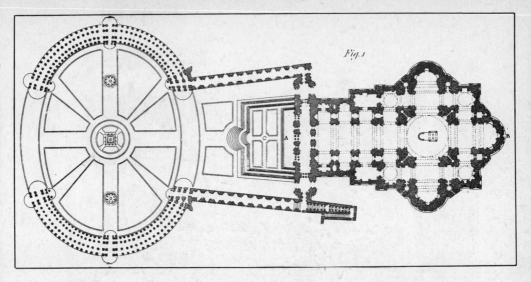

Fig. 1

Michelangelo tried to improved upon Leonardo's design by making the disks oval ("More esthetically pleasing," Michelangelo wrote in his journal). Leonardo, in Florence, sent a terse note to the young sculptor in Rome: "Whatsa matta you?" Leonardo wrote, "The diska drive, she'sa my idea. You keepa you hands off." Michelangelo eventually found another use for his design.

Early disk drives required one full horsepower to operate.

Some computer stores actually show disks being made, and the public is always intrigued.

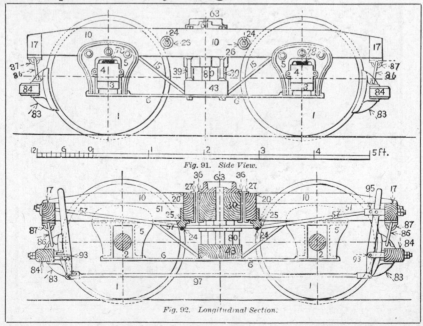

Fig. 91. Side View.

Fig. 92. Longitudinal Section.

Diagram of a dual disk drive. Please memorize all parts.

The making of a hard disk.

63

Inside the disk drive, the disks spin at many hundreds (floppies) or thousands (hard disks) of rotations per minute. A record/playback head moves across the disk's surface. These heads are known as **read/write heads.** Information is both read from and written on the disk by the read/write heads.

In addition to floppy and hard, there are two other kinds of drives available: **CD ROM** and **WORM.** A CD ROM disk is a laser disc (yes, a different spelling) that holds hundreds of megabytes of information—an entire encyclopedia, for instance. (I could toss in the gigabyte word here, kind of casually, you know, "CD ROM holds more than half a gigabyte," but I won't. They do hold *a lot.)* It is called CD ROM because it is the size of a musical compact disc (CD) and acts as a huge Read Only Memory (ROM). You cannot *write* any information to it as you can to a floppy or hard disk, but you can *read* from it.

A WORM (Write Once Read Many) disk is a laser disc of a different kind. Unlike CD ROMs, you can write information to WORM disks—once. It's like being a record producer and you're cutting the master record. WORM disks do not erase, so what you write the first time stays there. Because they hold so many megabytes of information, you could place the information from hundreds of floppy disks onto one WORM disk.

With disks, we have a way of getting information into RAM when we turn the computer on, and a way to store information from RAM before we turn the computer off. But how do we fiddle around with the information in between times? What we need are some **input devices.** That's where keyboards, joysticks, mice, track balls and scanners come in.

A **keyboard** is a board with keys on it, like the keyboard on a typewriter. Each key represents a letter, number, bit of punctuation, or symbol. Through the keyboard, almost anything can be communicated to a computer—words, numbers, symbols, which way the spaceship should go, when it should fire, and so on. Even graphics can be "keyboarded" in.

A keyboard.

Serious game players, however, will require a **joystick.** A joystick is a little box one holds in one's hand. A stick protrudes from this box, as does one or more buttons. If one pushes the stick up, the spaceship (or submarine or boxer or chess piece or Pac-Person) moves up the screen. When the stick is pushed down, the spaceship *et al.* moves down. The same is true of right, left, diagonals, and circles.

When the button is pushed, a missile is fired (or a torpedo is launched, or a punch is thrown, or a move is finalized). All this stick moving and button pushing has been observed to create the emotion of Joy in certain humans, hence the term joystick.

"A mouse! Give me a computer with a mouse!"

66

The Personal Computer

"Eek! A mouse!" Have no fear, a **mouse** for a computer is just another input device. It is a sleek, vaguely rectangular object that rolls on your desk. A wire protrudes from the mouse and is connected to your computer. (This wire corresponds to the tail of the mouse. It's a tenuous connection, calling this thing a mouse, but the name has stuck, and I guess we should be grateful it's not worse. It could have been *hand grenade*.)

When you move your mouse (pardon the expression), a blinking **cursor** (a little square) or an indicator of some sort (such as an arrow) on your screen moves likewise. If you move the mouse ever-so-slightly in a northwest direction, the cursor moves the same way, too. Mice have one or more buttons on them, and the buttons' use varies with the program you are using.

Mice serve much of the same purpose as joysticks, except their movements are more subtle, and the devices have a purpose beyond game playing. Mice are especially useful in manipulating graphics and are helpful whenever you need to delicately control the cursor, or move things not just up and down, but diagonally.

A **track ball** is a stationary (held in a "track" of some kind, I suppose, as a train on a track) ball that rotates in any direction. Like the mouse, if you rotate the ball up, the cursor goes up, and so on. Whereas the mouse moves around, the track ball rotates where it is. The one you like is a matter of preference. Most of the world uses keys on the keyboard to move the cursor around, but for those who want another device, most use mice.

Another input device is the **scanner**. This scans images or type already on paper. You can put a page into the scanner, and if the page has a picture or drawing, it is **digitized**—turned into digital images—and appears as pictures or drawings on your screen. If the page has text, scanners can read the text and—*voila!*—it is text

67

on your screen. As you can imagine, scanners save hours of retyping or redrawing.

Input devices—keyboards, joysticks, mice, track balls and scanners—get information into the computer. How do you suppose we get information out? You guessed it: **output devices.** These include monitors and printers.

THE CURSOR. The cursor is a square of light that tells you where you are on the video screen.

The **monitor** on a personal computer looks just like a television set—in fact, the screen on some (very) inexpensive personal computers *is* a television set. A wire connects the personal computer to the antenna of a television, and the computer literally broadcasts a signal to the TV.

A video screen.

Most computers, however, use dedicated monitors which offer better images than do moonlighting televisions. Monitors come in two types: **monochrome and color.**

Monochrome means you see one color against a black or white background. Most monochrome monitors produce either amber (orangeish) or green (greenish) characters against a black background because these colors are ("they say") easiest on the eyes. Black characters against a bright white background is the least preferred.

The inside of the picture tube is coated with **phosphor.** When an electron beam hits the phosphor, it glows. Phosphor is wonderful. I love phosphor. I love the sound of the name, and its derivatives. Phosphorescence, for example.

> *"Phosphorescence. Now, there's a word to lift your hat to. To find that phosphorescence, that light within, that's the genius behind poetry."*
>
> EMILY DICKINSON

But the days of phosphor are probably numbered.

The monitor is really a picture tube, the only vacuum tube used any more in computers—the only vacuum tube used anymore in almost *any* electronics. Computing is trying to eliminate even this: all laptops and many portables have **liquid crystal** displays. These are crystals that darken (they don't even *glow)* when the liquid around them is electrically charged. As you can tell, I'm not happy about this, but time marches on.

Let's move on to color monitors before I become depressed.

For games, graphics, and the education of younger children, color is certainly the way to go. For your own words and numbers, however, monochrome is less expensive. But color is so *pretty.* Color monitors come in **CGA,** which is OK for games—but don't try to do much serious work on one; **EGA,** which is wonderful for text and numbers; and **VGA,** for finely detailed graphics work.

The Queen of Phosphor.

Monitors are ephemeral. Like RAM, once the power is turned off, the video screen forgets. A more permanent method of "outputting" information is found in the **printer**. A printer, naturally, prints things.

A printer is known as a **peripheral**. It is so named because it is peripheral to the use of the computer—useful, but not necessary. At one time, almost everything other than CPU, ROM and RAM was considered peripheral. Now, most computers come standard with a keyboard, a monitor, a floppy disk drive or two, and often a hard disk.

Printers come in four basic types: **dot matrix, daisy wheel, ink jet** and **laser.**

Dot-matrix printers form characters with little dots, very much as do the signs on banks that tell the time and temperature. Dot-matrix printers use anywhere from 9 to 24 "pins" (each pin makes one dot) to create characters. The least expensive models are not the greatest for correspondence, while the more sophisticated ones are just fine. Besides characters, dot matrix can also print graphics.

Daisy-wheel printers type one character after another, just as a typewriter. With the advent of 24-pin dot matrix, ink-jet and laser printers, daisy-wheel printers are fast becoming a thing of the past.

Ink-jet printers spray ink in small controlled dots onto paper. This kind of printer has the advantage over the dot-matrix and daisy wheel in that it is silent. Ink jets perform graphics flawlessly, though a page heavy with graphics tends to come out of the printer damp—because of all the wet ink.

Laser printers offer the best of all worlds in printing . . . except price. They are fast, silent, and produce sharp type. Because they print with 300 or more dots to the inch, the graphics they create are also sharp. Laser printers, alas, are more expensive than the other three, but they're getting more affordable all the time.

Another popular peripheral for the personal computer is known as a **modem.** A modem attaches either inside the computer or outside the computer, and then to a telephone line. A modem allows one computer to be connected, over phone lines, to another computer. (The other computer requires a modem as well, of course.) When connected, information can flow back and forth between computers.

The process modems use to transmit computer information over ordinary phone lines is called *modulation*. (Modulation, by the way, also takes place with information before it can be broadcast over the radio. The "M" in AM and FM stands for modulation.)

A modem takes information from the computer, modulates it, and sends it over the phone line. A second modem at the other end *de*modulates the signal back into a form the receiving computer can understand. "Mo-dem," then, describes what a modem does—*modu*late/*dem*odulate.

A modem puts your computer in touch with the world. I'll discuss the practical benefits of this at various points throughout the book.

And there we have it—the personal computer.

Making phosphor.

Chapter 3

On Programs and Programming

All the stuff we discussed in the previous chapter—computers, printers, WORMS and such—are known as **hardware.** The stuff we use to make the computer do what computers do is called **software.**

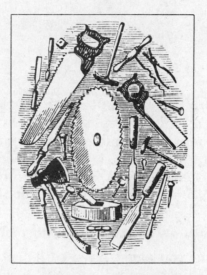

Hardware, circa 1957.

This hardware/software distinction is true of most electronics: a Walkman is the hardware, Michael Jackson is the software; a VCR is the hardware, *Field of Dreams* is the software; a television is the hardware, *Murphy Brown* is the software.

When we come to television, we come to another parallel between computers and "the rest of the world": television software is more commonly referred to as **programs;** so, too, is computer software.

To "program" your Walkman to play Michael Jackson, you slip in a Michael Jackson tape and push PLAY; to "program" your VCR to play *Field of Dreams,* you insert a videotape of *Field of Dreams* and push PLAY; to program your television to watch a television program, you turn the dial to the appropriate channel at the appointed time, push ON, and, *voila, Murphy Brown.*

Programming a computer (or, as they say, "running a program") to process words or write checks or play chess is about as complicated. Computer programs take more time to learn how to use because they are *interactive;* that is, they will do what you tell them to do (given it's within their capabilities), but first you must learn *how* to tell them. (More hints on how to make learning more fun later in the book.)

One thing you *won't* have to learn is **programming,** which, in computerdom, means writing a computer program. You no more need to know how to write a computer program to use a computer than you need to know how to make a movie to watch *Field of Dreams* on your VCR.

One of the great misconceptions that hovers around computerdom is that computer literacy has something to do with programming knowledge. I will sum up my reaction to that in one (polite) word: nonsense.

In a number of introductory computer courses offered by any number of night schools, business schools, junior colleges, and computer dealers, what is

With these friendly people selling programs, and all the people in the back room writing programs, why write your own?

3ᵇ Tibetisch.

	Figur	Benennung
Vocale		Kiku, i.
		Sciapkiu, u.
		Drengbu, e.
		Naro, o.
Accente		Nota Gutturalis
		Nota Palatini.
		Nota Narini.
		Nota Singularis
Interpunctionszeichen		
		Anfangszeichen
		Comma.
		Ausrufungsz.

1 2 3 4 5 6 7 8 9 0

5 Aethiopisch.

Figur						Bedt.
mit u	mit i	mit â	mit ē	mit ɛ	mit o	
hu	hi	ha	he	hɛ	ho	h
lu	li	la	le	lɛ	lo	l
lu	hi	ha	he	he	ho	h
mu	mi	sa	me	se	mo	m
ru	ri	ra	re	re	ro	r
su	si	scha	se	sche	so	s
schu	schi	scha	sche	sche	scho	sch
ku	ki	ka	ke	ke	ko	k
bu	bi	ba	be	be	bo	b
thu	thi	tha	the	the	tho	th
tju	tji	tja	tje	tje	tjo	tj
chu	chi	cha	che	che	cho	ch
nu	ni	na	ne	he	no	n
gnu	gni	gna	gne	gne	gno	ng
u	i	a	e	e	a	a
ku	ki	ka	ke	ke	ko	k
chu	chi	cha	che	che	cho	ch
wu	wi	wa	we	ve	vo	w
zu	zi	za	ze	ze	zo	z
ju	ji	ja	je	je	jo	j fr.
ju	di	dja	de	dje	djo	j
dju	dji	dja	dje	dje	djo	dj
gu	gi	ga	ge	ge	go	g
tu	ti	ta	te	te	to	t
tschu	tschi	tscha	tsche	tsche	tscho	tsch
tzu	tzi	tza	tze	tze	tzo	p tz
zu	zi	za	ze	ze	zo	tz
fu	fi	fa	fe	fe	fo	f
pu	pi	pa	pu	pe	po	p

7 Zend.

Figur	Werth	Figur	Werth
	a		z
	â		ñ
	i		t
	î		ṭ
	u		th
	û		d
	e (ĕ)		dh
	è		n
	ê		p
	o		f
	ô		b
	âo		m
	an		y z Anf.
	k		y id Mitte
	kh		r
	q		v z Anf.
	g		v id Mitte
	gh		w
	ń		ç
	ć		sh
	j		h
	ach		

6 Syrisch.

Benenn.	nicht anschl.	verdB. anschl.	v z S. anschl.	folg.
Olaph				
Beth				
Gomal				
Dolath				
He				
Vau				
Zain				
Cheth				
Teth				
Jud				
Coph				
Lomad				
Mim				
Nun				
Semcath				
Ee				
Phe				
Tsode				
Kuph				
Risch				

Some computer languages.

the first thing they may want you to learn? BASIC programming.

In any number of introductory computer books, what is the first thing they may want to teach you? BASIC programming.

In introductory computer shows, in introductory computer magazines, and during introductory computer skywriting expositions, what is the first thing they may present? BASIC programming.

Such a waste.

Learning BASIC is about as necessary to operating a computer as tuning engines is necessary to driving a car.

Not that learning the BASIC programming language can't be fun. Some people enjoy learning foreign languages. Some people enjoy jogging ten miles a day. Some people enjoy calculating *pi* to the 327th decimal place without a calculator. But to operate a computer, or to learn its operation, learning BASIC is an unnecessary expenditure of time and money.

There are professionals who write computer programs and television programs. Granted, it often looks as though some of them have missed their calling and should be writing for the other medium.

Some people enjoy writing for television, some people enjoy writing for newspapers, and some people enjoy writing for computers. This is fine. Everybody needs a hobby.

My point is that if you don't enjoy writing for computers, you don't have to. That point is seldom stressed, especially in introductory computer classes, books, videotapes, *et al.*

Teaching BASIC is a holdover from more than a decade ago when there were no programs for personal computers. If you wanted a computer program, you had to write it yourself. That time is long past, but the habit of teaching the language of programming remains.

If you're ever in a situation in which someone is trying to teach you BASIC programming against your will, write this simple BASIC program into the computer:

```
1 PRINT "I DO NOT CARE TO
  LEARN BASIC. WHAT'S NEXT?"
2 GO TO 1
RUN
```

This program will cause the computer to print, over and over, on the screen: "I DO NOT CARE TO LEARN BASIC. WHAT'S NEXT?" If the teacher does not laugh and/or have a "what's next," excuse yourself and go learn something practical, something truly basic, like tuning your car.

The best introductory computer class to take, if you like classes, is one in which you learn how to use the program you actually plan to use on your computer. Disk drives and screens and such can be learned in a very short time. What takes the time is learning, and mastering, the program you choose—be it word processing, spreadsheeting, accounting or blackjack.

If you don't like classes, the best "class" to take consists of: you, a computer, the program you want to learn, and a lot of time. We'll talk more about how to learn a computer program in the chapter, *Learning to Use Your Personal Computer.* When you know how to use a computer program, you know how to use a computer.

Computer
Manufacturer

Computer
Programmer

Computer
Writer

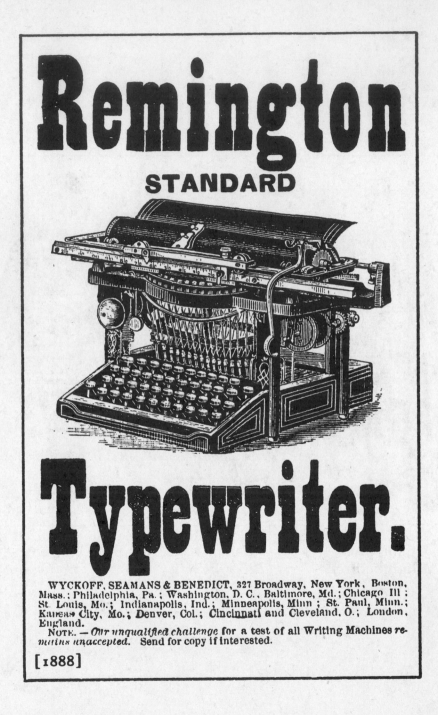

Remington
STANDARD
Typewriter.

[1888]

Chapter 4

Questions and Answers on Computer Basics

Since publishing my first computer book in 1982, I have received thousands of questions. (Actually, I have received thousands of *letters*. The questions tend to repeat themselves.)

This volume of queries suggests one of two scenarios: (1) I am such a knowledgeable writer that people assume I will have the answers to their questions, or (2) I am such a bad writer that people are forced to write and ask me things that should have been in my book in the first place.

I hope it is the former, but I fear it's the latter.

This chapter will attempt to answer the most frequently asked of these questions. It also includes some basic buying information (often, the reason people want to know about computers is so that they can buy the right one). More buying information can be found in the chapters on selecting and purchasing a personal computer.

To begin, allow me to quote a passage from the funniest letter I have ever received from a stranger:

> You live in Los Angeles? I used to live in Los Angeles. It was during World War II. My husband was there to establish a series of radar installations. We were speeding down the Pacific Coast Highway one night. My husband had to take a sighting of the North Star at a specific time. We were stopped by a policeman. "Go ahead and give me a ticket," my husband said, "but hurry—I've got to shoot Polaris." The cop looked at my husband funny, gave

him back his license and said, "Go ahead and shoot Phil Harris. I don't like him either."

And so, with a smile on our faces and a few basics under our collective belts, let's retire to the local pub for an informal after-class discussion, guided, as always, by the clear, white light of Polaris.

What's the difference between a PC, XT and an AT?

This has to be one of the most frequently asked questions. When IBM broke into the personal computer market in 1983, the company called its first machine the IBM PC. It came with 64K of Random Access Memory (RAM), upgradable to the then-whopping 256K of RAM. The PC used an 8088 CPU. When IBM threw a hard disk into the machine and tuned the computer a little, the company called its creation the IBM XT.

When a new generation of CPU was introduced, the 80286 (or 286 for short), a new generation of machine was developed for it at IBM. The machine was the IBM AT (for "Advanced Technology"). The AT ran almost 8 times faster than the PC or XT.

But microprocessor makers never rest, and since then, two more generations of CPU's (or **chips,** as they are often called) have appeared, the 80386 and the 80486. Computers using the 80386 chip run 15 to 20 times faster than the PC or XT—and the 80486, faster still. The newer the chip, naturally, the more expensive the computer.

I went into a computer store looking for a "PC" (my friend told me to look for "PC's") and before I knew it, the salesman was telling me about wait states and megahertzes and different kinds of chips. What the heck is all that stuff? What should I buy?

I understand your dilemma. Advertising has made big issues out of wait states and clock speeds (measured in megahertz) so that computer stores, too, have picked up on it.

Certain selling points in computers are overrated compared to other selling points. Wait states and clock speeds are two such overrated points.

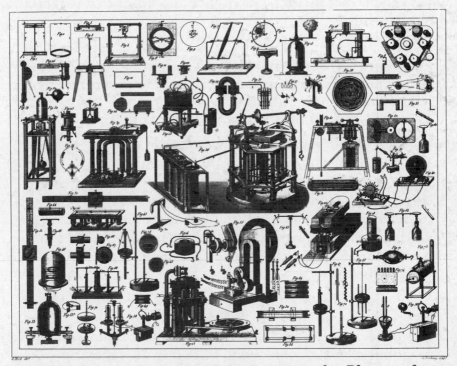

How every part of a personal computer works. Please refer to this diagram if you have any questions.

A **wait state** refers to a computer's internal circuitry as it relates to memory. Sometimes a computer's memory works faster than the rest of it. It's like a person whose thoughts whirl faster than his or her mouth. Out come non sequiturs. Wait states were invented for the memory to pause every now and then, so that the rest of the computer could catch up.

A computer with one wait state has one such beat, while two wait states indicate two beats. Computers with no wait states mean there are no pauses—the rest of the computer can keep up with the memory.

Clock speed refers to how fast a computer works. Computers do their work in clicks of a clock. This is rated in **megahertz**. (Just think of Ethel Mertz getting so large it hurts.) The higher the number, the faster the machine.

The original IBM PC's had a clock speed of 4.7 megahertz. The original IBM AT, a computer with a 286 chip, sped in at 6 megahertz. Now, 286 machines by a variety of manufacturers have clock speeds that are 10, 12, or more megahertz. As a rule of thumb, the faster the clock speed, the more you pay.

Clock speeds and wait states relate to each other. If the computer has a fast clock speed, but a slow everything else, then the overall speed of the machine is reduced. To give you a rough idea, a computer that runs at 10 megahertz with no wait states is roughly the same speed as another that runs at 12 megahertz with one wait state.

How fast a computer works also depends, to a great degree, on how fast the disk drive operates. (If the computer does not have a hard disk, then all the megahertz in the world won't keep things moving—because each time your computer accesses the floppy drive, it slows, on most machines, to a near halt—relatively speaking.)

Because hard disks are relatively inexpensive these days, most computers now have at least one. Hard disk access times are rated in milliseconds—28 milliseconds is a good, fast access time. The faster the access time, the faster the hard disk can work with the rest of the computer. Most people, in most uses, will never know the difference between 28 milliseconds and 60 milliseconds, so most people won't need to pay the difference. (Yes, of course: once again, the faster, the costlier.)

In sum, if you are concerned about speed, then the clock speed, wait states *and* hard drive are all important. The software program, Peter Norton Utilities, contains a utility called SI (System Information) which tests relative overall speed of computers, should you need to know. Most computer stores will have a copy of the program, and most mail order computer companies will tell you the "Norton Speed" of their various computers. (Make sure they tell you the speed *including* the hard disk.)

But speed is only critical for people with complex needs, such as massive spreadsheets or pages upon pages of desktop publishing. All other mortals will probably be quite happy with the less expensive "average" computers (which are light years faster than no computer at all).

Price, warranty, and the manufacturer should probably be higher on your list of questions than speed.

Do I need a hard disk when I buy a computer?

Back in the "old days" (the mid-eighties), getting a hard disk on a computer was an expensive option, $700 to $1,000 or more. It was a convenience, but, for most, not a necessity—two floppy drives were fine.

Nowadays, however, hard disks are so affordable—$200 to $300 more than a single floppy drive model—that you should seriously consider one. Not only are

"Since my baby left me,
Well, I've found a new place to dwell.
It's down at the end of Silicon Street
At Hard Disk Hotel . . ."

hard disks convenient and do they speed up computer operations, but also many new programs can only run on a hard disk. These new programs come not on a single floppy disk, but several. WordPerfect (a popular word processing program) comes on 12 disks, Ventura Publisher (a desktop publishing program) on 20, and Aldus PageMaker (another desktop publisher for the PC) on 20. Since these programs, and many more, can only run on a hard disk, the trend in software is toward hard-disk-required use.

What is DOS?

DOS stands for Disk Operating System, a set of programs that comes with most IBM-compatible computers. The basic function of DOS is to tell the computer how to store information on disks, and, equally important, how to find it again. DOS is also known as MS-DOS or, if it comes with a genuine IBM machine, IBM-DOS.

DOS—which rhymes with "dross"—also includes dozens of "utility" programs for doing a variety of "housekeeping" tasks around your computer.

The manual for DOS is less inviting than a telephone directory, and thicker than most. The manual (or "documentation" in Computerese) you can set aside. I suggest purchasing a book that puts the arcane DOS commands into relatively plain English.

Some of these commands you can avoid by using one of the DOS "shell" programs. These are programs that put a comfortable shell around DOS and keep its odd syntax at a safe distance. Two are WindowDOS and XTree. They simplify copying, deleting and renaming files—and so much more.

What's OS/2, and do I need it?

OS/2 is the next-generation operating system (Operating System/2) developed by Microsoft, the same people that gave us MS-DOS. (Every IBM-compatible computer has MS-DOS. If MS-DOS was written by Microsoft, can you guess what the MS stands for?) OS/2 was supposed to sweep the nation, but a few interesting factors are keeping its popularity at bay.

One is old-fashioned Future Shock. Computer advances spill weekly from Silicon Valley, and we, the computer users, are not keeping up. Too much, too soon. Intel, the company that developed the original 8088 processing chip for the IBM PC, has already developed the FOURTH generation processor, the 80486 chip. At the same time, Microsoft is still trying to peddle the second generation operating system (OS/2, to repeat myself). We, the computer users, however, basically find good old MS-DOS satisfactory. So many advances in technology are making buyers confused with too much of the new, and they're taking a "wait and see" attitude. Some call it Future Shock. I call it good buying practices, also known as common sense. Buy your first computer in haste. (*Any* computer is better than no computer.) But buy your *second* computer at leisure.

OS/2 offers multi-tasking: you can run two or more programs at once. OS/2 can also work with more memory, up to 16 megabytes (that's about 16,000K), while MS-DOS has a limit of 640K.

These nice features come at a price, of course. OS/2 requires *at least* a computer with a 286 chip. A 386 chip is recommended to use OS/2's full power. This means a more expensive computer. OS/2 is also, as they say, memory hungry. What MS-DOS would consider a generous repast—640K, say—OS/2 hardly considers an appetizer. When you invite OS/2 to dinner, think in *megabytes* of memory. Memory (RAM) is not as expensive as it once was—it is, in fact, relatively cheap these days. But extra cost is extra cost, and most don't need OS/2's power, so most are not using OS/2.

We old-time computer users have been pushing old MS-DOS to the limit, tricking it into using more than 640K of memory. We will need another operating system within a few years, one that lets us add more **memory resident programs** (programs that work from memory, not from a disk, making them instantly available for whatever instant tasks we ask them to perform) and whatever else we want to throw into our computers. That operating system will probably be OS/2. You can wait, there's no hurry. We'll all catch up eventually.

Sometimes when I am using my modem on my computer, I get disconnected. I happen to have call waiting on my telephone and was wondering if that might be affecting my modeming.

Indeed. If someone is trying to call you while you are modeming, call waiting's "beep" can cut off your transmission. I, too, found this out the hard way. One day I was modeming a file, and beep! I was disconnected from the distant computer.

With a few calls to the phone company, and several hours on hold (well, it *seemed* like several hours), I found a solution. If you're making a call that you don't want interrupted, first dial *70. You'll get another dial tone. Now dial your number and speak (or modem) undisturbed.

If you're wondering if the asterisk on your computer keyboard (just above the number 8) is the same as the asterisk on the telephone, it is. In my communication software (the program that "interfaces" between my computer, my modem and the other person's computer and modem), I preface all numbers I dial with *70. (I've tried this in California—I can only hope it works in Poughkeepsie and everywhere else. With deregulation, who knows . . . .)

When you hang up or place another call, call waiting goes back into being.

I was going to buy a FAX machine, but someone told me to buy a FAX card instead. Is it true? Can my computer FAX?

The facsimile (FAX) machine revolution has been swift and quiet. While many computer magazines and newspapers devoted much space to communication using modems, FAX appeared like a periscope at sea. I first became aware of its popularity when two people in one week asked me something I had never been asked before: what's my FAX number?

FAX cards install as would an internal modem. You simply insert the FAX board into a free **expansion slot** (an area inside a computer where various **expansion boards** or **cards** can be added—not as intimidating as it sounds, and most computer stores will install the boards at a nominal cost), plug in a phone cord, and finish setting it up using the installation software that comes with the board. Your computer will need nearly 400K of free memory, a hard disk and a **graphics adapter** (as the term implies, it adapts the computer to receive and store information as graphics—as opposed to text or numbers). Your computer will then read incoming FAXes as a graphics file. Your printer needs to be able to print graphics, which means you must have either a graphics-oriented dot-matrix printer or a laser printer with a lot of memory. If you want to send FAX's of signed documents, newspaper clippings and things you haven't typed into your computer, you'll need a scanner. In short, if you're set up for desktop publishing, you'll have what you need to FAX with your computer.

The problem with computer FAXing is size: the files created by the incoming FAXes are huge. A single-page letter, which takes up maybe 2K of room as a letter, consumes a whopping 30K of disk space as a FAX. A single page FAXed from afar with intricate graphics can take almost 100K!

This is because the incoming FAX is saved as a graphics file, not as a text file. (Graphics take up far more room than text.) The computer treats it as a graphics file, too: you can edit it with a graphics editing program, but you can't edit it with a word processor.

Once a FAX comes in, you can read it from your screen—but if you want to print it, plan to wait: it takes about five minutes per page—and that's on a laser printer. The good news is that it will print in the **background**; that is, while it is printing the FAXes, the computer (although not the printer) is free to do any other task.

The FAX board shines, however, when you are *sending*. You can FAX a memo in a matter of moments. If you have a letter going to a long list of recipients, the FAX board will send them, one after another, automatically—while you use your computer to do something else.

Dedicated FAX machines are the interim step between regular mail and electronic mail. People like the fact that they put paper in and take paper out. It's comforting. Reassuring. And dialing a phone number— well, that's American.

That offices word-process a letter, print it out, and FAX it to another office that also uses computers, I find amusing. It's not as wasteful as, say, typing a letter on a typewriter vs. word-processing a letter on a computer, but it's not necessary—except that FAXing is the standard of today, which makes it necessary.

How often should I clean the heads on my disk drives?

Oh, about as often as you wash your car. For heavy use, once a week is fine, but only if you don't have a hard disk. If you have a hard disk, and if you're like me, once every few months will have to do.

The only heads you clean are the ones on the floppy drives. Hard drive heads never actually touch the disk (they float a micromillimeter above the drive on the cushion of air produced by the hard drive's rapid rotation), so there's no need to clean them.

Floppy drive heads do touch the surface of the disk, so require occasional cleaning. If you have a hard drive, you probably don't use your floppy disk that often. In that case the heads, naturally, need to be cleaned less often. If you have a one- or two-floppy drive computer, frequent cleaning of the heads is essential.

Cleaning the heads on a disk drive is a simple, two-minute procedure. Head cleaning kits cost from $15 to $30. (The more expensive kits are usually not better, just more expensive.) One kit can clean heads dozens of times.

We have many power failures in this area (one last week for over four hours). What would happen in this case to a computer?

Disaster. Whatever was in the memory of the computer (RAM) would be no more. There are two solutions—although "preventatives" is a better word.

First, if you live in an area of occasional power failures or severe fluctuations (it takes only a second of reduced power to erase RAM), get into the habit of saving information onto your disk regularly.

Once information is on a disk, it's safe. Power failures do not affect disks. After the power is restored, you simply read the information from the disk back into the computer's memory and continue working.

If you have frequent power outages and fluctuations, or if you don't want to have the specter of no power dangling over your work, you'll probably want to invest in a back-up power supply.

These are battery packs that plug into the wall and automatically supply about five minutes' worth of electricity whenever the power goes out. These five minutes will provide you plenty of time to save what you have in memory onto disk.

This is not an inexpensive solution: about $500. A less expensive solution would be to buy a computer that can operate on DC (battery) current. (All laptop and most portable computers have battery options.) You can operate your computer from a battery all the time, using the AC (household) current to supply constant power to the battery.

When the power goes, you can light a candle and keep on computing, knowing you have an hour (or two hours, or whatever the life of the battery is) before you'll have to stop.

It gets hot here in the summer. Will I have to buy an air conditioner after I get a personal computer?

If you're asking me, get the air conditioner *before* getting a computer. I am of the opinion that air conditioning is a far more significant contribution to civilization than personal computers. But that belief comes from my disdain for temperatures above 70 and below 68.

The idea that computers need special humidity and temperature-controlled environments comes from the Old Days (say, twenty years ago) when computers were few and could afford to be prima donnas.

Today's personal computers are a hardy breed. In terms of heat, the general rule is that if you can stand it, the computer can stand it.

Naturally, as with any piece of electronics, keep your computer out of direct sunlight (even when not in use). Keep your disks out of direct sunlight, too. Disks are, in fact, far more susceptible to damage from heat than computers.

If it gets very hot where you live, check the maximum operating temperatures of disks and computers before you buy. If you're in doubt, buy an air conditioner. Not for your computer—for yourself.

I am a grandfather and my grandchildren have a computer. How can I prepare myself to understand and use a computer?

Bless your heart for even *wanting* to understand. It seems as though the old and the young are taking to computers like ducks to water. It's us middle-aged fuddy-duddys who are having all the trouble.

I think you have the finest resources available for understanding computers: your grandchildren. Sit down with them and their computer and get involved. Ask questions, try things out, have fun.

When I was young, I spent weekends with my grandmother helping her in her pizzeria. I remember those weekends as some of the most wonderful moments of my childhood.

Grandchildren and grandparents have a special bond, one which is strengthened by time spent together. So forget the computer books. Go visit your grandkids and learn how to play Donkey Kong. ("Donkey Kong?! Oh, Grandpa, nobody plays *that* anymore!")

I am retired and took a Community College beginners' course on computers about two years ago. The only familiar and interesting word I heard during the course was a homophone, which I assumed was a bawd, but disappointedly learned was a baud.

I know just how you feel. (**Baud,** by the way, is the speed at which something is transmitted from computer to printer or from modem to modem: the higher the baud, the faster. Hummm. Maybe baud and bawd have something in common after all.)

I am absolutely baffled by what is happening when I turn on ("boot up") my computer. I have to wait about 30 seconds as the machine prepares itself. Before I get my main menu, the screen is abuzz with activity, none of which I understand.

When you turn on an IBM or compatible computer, the machine automatically looks for information in the CONFIG.SYS and AUTOEXEC.BAT files.

"Say, what?"

Let's start at the beginning. When you turn on your computer, it has to "boot up." It searches for the operating system, MS-DOS. Once it has read DOS into its memory, the computer looks to see if you have two specific files: CONFIG.SYS and AUTOEXEC.BAT.

CONFIG.SYS is the machine's configuration file ("Configure System"). The machine looks to this file for special commands, such as, "Do you have any special equipment attached to your computer it would be good for your computer to know about?" It is a file you probably will never have to touch. If a word processing or other kind of program requires a CONFIG.SYS file, it will probably make one or adjust the one you have automatically. If your computer does not contain a CONFIG.SYS file, that's okay—you probably don't need it.

AUTOEXEC.BAT is a type of "batch" file. *("Auto*matically *Exec*ute this *Batch*" of commands to my computer.) Any series of commands that you want performed automatically every time you turn on your computer can be placed in the AUTOEXEC.BAT file.

If you almost always use your computer for word processing, for example, you can add the command that starts your word processing program in the AUTOEXEC.BAT file and, presto, whenever you turn on your computer, the word processing program of choice starts itself (or so it seems).

What are "expanded" and "extended" memory that I keep reading about in computer ads?

Most personal computers now sold come with a standard memory size (RAM) of 640K. Some models might have a little more or less. DOS, however, can use a maximum of 640K. This limit is also called **conventional** or **base memory.** If you are buying an IBM or compatible computer with more than 640K of RAM, you will not be able to use the extra memory without supplemental software.

Memory above 640K is called **extended memory.** The intent, originally, of extended memory was that software would be developed to use it.

Software developers found that creating programs to use the extended memory was risky. Why develop a program if no one had the extra memory in the first place? Because DOS did not normally address extra memory, the developers would have to fool the machine into using it, and someone needed to develop a standard.

It turned out that the giant companies of Lotus, Intel and Microsoft got together. Lotus and Microsoft said, "Let's create a standard. If people had extra memory to use, then we could make future versions of our spreadsheets, word processors and the like to use that extra memory," and Intel said, "And we can sell them the memory."

The standard they developed they called **expanded memory,** a term so close to "extended" as to be genuinely confusing—but that's what computer terminology is all about, isn't it? Their standard is also called the LIM Standard, for Lotus, Intel, Microsoft.

It turns out the three companies did a good thing, because more and more software developers have created software that can address expanded memory.

Many programs can work more quickly and efficiently with expanded memory.

If you put extra memory chips (yes, memory comes in chips, too) into your 286 or 386 computer, you only have "extended memory" for which there is little software. You need *expanded* memory, not *extended* memory. Fortunately, there are programs that turn extended memory into expanded memory, and do so without your even knowing about it. (Running one of these programs is an example of the sort of thing you can have AUTOEXEC.BAT do each time you start your computer.)

I just bought a computer (an AT compatible), and a friend gave me copies of his software. (Thank heavens—the computer was so expensive.) Should I feel guilty?

Should you feel guilty? Who do you think I am? Dear Abby? Father McWilliams? As my friend John-Roger often points out (usually to me), "I'm not the keeper of the 'shoulds.'"

I do, however, have a point of view.

You go to a computer store and see that computers cost, say, $2,000. For that, you could get five full-featured dishwashers, or 165 trips to a first-run movie theatre with a date, or a hell of a week in Hawaii (date optional). But you want *that* computer; you know it'll be great.

Then the salesperson asks with a smile, "What software would you like with that?" You mention word processing to start, and he suggests one of the popular programs which lists for around $500, but he'll sell it to you for $300. $300? That's one Sears dishwasher (on sale), or 25 trips to the movie theatre with a date, or a hell of a weekend at the local TraveLodge (date mandatory).

Then you start to get a little steamed. Did this salesperson apprentice at a used car lot? "You want this car with *wheels?*" Hey, at $2,000, computers should come with software!

Hardwares, softwares, who cares?

The salesperson makes it worse by mentioning a spreadsheet program, a data base program (for keeping lists) and a program for managing your money (that you now no longer have). How much is this $2,000 computer going to cost?

Your anger subsides when your friend leans over and whispers that he has software he'll *give* you . . . That's more like it. You'll show these overpriced computers a thing or two—you have *free* software. (Never mind that the software programmers have spent years toiling at designing their programs and that they don't work for the computer companies.) You will have your computer and the programs, too.

On the other hand, I realize buying software is akin to buying miracle health formulas. You hear the salesperson tout the benefits, and read ads that sound as though this program were written in Lourdes—but

until you use it, you won't discover how really good or, all too frequently, *bad* it really is.

In understanding all these points of view, I don't get upset when I hear that a friend has loaned a program to someone to try out. I do feel, though, that if you start using a program a lot, you should (oops! a "should"! I shouldn't do shoulds, should I?) pay the piper (or programmer) and buy a legal copy.

After all, the program is helping you be a better writer or accountant or whatever, and you should (all right, I confess: I'm addicted to shoulds) reward the people behind it. In addition, almost all software companies keep improving their programs and sell updates to registered users at quite reasonable prices. Lastly, as a registered user, you receive software support. When you have a question, you can call someone (sometimes for free, sometimes not). Frustration is common in learning a program; to be able to call someone and vent some of that—and learn a thing or two—is worth the price.

We'll have more questions, and gallant attempts at answers, at the end of other sections.

At this point in the book you can forge ahead and read it all, or you can skip ahead to the computer use you might find most suitable—business, word processing, desktop publishing, computers for people with disabilities, etc.

Or, if you already know how wonderful computers are for these things, you can go to the section on selecting and learning a PC.

Or, if you're like me, you can skip right to the section called *Utter Nonsense*.

The choice is yours. Enjoy.

PART II

The Personal Computer in Business

"And then we're going to put the printer over there in
that building. Would you like to see?"

Chapter 5

The Personal Computer in Business

Personal computers are the best thing to happen to business since, well, computers.

There is no doubt that big business is happily addicted to big computers. Each day, large computers in large businesses do the work of three *trillion* clerical workers. Three trillion. (A short while ago, most of us had no idea how large a trillion was. Thanks to the Pentagon, however, we're starting to get the idea.)

If those three trillion workers went on strike, that is, if someone pulled the plug on all the large computers, big business would not grind to a proverbial halt—it would stop cold.

But this is not a section about the slaughter of three trillion innocent workers (*The Day the Computers Stood Still);* it is a section about what the newest addition to the computer family, the personal computer, can do for your business.

No matter what size business you own or work for—large, small, and all points in between—you've probably wondered: Is a personal computer a worthwhile investment? This section will help you decide. (The answer, by the way, is likely to be "yes.")

The practical uses of personal computers in business are here today. They are powerful, dependable and inexpensive. In word processing, accounting, cost projection, inventory control and several other key areas of business, a personal computer will pay for itself in less than six months.

People ask, "Should I buy a personal computer for my business now, or should I wait?" That's like asking, "Should I buy today's newspaper, or wait for tomorrow's?"

Today's newspaper pays for itself today; tomorrow's pays for itself tomorrow.

Today's computer, used in business, pays for itself today. Tomorrow's computer will pay for itself tomorrow . . . and today's computer will still be on the job.

In the world of business, there's been nothing like the personal computer since the early 1950's, when the computer advances of World War II were finally made available to American business. The difference today is that personal computers are not just for big business, they're for every business. And personal computers can be something the big computers never were: fun.

Maybe we need a better analogy. "Personal computers are the best thing to happen to business since, well, computers" is a catchy opening line, but for a closing line, we need something more accurate.

We need to find an instrument that forever changed the face of business, yet was inexpensive enough for nearly every employee to have. A business tool that became so popular, every home eventually got one. A machine that sat on virtually every desk, and became so commonplace as to be ignored.

How about, "Personal computers are the best thing to happen to business since the telephone"?

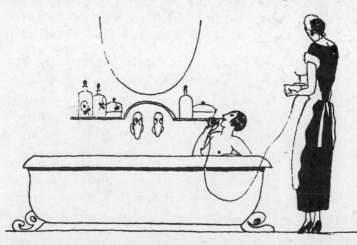

The Telephone of Tomorrow

Private business is always the pioneer, the trail-blazer and pathfinder—for government and public. And private business is making wide and clear the once hidden road to Tomorrow's Telephone—to the ultimate developement of wire communication—to the Automatic Telephone.

Business must avail itself of all things most efficient—of all things simple and sound to the core—of all things making for certainty, economy and high morale—in short of the best as soon as it appears.

Business cannot afford to do otherwise. That is why business in America—wherever that business is dealing with large problems and mighty forces—has blazed the way for Tomorrow's Telephone by investigating the Automatic, buying the Automatic, using the Automatic.

Governments abroad and at home are already traveling the clear road blazed by private enterprise.

England, France and Germany agree on this one point: That the Automatic Telephone must be used for government service because it is the type to which all telephones must eventually rise.

Our own War and Navy Departments, the United States Naval Torpedo Station, the fortifications at Sandy Hook, the Arsenal at Springfield, have used the Automatic Telephone for years and are each year adding to their equipment.

A few weeks ago the Federal Reserve Bank of New York bought the Automatic because the directors decided to transform their business telephones from a liability to an asset. They saw what many another great business has seen—that the Automatic Telephone is the only one giving 24-hour, 365-day secret service for a minimum labor and investment cost.

The Bethlehem Steel Company, the Alfred Du Pont Estate, the Tonopah Mining Company, Armour and Company, Mayo Hospital at Rochester, Minn., Sears, Roebuck and Company, The Great Northern Railway, the University of Chicago, the Baldwin Locomotive Works and hundreds of others have installed the Automatic Telephone and are constantly adding to the original installation.

Everywhere the signs read plain. Everywhere the trails and roads of telephony lead toward Tomorrow's Telephone, the Automatic. An unusually interesting and valuable booklet, "Your Telephone—Asset or Liability," has been prepared especially for the use of the executives of the larger business concerns and public institutions. A copy will be mailed on request.

*"The findings of the committee are unanimous,
Sir: If you want any more declarations, you'll
have to buy us a word processor."*

Chapter 6

Word Processing in Business

Someone once said, "If you're in business, you're a professional writer." There's a certain truth to that.

Consider, for a moment, the importance of the written word in business: letters, memos, reports, contracts, catalogs, brochures, notices, newsletters—the list goes on. (Did I mention lists?) Numbers may be important for keeping score, but you wouldn't know which score belonged to which team if it weren't for words.

Businesses are made up of people, and people communicate using words. The mastery of words can make the difference between a sale and no sale, between a raise and no raise, between a negotiated settlement and a court battle, between credit and no credit, between well-informed employees and my employees, between clarity and confusion, between communication and misunderstanding.

As you probably already know, word processing uses a computer's power to store and manipulate information. Rather than writing or typing directly onto a

piece of paper, you enter the words, through the keyboard, directly into the computer. They are displayed on the video screen, and can be moved about, changed, deleted, and added to at will.

Only after the text has been corrected, revised, and considered perfect does the printer "type" the processed product on paper. If the printed copy indicates the text was not all that perfect, changes can be made and another copy printed.

Before I get caught up reinventing the wheel here, let me direct you to the next section of this book, (PART III), which is entirely devoted to word processing, especially the chapter on word processing in the office.

Know for now that word processing alone would justify the purchase of a personal computer for almost any business. But there's more, lots more, a personal computer will do for business, and that's what the following chapters will discuss.

113

An Ode to Accountancy, prepared for us by Gerald B. Mellon, C.P.A.

Chapter 7

Accounting

Whatever personal analogy you use for business, accounting is essential. If business is a game, accounting is a way of keeping score. If business is a matter of life and death, accounting tracks the vital signs.

In the 1950's, computers and accounting took to each other like ducks to drakes (as Quentin Crisp would say). The data processing department owned The Computer, and all it wanted to do with The Computer was accounting. For a while, it looked as though it would have its way. But word processing snuck in here, cost projection crept in there, and soon the monogamy was over, although the computer-accounting love affair continued.

The speed and efficiency with which personal computers handle the accounting needs of some small-to-moderate-sized companies is nothing short of amazing. As they did to slide rules, computers make general ledger books a thing of the past.

Personal computers work best when information must be figured, refigured, shuffled around, and figured again. Sound like the way numbers work (or you wish they would work) in your company?

Take invoicing, for example. To write an invoice manually means a certain amount of calculation, looking up of information, and repetitive typing. On a computer, the figuring and looking-up takes place automatically, and the repetitive typing is eliminated.

On a computer, the date is added to the top of the invoice automatically. Your computer knows the date and time because you either typed in the information when you turned on your computer, or your computer has a **clock-calendar** (a chip that remembers the time and date and tells your computer that information whenever asked). For your invoice, you don't have to type that information at all.

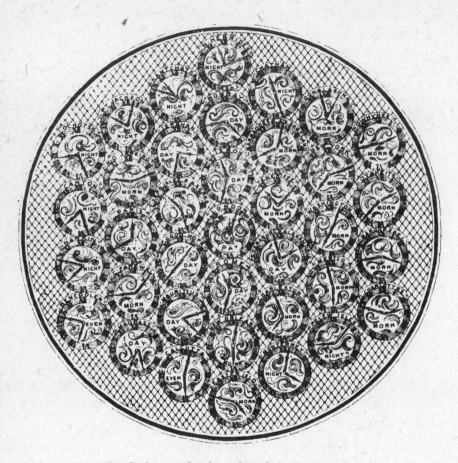

Disk for a clock-calendar program.

In computerese, anything that is set like this is known as a **default** or the **default value**. The date can be changed, of course, by simply typing over the defaulted date.

Each customer is assigned an identification code (either a name, number, or combination of the two; it's your choice). By entering the code, the computer automatically adds the customer's name, address, zip code, other shipping information, discount schedule, payment terms, sales tax (if they are subject to sales tax), and any other information you entered when you set up the customer account.

Each item in your inventory is also assigned a code (again, any collection of letters and/or numbers.) To add an item, all you need enter is the item's code. The retail price, extended retail price, and discounted price are automatically displayed. You continue entering product codes and numbers of products ordered until the order is complete.

With the push of a button (maybe two), the invoice is calculated, tax and shipping (if applicable) added, and a grand total arrived at. When printed, a packing list and shipping label can be generated along with the invoice.

It's obvious how much time this would save a company that does a fair amount of invoicing. With a manual invoice, the keystrokes can be measured in the thousands. With a computer-written invoice, the keystrokes can be measured in the dozens. And as all calculating is done by the computer, your company saves time *and* errors.

But that's just the beginning. The time saved when various accounting programs (accounts payable, accounts receivable, invoicing, inventory, general ledger) are linked together is even more impressive.

When computer programs work together and share information, they are known as **interactive.** If the invoice above were part of an interactive accounting system, the following could take place while the invoice was being written:

• When the customer code is added, the program checks with the accounts receivable program. Is the account past due on a previous order? Does this invoice bring them over their credit limit? If so, the computer will beep and let you know.

• When the code is entered, the computer checks with the inventory program to see if the items are in stock. It's easier to back order when the original invoice is being written.

• If the items are in stock, the computer removes them from the inventory records. No need to post them later. It will also let you know, while entering the invoice, when you fall below minimum stock levels, and when it's time to reorder.

• The sales of all items are listed, both in dollar amounts and number of units sold.

• Any sales tax collected is added to a special tax account. When it's time to pay the State what you've been collecting for it, you'll know exactly how much.

• The invoice information can be posted to the general ledger.

All this activity, which would take eight or more steps with traditional bookkeeping, takes place inside the computer automatically. (I somehow want to say "magically.")

Here are some thoughts on accounting with personal computers:

1. The first person to talk to is your accountant. He or she may or may not know much about computers,

but your accountant knows accounting, and your accountant knows your business.

Tell your accountant you're thinking about buying a computer, and ask if he or she thinks your accounting needs would be served with one. Every good accountant I've talked to will read at least one book on personal computers before giving an answer.

Your accountant may have an accounting package he or she has tried, uses, and recommends.

The descriptive literature from companies that publish accounting software is usually bilingual: it is written in computerese and in accountancy. Ask your accountant to translate it into English for you.

2. Accounting software is often the most intricate, expensive, and difficult set of programs you can buy. The quality of accounting programs varies enormously, as does the price. (A complete set of interactive programs can cost $99 or $4,000; specialized programs—medical accounting software, for example—can cost even more.)

Take your time selecting and purchasing accounting software. If you're in a hurry to save money, it could cost you a lot.

3. There may be accounting software written especially for your kind of business. This is known as **vertical market** software. Sometimes it's advertised in whatever trade journal covers your business, or you might check with your national trade association.

Some of this software is good (medical billing will fill out all insurance forms, for example), and some is ordinary accounting software with some module names changed to confound the innocent. Ask for a list of businesses using a specific manufacturer's software and give them a call.

4. If you want a full set of interactive accounting software, it's a good idea to start with the general ledger module. Narrow your general ledger choices to the ones that (A) meet your current and projected accounting needs, and (B) have a complete set of integrated accounting modules.

From your narrowed list, look next at the accounting module you'll use most: accounts receivable, accounts payable, inventory, etc. (Invoicing programs are sometimes incorporated in accounts receivable programs, and sometimes not.) The power, features, and ease of use of these modules can vary dramatically from manufacturer to manufacturer.

This should narrow your list even more. Then look at the power and features of the other modules. This should eliminate a few more. Throughout all this, keep in touch with your accountant.

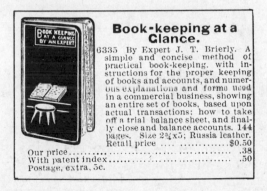

Book-keeping at a Glance.

6335 By Expert J. T. Brierly. A simple and concise method of practical book-keeping. with instructions for the proper keeping of books and accounts, and numerous explanations and forms used in a commercial business, showing an entire set of books, based upon actual transactions: how to take off a trial balance sheet, and finally close and balance accounts. 144 pages. Size 2¾x5; Russia leather. Retail price $0.50
Our price.. .38
With patent index........./................... .50
Postage, extra, 5c.

Of the remaining contenders, rate them according to three factors: (1) ease of learning, (2) ease of use, and (3) support. Let's look at each individually:

• **Ease of learning.** Does the program follow standard bookkeeping formats? Will you, or the person who keeps your books, be able to go from paper to disk easily? ("Easily" is not the right word. It will not be easy. "Without major trauma" is the most one can hope for.)

• **Ease of use.** Even more important than ease of learning is ease of use. Do all the programs interact smoothly? Is entering information easy? (Yes, here it should be easy.) Are the programs flexible enough to meet the specific needs of your business? Does the fact that it was easy to learn make it, once learned, difficult to use?

• **Support.** Is there a phone number you can call when you need help or have questions? (Yes, you will need help, and yes, you will have questions.) If so, try calling it. Is the line always busy? Is this help free and unlimited? If not, can help be purchased? (Unless he or she keeps the store's books on the program, the salesperson at the computer store will probably not be able to provide the detailed, expert advice you will need.)

5. If the program has monumental bugs, or does not meet your accounting needs, can it be returned for a refund, or at least full credit toward another accounting program?

6. Safe accounting practice dictates that you keep dual books for at least six months. This is "just in case." (See *The Drawbacks of Personal Computers* chapter of this book.) The idea is to go through at least two quarterly periods, compare the electronic books with the paper books, and make sure they are *the same*.

If you get through two quarters and the paper matches the electronic, then you can safely retire the paper (or the electronic, if everyone finds the "old way" better).

If the books do not match, find out why, correct the error(s), and go through two more quarters. (If your accounting needs are slim, and your accountant approves, you might want to try three month-end comparisons and one quarterly, and if all four match, change over then.)

This means you should not look for accounting on personal computers to save you either time or money for at least six months. It will, in fact, cost you more to keep a double set of books than to keep the single set you already have.

7. Back up accounting data regularly. (See *The Drawbacks of Personal Computers* chapter of this book.)

8. Remember that accounting software will not solve all your problems, that compromises will have to be made, and that panaceas went out with Greek mythology.

Personal computers offer the small business-person, for the first time, the accounting power that big businesses have had for forty years. A few dozen of those terribly inexpensive three trillion clerical workers can now come to work for you.

Chapter 8

Spreadsheets and Graphics

One of the primary reasons personal computers have achieved the degree of acceptance they have in business, especially big business, is electronic spreadsheeting.

Spreadsheeting has been an essential part of financial decisions for decades. The electronic adding machine made it easier. The pocket calculator made it portable. (It was hard to fly in the mid-1970's without seeing at least three or four young executives, hunched over their legal pads, calculating away.)

In the late 1970's, VisiCorp introduced a $200 program, VisiCalc, that allowed a $2,300 Apple computer to do something very few $1,000,000 mainframes could do: spreadsheeting. If one variable in the spreadsheet changed, all the related variables would change— instantly, electronically, automatically.

It was astounding. Hours—days—of figuring reduced to seconds. Managers, decision makers, and cost projectors across the country snapped up Apples with VisiCalc—as well as other personal computers running the VisiCalc imitators, dubbed VisiClones.

Today, VisiCalc is all but forgotten, and a more powerful breed of computers and financial projection programs continues to revolutionize the way business decisions are made. (Even the most novice of computer novitiates knows that 1-2-3 is a computer program—it's the most popular of the IBM-based electronic spreadsheets.)

For those who do not know what spreadsheeting is, electronic or otherwise, allow me this brief explanation.

Spreadsheets are made up of rows and columns of numbers. If you were figuring a profit-and-loss statement by month, each month's figures (sales, cost of goods, overhead, etc.) would be a vertical column. The individual items would be horizontal rows. Some items in each row would be fixed costs, such as rent, and some would be variables, such as commissions.

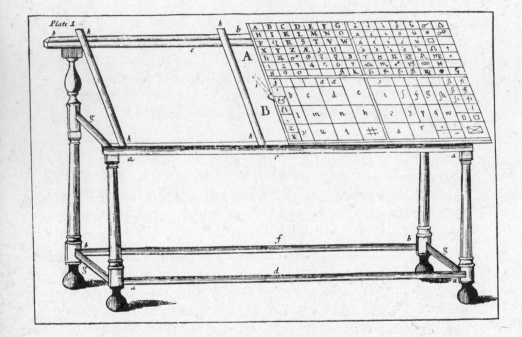

Once these figures were entered into a computer, the program could answer an infinite number of "What if?" questions: "What if the growth trend from last year continued for the next six months?" "What if we increased salaries by 10%?" "What if the cost of goods increased by 2%, but sales increased by 4%?" And so on.

Electronic spreadsheets are helpful when deciding at what point a project will become profitable. "How many improved widgets will we have to sell before the improvements are paid for?"

In the film, *Catch-22,* Milo Minderbinder explains that he is making a fortune buying eggs at three cents each and selling them for two cents each. "How can you possibly make money buying eggs at three cents each and selling them for two cents each?" someone asks. "Volume," Milo responds knowingly.

An electronic spreadsheet could tell Milo just how much volume he'd need before turning a profit.

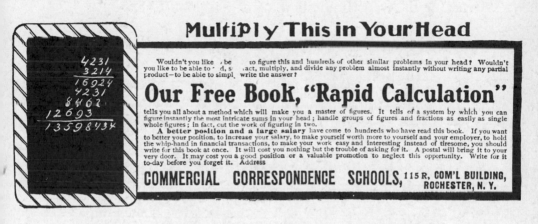

Graphics

Of course, rows and columns of numbers are impressive to those who work with rows and columns of numbers. But what happens when you want to impress clients, backers, bosses, and the rest of the world?

That's where statistical graphics come in.

What once took art departments hours to create, personal computers can draw in seconds. Pie charts, bar graphs, sales curves—all the standard visual presentations business uses to illustrate numbers.

Just enter the data, and the personal computer will draw a pie or a graph or a curve on the screen. Push a button, and the printer will print it. Most programs allow you to use the data already entered in the electronic spreadsheet.

Computers can do other kinds of graphics, too. Designers, architects, engineers, and manufacturers find personal computers invaluable. A widget can be examined from all angles, for instance, modified, put through various tests, corrected, and tested again, all inside the computer. The specifications for the New Deluxe Wonder Widget can be printed out, along with a drawing of what the little marvel will look like.

CPU at work: "Get that bar graph to the screen right away. They're waiting for it up in sales."

Weeks, perhaps months, of drawings, prototypes, tests, and "back to the drawing board" are reduced to an afternoon in front of a video screen. This is performed with **CAD-CAM software** (Computer Aided Design–Computer Aided Manufacturing).

Since the rise and shine of desktop publishing, pictures and drawings can be created or scanned, then edited, sized, otherwise manipulated and dropped into the text. (Any kind of illustration done on computer, by the way, is called a **graphic.**) We'll peek in on this kind of graphic later when desktop publishing is discussed in Part IV.

"We sure could use a data base, Leo."

Chapter 9

Data Bases

A data base is a collection of information (a *base* of *data*). Data base management programs allow you to call up pieces of that information, at various times and in various orders.

Let's assume, for example, that you have 10,000 accounts spread across the country. If you were to put all of your customers' names, addresses, and sales histories on one long sheet of paper, you would have a list. It might be in alphabetical order, or arranged by state, amount of spending, value of the Christmas card they sent last year, or by any other variable.

This list would be valuable (it's good to know who your customers are), but limited. What if you wanted to find all your customers in Cleveland? If the list were in alphabetical order, it would take some searching. And the longer the list, the more searching it would take.

If, however, you were to put these customers into a computer, under the control of a data base management program, you could ask for all customers in alphabetical order. You could ask for them in zip code order. You could ask for your top 25 customers in sales. You could ask for your 100 fastest paying customers. Or you could ask for all your customers in Cleveland.

Any piece of information in your data base is known as a **variable** (first name, last name, company name, address, city, state, zip, favorite color, etc.). When you ask the program to look for a variable, this is called a **search.** When it rearranges the order of variables, it's called a **sort.** It's this ability to search and sort variables that turns a list into a data base. (And turns a data base into any number of lists.)

But the real power of data base management comes when you *combine* searches and sorts. You can ask for all your accounts in Cleveland rated by sales volume. You can ask for your best paying Minnesota accounts in zip code order. You can ask for all accounts with more than $1,000 in sales last month, except those in Minnesota and Cleveland, listed in alphabetical order.

It's this type of activity—searching and sorting—to which computer advocates like to point when touting the computer's superiority over humans. They argue:

A personal computer can sort a list of 10,000 names and addresses into zip code order in from one to ten minutes (depending on the computer). It can take the same list and re-sort it into alphabetical order in one to ten minutes. It can separate by state, and list alphabetically within each state in one to ten minutes.

"Ignorance is bliss."

A total of three to thirty minutes. "Can you imagine how many days—weeks—these three tasks would take a human?" the advocates ask.

That's true, but in most companies, extensive sorting and searching does not go on all that often: it's too time consuming and too expensive. A personal computer will not *save* you weeks of time, but it can *provide* you with weeks of time.

As a manager, you might have wondered who your top ten accounts in Cleveland were. You know the top one or two, but who's number eight? If your accounts receivable list is in alphabetical order, you might have decided that the hours of work necessary to separate the Cleveland accounts from all the other accounts, then to rank those accounts in sales-volume order, was not worth the time. (Especially if you had to do it yourself.)

If, however, the answer to this question could be had within ten minutes, and during nine of those ten minutes you or your workers were free to do something else, you might decide to satisfy your curiosity. It may produce some valuable results. (Maybe the top one and two are not one and two after all.) The investment of time is minimal, so the payoff need not be that great.

Once the data has been searched out, selected and sorted, the information can be used with other computer programs (providing, of course, you bought compatible programs). The data could be used with the word processing program, for example, to send personalized form letters. (You may want to keep in touch with your fastest—and slowest—paying accounts.) Or it could be entered into a spreadsheet of who buys what when.

Any kind of information can be entered into a data base. The data base program you get should reflect the kind of information you want to manage, and the way you want to manage it.

Precise, predictable facts make up one kind of data base. An address file is a good example of this. A last name is always a last name, and it's correctly spelled only one way; a zip code is a zip code is a zip code.

These data bases file the variables in a particular order. In our mythical data base of 10,000 customers, the second variable in the file is *always* the last name, the eighth variable in the file is *always* the zip code, and so on. These are known as **fields.** If someone's zip code is not known, that field is left blank.

When you search through this data base and ask the program to find someone by the last name of "Schwartz," the program looks in the second field of variables until all the Schwartzes are found.

What happens, though, if you want to put a series of quotations into a data base, or a collection of photographs? Here you need a data base that stores information in a different way.

Some programs let you create fields of any length. The words that you place in a field do not have to be in any particular order.

For example, you might create a data base of your photographs. "Photo #1256" might have such special comments as "waterfall, Canada, color, nature," and hundreds more, all placed in random order. Any time you ask for photos of a waterfall, or scenes of Canada, or a shot of nature, "Photo #1256" would be listed.

As in other good data bases, you can also combine key words. Only those bits of information that match all categories will appear.

If you were a classical music buff and entered your record, CD and cassette collections into a data base, the program could tell you how many hundred recordings of Beethoven's Fifth Symphony you had by your simply typing "BEETHOVEN" and "FIFTH SYMPHONY." The several you might have by Toscanini could be found

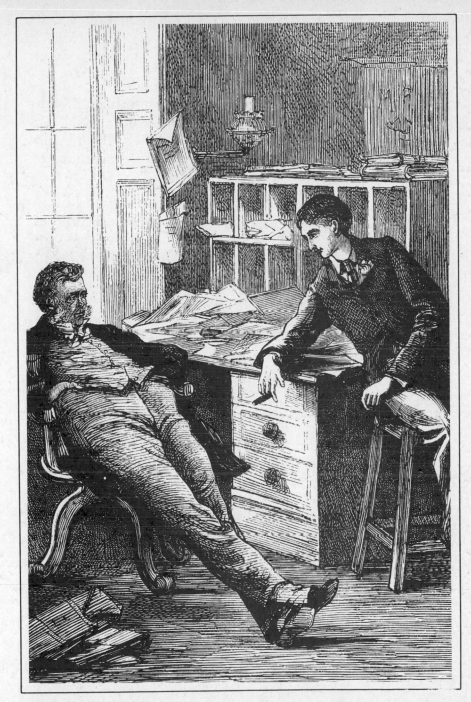

"Some guy told me he could install a data base management system. I wrote his name down somewhere, but I can't seem to find it."

by typing in "BEETHOVEN" and "FIFTH SYM-PHONY" and "TOSCANINI."

You could ask the program to search through your electronic address book and find all of your FRIENDS living in CLEVELAND who own a COMPUTER. Only those entries with the key words "friends," "computer" and "Cleveland" would be presented.

Because your fields can contain one bit of information, or many bits, this type of data base can combine both objective and subjective labels. In other words, you can have strict or less-than-strict fields with varying types of information.

Database programs are marketed under a variety of names. The title, or description, usually has something to do with "data management," "resource control," or "information manipulation."

Some are general, all-purpose data bases; others use the search and sort functions for specific purposes, such as filing programs, sorting programs, and mailing-list programs.

The more powerful and flexible a program is, the longer it takes to master, and the more disk space it will require. If your data base requirements are simple mailing list management, that can be done with a far smaller investment of time, money and disk space than an ultra-powerful program. If, on the other hand, you need many variables relating to many other variables from several different areas of your business (and/or life), then the investment of time and money in a full-scale data base program has its rewards.

The most powerful data base programs are called **relational** because you can interconnect separate data bases to each other. For instance, you might have an address data base and an accounts-payable data base. You might also have an invoice data base. With a relational data base program, if you look up Herbert Hoover in the address data base, you can, in one keystroke, also zoom into the other data bases to see if he turns up there, too. (And if he does, your accounts receivable are in enormous need of updating.)

Data bases that can search using the operating words AND, OR and NOT are deemed to have **Boolean search** (named after George Boole, a 19th-century mathematician). Not everyone needs Boolean search, but for large data bases (over a few thousand records), the ability to say AND, OR and NOT helps pinpoint your searches.

We live in an information age, and the ability to manipulate and manage information in this age is power.

"I put all my papers on a disk so I could find everything, and now I can't find the disk."

Chapter 10

Information Services

Money banks store money and information services—once known as data banks—store data.

Information services have large computers that store large amounts of information. The companies that maintain these banks of information charge by the hour to "access" their data. (Computerese believes that all nouns are really closet verbs, desperately seeking liberation.)

You connect your personal computer to the large computer through a modem and a telephone line. As discussed previously, the modem translates your computer's signals into little beeps and boops that can be sent over phone lines. A modem at the other end retranslates the beeps and boops into signals the other computer can understand.

Modems for personal computers are available in three popular speeds: 300, 1200 and 2400 baud (and soon, 9600 baud will be affordable). One baud is one bit per second. A 300-baud rate would send information at 300 bits per second, or roughly 30 characters per second. (In telecommunication, a blank space counts as a character.) A 1200-baud modem operates four times as fast, about 120 characters per second, and a 2400-baud modem at about 240 characters per second. Because the cost of modems has dropped so much in the past few years, few people bother with a 300-baud modem anymore; 1200 is an economical choice.

Because information services charge five to several hundred dollars per hour, a 2400-baud modem might well be worth the investment if you plan to access a lot of information from these services. When you consider what you'd be paying someone to sit patiently

The Source and CompuServe—two popular data banks.

while a slower modem casually chatted with this distant computer, and when you consider the amount of extra time a "company computer" is tied up, then 2400 baud seems the only way to go for business telecommunicating. (A 2400-baud modem will communicate with 1200-baud modems just fine—at 1200 baud, of course.)

Information services offer a wide variety of groupings—also known as data bases—several of which are almost certain to be of value to your business. Here are just a few of the categories available.

• **Stock market quotations.** Some services offer up-to-the-minute quotes; others are on 15-minute delay. Up-to-the-minute costs more. (So what else is new?) Some services let you place buy-and-sell orders from your computer.

• **Stock information.** News that might affect stocks, stock histories, background information, and so on. One rates 4,000 stocks by performance in 58 categories (earnings per share, P/E ratios, etc.). Also, information on commodities, bonds, money markets, metals, government paper, commercial paper, fly paper (airline loans), and more.

• **AP and UPI Newswires.** Stories are available minutes after being filed. Read Thursday's column on Tuesday. Check the weather at your destination. Find out the details of a late-breaking story even before Dan Rather.

• **Newspapers.** Special editions of *The Wall Street Journal, The St. Louis Post-Dispatch,* and others. Also, complete editions (except crosswords, weather, stock market quotations, and horoscopes) of *The New York Times, The Wall Street Journal, The Washington Post,* and *The Christian Science Monitor,* among others.

• **Newsletters.** Thousands of dollars' worth of newsletters for the price of online time.

• **Magazines.** Abstracts from *Time, Newsweek, Motor Trend, Forbes, Harvard Business Review, Venture,* and over 500 other popular and business journals. You can search any of these using key words. (All articles containing "GOLD" and "BUSH," for example, can be found.) In one service, issues from 1959 on are available. Complete articles can be mailed to you, or sent immediately via FAX machine. Also available are key word searches through more than 150,000 *Barrons* and *Wall Street Journal* articles dating back to 1979. Some services offer the full text of *Consumer Reports* and other magazines.

• **Travel.** Make, check, or confirm airline, hotel, car-rental, and other reservations.

• **Health information.** Both emergency and non-emergency information of a medical nature.

• **Business information.** General news and its effect on business. News about business. Press releases from major corporations.

• **Legislation.** Information on legislation that might affect business or stocks.

• **Agriculture.** Comprehensive index to worldwide sources of information on agriculture and other related topics, including nutritional research, animal studies, botany, forestry, and more.

• **Calculations.** Use the programs at the information service to amortize mortgages, calculate compound interest, work out loan repayment schedules, and so on.

• **Encyclopedias.** Both the *World Book* and *Academic American* Encyclopedias are online. You can search by using one or two key words. "PETROLEUM" would list all articles with the word "petroleum" in them. "PETROLEUM and MEXICO" would list only articles with both words.

142

• **Research.** In addition to the encyclopedias and magazines listed above, a vast array of other research resources are available from specialized information services. These data banks, once available only to professional researchers and corporate librarians, are now available to all.

• **Wall Street Week.** Complete transcripts of the four most recent PBS shows.

- **Yellow pages.** Scans over two million listings from 4,800 phone directories. Don't quite remember in what city the Ajax Cement & Monument Company is located? This will tell you, along with the address and phone number.

- **Books in print.** Subject, author and title of every book the R. R. Bowker Company can track down. Search for the book you want by any of the three classifications: author, title or subject. You can also find out the title and location of any book in the Library of Congress (from 1897 to present, give or take a few months.)

- **Biography.** Information on more than 2,000,000—count 'em—2,000,000 famous people. I didn't know there *were* 2,000,000 famous people. Could you be one of them? ("Rittenhouse, Henry Paul; Assistant Sales Manager, World Wide Wickets, 1979 to present. Born of humble origins in Cleveland, Ohio . . .")

- **Career placement.** Students and experienced personnel place their resumes in the data bank, and personnel directors look at them. Object: employment.

- **Statistics.** Data on industrial production, labor force, food consumption, and other statistical information from 130 countries.

- **Magill's Survey of Cinema.** Complete text articles covering over 800 notable films and brief entries for thousands more.

- **The Bible.** Includes the complete text of the modern-day revision of the 1769 edition of the King James version. If you need to search for a Biblical quote, this is one way.

- **Advertisements.** A listing of all ads, one-quarter page or larger, appearing in 148 U.S. consumer magazines. Who placed more, Wheaties or Cheerios?

• **Science, math, etc.** Heavy-duty medical, chemical, engineering, physics, astronomical, electrotechnical, etc., journals. Also, millions of patent abstracts.

• **The Government.** Everything you want to know about Federal Government: bills pending, Senate hearings, government publications (over 100,000), court decisions, executive orders, *The Congressional Record* and, yeah, once again, *The Washington Post.*

• **Dissertations.** Get this: A complete listing of every American dissertation accepted by every accredited university since 1861. Imagine what this information will do for your company's sales! This alone is worth the price of a computer.

Information services are also helpful in electronic mail and teleconferencing, which are discussed in the next chapter.

The above is a small sampling from the smorgasbord offered by data banks, and more services are being added daily.

For more information on information services and telecommunication in general, let me recommend *The Complete Handbook of Personal Computer Communications—The Bible of the Online World* by Alfred Glossbrenner, and his equally helpful *How to Look It Up Online.* They both give a clear, concise, amusing view of how to get computers to talk to each other, and the value humans can gain from that interaction. (St. Martin's Press, New York; 800-221-7945.)

You can also contact the information services directly. (Addresses and phone numbers of the major ones are listed in Glossbrenner's books.) Most will send you full-color brochures designed to convince you that your life up to this point has been somehow incomplete, and wholeness can only be found when your computer is attached to their computer. There are religious overtones to some of these presentations. Read Mr. Glossbrenner for a more balanced view.

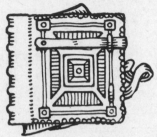

The power of information services can be brought home even without a modem. With a CD ROM player, you can have hundreds of megabytes of information all on a compact disc. Yes, the same laser technology that brings you your favorite music on CD's and your favorite films on laser discs can be part of your computer.

One of the most popular programs on CD ROM disk is the Groiller *American Academic* Encyclopedia. (And the complete encyclopedia uses only one-quarter of the capacity of one disk!) CD ROM, although heavily laden with potential, is still in its infancy. This is because the drives and the disks remain relatively expensive.

The *American Academic* Encyclopedia is fun. You can search all entries in the encyclopedia by a single word or collection of words. "WAR" and "CIVIL" would get you all entries on civil wars of any kind. "WAR" and "CIVIL" and "UNITED STATES" would get you all articles on civil wars in which the United States was involved.

I used it to help research a book on strokes. In addition to basic information of the medical kind (the kind I was looking for), there were articles on two and four stroke engines, golf strokes, tennis strokes and calligraphic strokes. I also noticed that the encyclopedia's writer on American history was more than partial to the phrase, "With one stroke . . . ", as in, "With one stroke, Jefferson's purchase of the Louisiana

territory more than doubled the size of the United States."

The value of this search was surprising. It listed, for example, people (famous and less so) who at some time in their lives suffered a stroke. The word "stroke" was in the encyclopedia entries on their lives (Walt Whitman, for example, or Louis Pasteur), and the CD ROM program found it. The medical section on strokes might never have mentioned it, and to visually peruse every biographical entry in the encyclopedia would have taken weeks. It would, in fact, not have been worth doing. But I'm glad I have that list of names.

The speed with which the CD ROM goes through the text, lists all articles with the key word(s) in them, and displays the first article is remarkable: a matter of seconds. Going from one article to the next takes a second, maybe two at the most. Text can be read on a screen, sent to a printer, or sent to a regular floppy or hard disk file. There it can be edited using a word processor and incorporated into other text. It's a great (and fun) research tool, and heralds the future of "personal" information storage and retrieval.

The World Book is also available on CD ROM in a package called Information Finder. It has all the features of the *American Academic,* plus an on-line dictionary. Puzzled about a word in the text? Put the cursor over the word, touch a button, and the definition appears.

The full text of many newspapers and magazines is available on CD ROM disks, as is *The Chicago Manual of Style,* unabridged dictionaries and more. For another look at CD ROM, please have a look at the chapter, *A Research Library Etched by a Laser*, in the next section (*Word Processing*).

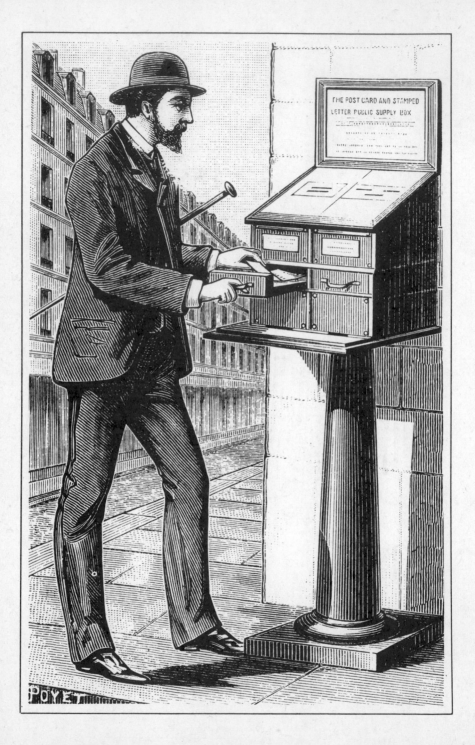

Chapter 11

Electronic Mail and Teleconferencing

Electronic mail can get a letter across the country in seven seconds, not seven days. All it takes is two personal computers, two communication programs, two modems, and two telephone lines.

A modem will send and receive an average letter in less than a minute. Many modems now come with **auto-dial** and **auto-answer** capabilities. With one of these modems at each end, one computer will automatically dial the other, make a connection, transmit the letter, and hang up in less time than it would take to address an envelope.

At the receiving end, the letter is stored on a disk. It can either be read from the screen, or printed out and read on paper. (I find reading anything longer than a one-page letter on a video screen tedious. This applies only to new information: I don't seem to mind the screen at all while word processing.)

Some computers can receive mail while they're in use. Others can be set to send out letters after hours,

when the computers are not in use, and when telephone rates are lowest. (Like a FAX, the only real cost in sending electronic mail is telephone time.)

Subscribers to The Knowledge Index and Compu-Serve (two popular data banks) can leave electronic mail for any other subscriber by simply knowing his or her identification number. MCI Mail and Easy Link are two services devoted entirely to electronic mail. You can reach other members either with their number or by typing their name. All services charge for electronic mail, but the call is local on both ends.

If the recipient of your message does not have a computer, or does not have compatible communications software, or does not check his or her electronic mailbox regularly, personal computers can help speed the message in a more traditional way. Mailgrams, FAXes, telexes and plain ol' letters can be sent using the services. For the latter, they print, stamp and post your letter. (It costs about $2, but it's mighty convenient.)

Teleconferencing

Teleconferencing allows anyone with a personal computer to join in a conference. Conferences can either happen in "real time," or over a period of time.

Real time conferences mean that all participants are online at the same time. Someone types something in, and everyone reads and responds. This sort of "meeting" has certain advantages over traditional face-to-face encounters.

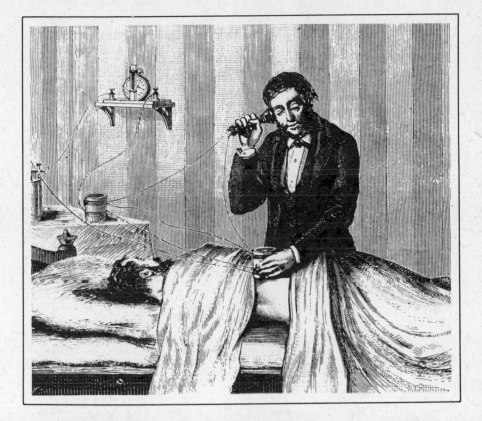

"Hello, Ma? This is Alex. Yeah, the new phone works just fine. We have a few bugs to take care of, but Watson and I are working on those right now. Talk to you later. Bye!"

First, it can happen over long distances. No need to fly everyone in, or arrange for elaborate phone connections. (With phone conferences, the value tends to decrease and the confusion tends to increase with the addition of each new participant.)

Second, everything said is on record, word-forword. No more, "What I said was..." or "If you'll recall, that idea was mine."

Third, participants who tend to be long-winded and dominate meetings will have to learn either speed-typing or how to condense their comments. (The latter, one hopes.) Conversely, participants who sit back in meetings due to shyness or fear of public speaking, tend to be more active when there's only a video screen and a keyboard to face.

Finally, teleconferencing slows the pace of a meeting, so that participants have time to think about what's being "said," and consider responses more carefully before making them.

In addition to real time conferences, there are conferences that take place over time. Participants log on at any time, read what's been said since their last log on, make whatever comments they have, and sign off. Before signing off, a copy of what's transpired thus far can be placed on disk for future reference.

This system is particularly good for product development, brainstorming, troubleshooting, problem solving, coauthoring, mastermind groups, or for ongoing projects of any kind.

Like the telephone, as the number of people who use personal computers grows, and as these personal computers "talk" to each other more, the greater the power each computer has.

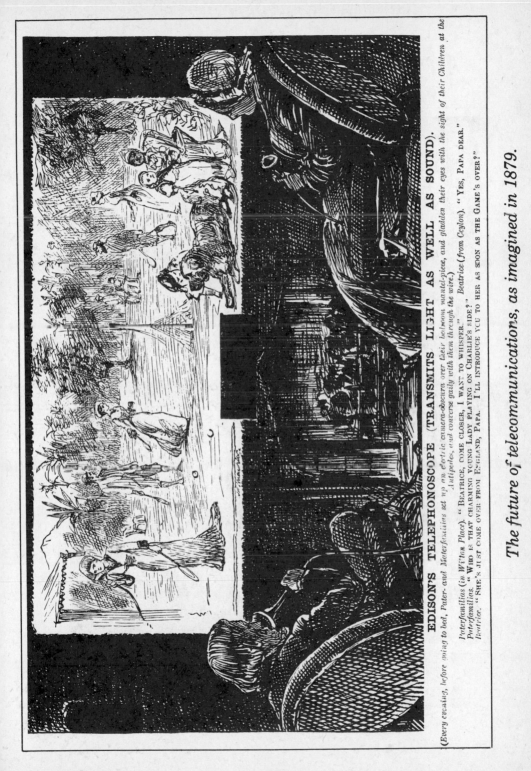

EDISON'S TELEPHONOSCOPE (TRANSMITS LIGHT AS WELL AS SOUND).

(Every evening, before going to bed, Pater- and Materfamilias set up an electric camera-obscura over their bedroom mantel-piece, and gladden their eyes with the sight of their Children at the Antipodes, and converse gaily with them through the wire.)

Paterfamilias (in Wilton Place). "BEATRICE, COME CLOSER, I WANT TO WHISPER." Beatrice (from Ceylon). "YES, PAPA DEAR."
Paterfamilias. "WHO IS THAT CHARMING YOUNG LADY PLAYING ON CHARLIE'S SIDE?"
Beatrice. "SHE'S JUST COME OVER FROM ENGLAND, PAPA. I'LL INTRODUCE YOU TO HER AS SOON AS THE GAME'S OVER?"

The future of telecommunications, as imagined in 1879.

155

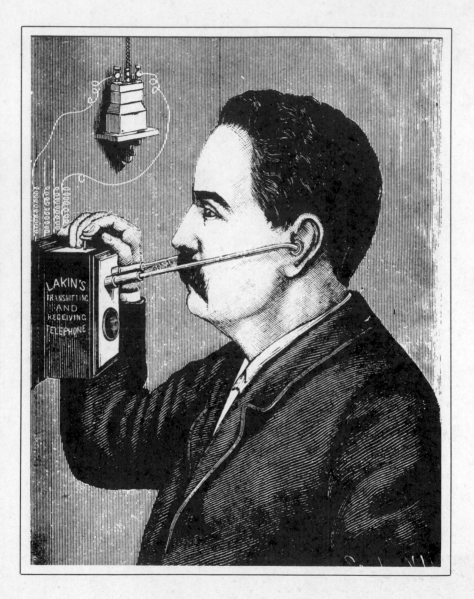

Chapter 12

Networking

"You have meddled with the primal forces of nature, Mr. Beale, and I won't have it, is that clear? . . . There is only one holistic system of systems, one vast and immense, interwoven, interacting, multi-variate, multi-national dominion of dollars!"

Those happen to be my favorite lines from the movie *Network*, written by the late Paddy Chayesfsky. We're not going to talk about those kinds of networks here, but we are going to talk about LAN.

LAN stands for Local Area Network, meaning two or more computers connected by wire so they can communicate with each other. I suppose someone threw in the word "local" to emphasize that the computers are nearby, generally in the same office or building.

In 1983, I connected together all the computers in my company, Prelude Press. It took the installer two days to set up the system. (The founder of the company himself was the "installer." He crawled around on his hands and knees while the rest of us stepped over him and occasionally offered him a glass of water when sympathy overtook us. He sold his networking system a few years later—for $30 million.)

I was curious about LAN's and wanted to see if my employees found a network useful. Not really. They could type little notes to each other ("Hey, let's go to lunch!"), but they still needed their own software for each machine.

Since then, software developers have created special network versions of programs. (Which is not the same as the "network" version of *Network*, which has all the nasty words removed by the network censors.) In a software network, one computer with a hard disk becomes the "server" and holds the software. The other computers (called "terminals" or "nodes") access the software over the wire from the server.

When hard disks were more expensive, networks offered an office the advantage of needing to buy only one hard-disk PC. The other computers that became nodes only needed floppy drives for back-up purposes. Now that hard disks can be added for $300 to $400 each,

Here, the delicate strand of cable necessary for networking personal computers is run through an office building.

> ## Estimate for Half Mile Private Line.
>
> 24218 Two No. 24208 instruments, wound with
>   fine wire, at $3.50.................................$7.00
> ½ mile No. 12 B B Galvanized Iron Wire, 85
>   pounds, at 9c.. 7.65
> 14 Pony Glass Insulators, at 5c 70
> 15 Oak Brackets, at 3c..............................   .45
> 5 Cells Gravity Battery, at 65c................... 3.25
> 2 pounds Office Wire, at 40c......................   .80
> 2 pounds Blue Vitriol, at 9c...................... 1.08
>
> $20.93
>
> The above estimate is for a practical working line,
> not a toy.
> Quotations given on main line relays, combination
> sets, sounders, keys, etc., upon application. We can
> furnish anything used in telegraphy at a discount from
> usual prices. Electrical supplies of any kind quoted
> upon request.

that advantage is gone. (It costs about $200 a piece for each computer to be connected to a network, including the price of installation and a special board for each computer.)

Why are networks still being installed? It's the software and the printers. Accounting departments find it far cheaper, on a per-computer basis, to buy network versions of software than several copies of a stand-alone version.

Also, clusters of computers can share the same printer, which *is* an advantage when that printer is a fast and reliable laser printer.

Networking is also valuable when the same information needs to be updated and accessed by several people (and computers) at once. (Ticket sales, for example, so that seat E-104 does not get sold to two different people ten minutes apart.)

Depending on the setup, each computer which runs virtually independently, can have access to other people's machines over the network. Thus, the boss could log onto the bookkeeper's computer and worry about accounts payable without ever having to leave his or her office. The boss might also run a data base program in the sales computer. Memos might be sent as entire files to everyone's machine.

On the down side, says a friend who works at an office with a network, programs may run significantly slower than stand-alone versions. His word processor dawdles compared to the same software in a stand-alone version. When he has to spell-check or use the thesaurus, he sometimes gives up because of the lack of speed.

Also, his office had a power surge in the lines a few weeks ago. One computer's power supply short circuited and zapped the whole system. Forty computers were instantly rendered useless for the rest of the day. Luckily, the zap did not melt anything; it just temporarily paralyzed the system.

The only advantage my friend finds to the network is that he can send messages up to 40 characters long to his coworkers. ("Hey, let's go to lunch!")

Think of my friend whispering in your (Caesar's) ear that not everything is so great. Then balance that against the real advantages—smaller per-machine software expenses, smaller printer expenses, and the ability to share data bases and to get files from other computers.

What happened to my friend's network? Well, when the accountants discovered the insurance might not cover the cost of repairing 40 computers, did they run to the windows, throw them open, stick their heads out and scream, "We're mad as hell and we're not going to take it anymore!"?

Of course not. They're accountants.

Telephone service, a public trust

An Advertisement of the
American Telephone and Telegraph Company

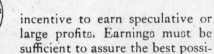

THE widespread ownership of the Bell Telephone System places an obligation on its management to guard the savings of its hundreds of thousands of stockholders.

Its responsibility for so large a part of the country's telephone service imposes an obligation that the service shall always be adequate, dependable and satisfactory to the user.

The only sound policy that will meet these obligations is to continue to furnish the best possible service at the lowest cost consistent with financial safety. There is then in the Bell System no incentive to earn speculative or large profits. Earnings must be sufficient to assure the best possible service and the financial integrity of the business. Anything in excess of these requirements goes toward extending the service or keeping down the rates.

This is fundamental in the policy of the company.

The Bell System's ideal is the same as that of the public it serves—the most telephone service and the best, at the least cost to the user. It accepts its responsibility for a nation-wide telephone service as a public trust.

An ad for the telephone. A <u>very old</u> ad for the telephone.

Chapter 13

Personal Computers in Small Business

Whom do you suppose gets the benefit of those three trillion workers generated by the large computers of this world? Indirectly, of course, we all do; but directly, the one who has profited most from this inexpensive labor force is big business. Big business is, after all, big enough to afford and operate big computers.

During the 1950's, the entry-level price of computing was around $1,000,000—and that's a million dollars when a million dollars was *a million dollars*. Technological breakthroughs continued, and by the early 1960's, a business could have a computer installed for about $200,000. In the early 1970's, this price was hovering around $100,000.

For most small businesses, any of these prices were—and still are—prohibitive. Beyond that, most small businesses could not use a large computer profitably. The word and data processing needs of a small company simply could not justify the expenditure of $100,000.

Some tried anyway, and the history of small business in the 1970's is laden with stories of small companies going under because they bought a computer. These disasters created a fear of computers in the small business community that continued until fairly recently.

But this fear is now all but gone, just as the fear of computers in the general population is diminishing day by day. The instrument of this change is the personal computer.

Personal computers first appeared in the mid-1970's. They were toys and tools for hobbyists. As the seventies progressed, certain hobbyists, who also happened to own small businesses, began using their "microcomputers" on the job. Programs were written to do accounting and word processing and inventory control. These programs were traded, sold, and improved.

Soon a non-hobbyist small businessperson could buy a personal computer, a printer, a few programs, and—with no small degree of trial-and-error—assemble something resembling a small business computer. These people were the explorers.

By 1980, the small business pioneers had come along. Some were amazed by how much small computers could do, others were disappointed by how little. There were precious few books on the subject, almost no computer stores, and learning came hard. A small businessperson had to really *want* the benefits of a computer, and be willing to endure life on the frontier. Some did, and they were rewarded.

Soon the wind shifted; the rumors began to change. Rather than stories of small companies failing because they bought a computer, there were tales of small businesses being *saved* by the purchase of a computer.

The changes in personal computers since 1980 have been astounding. Someone estimated that if the aeronautics industry had progressed as quickly as the computer industry over the past 40 years, airplanes would cost a few hundred dollars and fly around the world seven times on $5 worth of fuel.

Big computer companies are selling small computers to small companies, and small computer companies are becoming big computer companies by selling small computers to big companies. It's still the frontier, so don't expect that purchasing and operating a small computer will be as easy as buying a pick-up truck—but at least there are hotels on the frontier, and towns, and indoor plumbing and the occasional flush toilet.

𝒯ʰᵉ **FIRST FLUSH**

Let's take a look at some of the uses of personal computers we've already discussed and see how they might apply—or not apply—to the small business.

• **Accounting.** This can be one of the most powerful uses of personal computers in a small business. For less than $10,000 (sometimes far less—as little as $3,000, complete with laser printer), the small business can have the advantages large corporations had to pay $1,000,000 for back in the 1950's.

Now, small business can have as much control over its numbers as big business. Not only are computers faster than manual systems—especially if you do a lot of invoicing and/or have an intricate inventory to maintain—but the reports generated by the accounting program can be invaluable. And there's nothing like an up-to-date, complete set of books at tax time.

"What do you think, Maggie? You think we need a computer?"

• **Word processing.** Here, too, what once cost much more (about $20,000 fifteen years ago) now costs much less (around $2,000). If you or anyone in your company spends more than two hours per day at a typewriter, the word processing power of a personal computer would pay for itself in less than a year. (If you already have a personal computer for, say, accounting, the $300 invested in a good word processing program would pay for itself in about a month.)

Not only will word processing speed the correspondence and reports and other activities now under the domain of a typewriter, but you'll find yourself using other features—personalized form letters, for example—that were never economically feasible before.

• **Electronic spreadsheeting.** Here the usefulness will depend on your business. Large corporations used to hire small computers—known as junior executives—to do this very work. It was expensive, but they must have thought it was worth it.

Electronic spreadsheeting is such a new tool for small business that the use for it has, in many areas, yet to be created. To get a simple cost projection was not worth an hour—much less a day—of a small businessperson's time. If, however, the same projection could be calculated in a minute, then playing the game of "What if?" might prove valuable.

For some small businesses contractors, for example, or anyone who must prepare frequent estimates—the electronic spreadsheet power of a personal computer could pay for itself in a short time. For other small businesses, it might be worth using only if the computer has a more practical function. For still others, electronic spreadsheeting holds no value whatsoever.

A careful look at electronic spreadsheets, how they work, and what they do, should help you decide in which category your business fits.

• **Data bases.** Like electronic spreadsheeting, data bases will be invaluable to some small businesses, marginally useful to some, and useless to others.

For some, the data bases automatically created by the accounting or inventory programs might be all they need. For others, a simple mailing list program will suffice.

But if the management of information and its instant retrieval is important to your company, or you deal with information that must be intricately cross-referenced, then a data base program is a must.

• **Graphics.** Maybe yes, maybe no; again, it depends. If a pie chart or bar graph might help sell your product or communicate how things are going, then this feature is valuable. The same is true for desktop publishing.

• **Information services.** If stock market information, research, news, or any of the many things information services offer is important to your company, then being "online" with a data bank or two will be of frequent (and, in some cases, constant) benefit.

It's hard to imagine a small business that, at *some* point, couldn't make use of at least one of the information services' many services.

• **Electronic mail and teleconferencing.** Another gray area. My guess is that most small businesses will not use electronic mail—primarily because most other small businesses are not using electronic mail. FAX is the "modern" way to zap information from place to place.

• **Networking.** This will no doubt prove important to many small businesses. If you only have one personal computer, of course, there's no need to network. But, like telephones, personal computers tend to multiply in small offices. As soon as there's more than

One of the many small businesses that use a personal computer and pass the savings on to the customer.

one computer, the advantages of networking become obvious.

If a company has three personal computers—one in accounting, one for the secretary, and one for the boss—there may be a lot of disk swapping to exchange information.

With a good networking system, however, the boss could check the inventory status of any item, find out the bank balance, or read a dictated letter, all without leaving his or her office—and without disturbing anyone else's work. The secretary could enter a phone order directly into the accounts receivable program, run a spell-check program on a report the boss is writing, or remind the boss of an impending meeting.

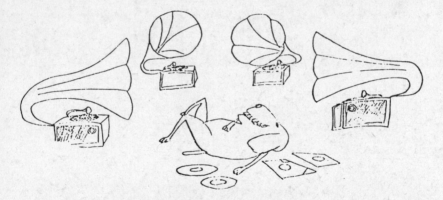

The best thing about a personal computer is that it does all of the above on one machine. You do not need to say, "Well, we have word processing needs, but I can't see spending $3,000 on that," or "We have bookkeeping, but it only takes an hour or two a day to do it by hand," or "It would be nice to have our inventory under control, but we do all right."

It's not as though you were spending $6,000 on an accounting machine, and another $3,000 on a word processing machine, and another $3,000 on an electronic spreadsheet machine, and another $2,500 on an electronic mail machine.

Fortune's Ladder,

(TO BE READ FROM THE BOTTOM.)

The drift of this Ladder to well comprehend,
Take a Paddy's advice, and *begin* at the *end*.

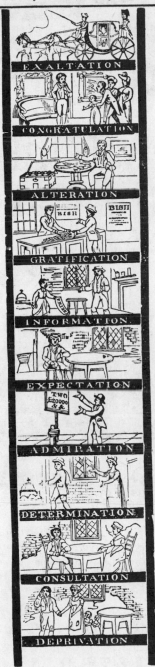

Ford

Today's High Peak *in* Motor Car Value

T H E   T O U R I N G
Black. All-steel body. One-man top. Weather-
proof side curtains opening with all four doors.
Four cord tires, nickeled head lamp rims, wind-
shield wiper. Starter and de-
mountable rims $85 extra.
Balloon tires $25 extra. *Price*
f. o. b. Detroit. **$290**

F O R D   M O T O R   C O M P A N Y

D E T R O I T

Personal computers are like the old Model T. If you were a farmer, you could buy one to go to town; and if you took the back seat out, you could deliver produce with it; and if you jacked it up and attached a belt to the rear wheel, you had power for your threshing machine. None of these alone might be worth $450, but all three combined in one machine—*that* was a farmer's dream.

"FINE LARGE CUCUMBERS!"

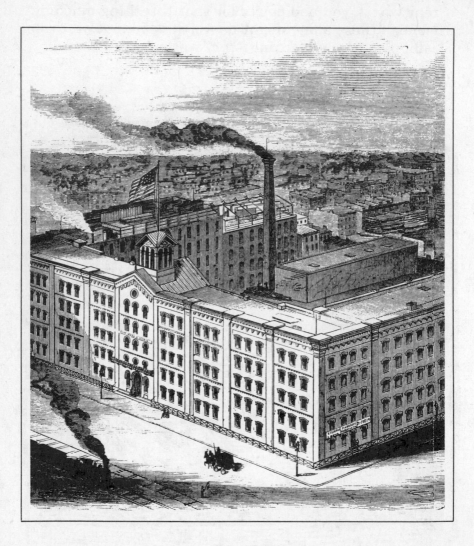

Chapter 14

The Personal Computer
in Big Business

Computers have been a part of big business as long as there have been computers. Going back even further, our very system of writing was not developed to record the beauty of a sunset, but to keep track of grain transactions.

Prior to 1975, computers were big things. They consumed more floor space than any other part of most large corporations (except the executive suites). The idea of a whole computer that sat on a desk? No. This was decidedly *not* big enough for big business.

The first personal computer was sold in 1975. It was in kit form. It appealed to hobbyists. It seemed to have about as much application to big business as ham radio.

Over the next few years, microcomputers grew more powerful and less ugly. When electronic spreadsheeting was invented, personal computers, like pocket calculators, finally had something practical to offer big business.

Big business did not, as a whole, immediately embrace this new office machine. In the first place, an Apple II (which was the only computer at the time that could run VisiCalc, the only electronic spreadsheet at the time) did not have what you would call a sophisticated design. Exposed cables of various colors and shapes connected monitors and disk drives. It was not an item most managers would want on their desk.

Further, many corporations decided that everything having to do with computers was the domain of

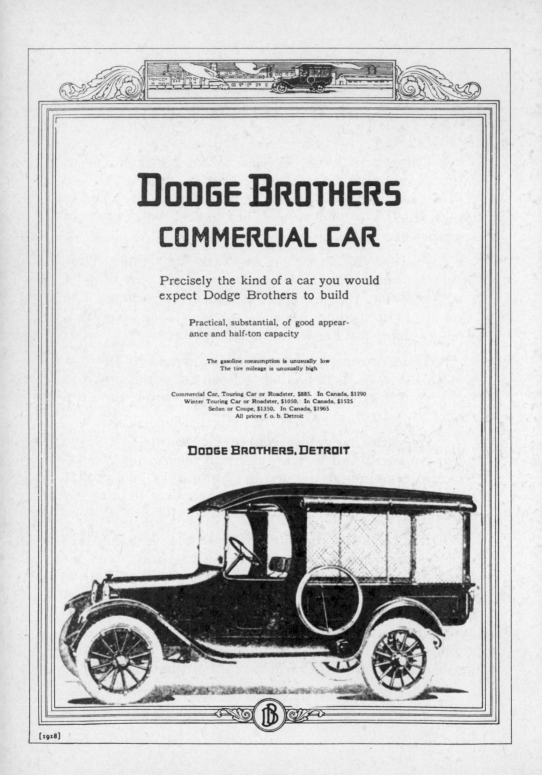

DODGE BROTHERS
COMMERCIAL CAR

Precisely the kind of a car you would
expect Dodge Brothers to build

Practical, substantial, of good appearance and half-ton capacity

The gasoline consumption is unusually low
The tire mileage is unusually high

Commercial Car, Touring Car or Roadster, $885. In Canada, $1290
Winter Touring Car or Roadster, $1050. In Canada, $1525
Sedan or Coupe, $1350. In Canada, $1965
All prices f. o. b. Detroit

DODGE BROTHERS, DETROIT

[1918]

176

the DP (data processing) department, where more than enough money was being spent already.

This philosophy was prevalent in the early 1980's, as I discovered just before appearing on a business-news TV program. I was in the greenroom with the show's other guest, the president of a mid-sized corporation. I told him I was the author of a book on personal computers.

"We have a large computer," he said, and rattled off a string of numbers that, I suppose, would have impressed me, if only I had known something about large computers. "We don't have any need for personal computers."

I could tell by his tone of voice that he was of the opinion that nothing "personal" should take place in or around a corporation, particularly his own.

"Personal computers can serve some practical needs, even for a business that has several large computers," I explained, trying to sound as little like a computer salesman as possible.

"I'm told our computer is working at only 47% capacity," he explained. "There's no need to buy another computer until we use the remaining 53% of the one we own." Certainly, he felt, that stroke of logic should end the discussion once and for all.

Unfortunately, that argument made about as much sense as saying that he wasn't going to buy a company car until the company truck was being used 24 hours a day. Since he was barely tolerating my presence as it was, I thought I would use an indirect approach.

"Does your computer do word processing?" I asked.

"No. Our secretaries don't need word processing. They're all excellent typists." He seemed irritated, as though the suggestion of word processing impugned the quality of his secretarial force.

"Your accountant is good at math," I said, "but I'm sure he uses an adding machine." That was too direct.

"If we wanted word processing, we could have word processing," he said through narrowing eyes. "I'm told that we could program our computer for word processing, and add five terminals and two printers, for only $75,000."

"*Only* $75,000?" I was not used to hearing words like "only" put in front of amounts like "$75,000." "For $15,000 you could buy five personal computers, five word processing programs, five printers—and the computers could have big names on them: IBM, NEC, Digital."

There was a silence in the room. I hadn't felt anything like it since the generation gap fifteen years before.

"That may be," he said, "but my secretaries don't need word processing, and we don't need any more computers when the one we have is working at only 47% capacity." He returned to his *Barrons*. I was dismissed.

After meeting this man, the stories I had heard about personal computers in large corporations became believable—stories of managers having to put in requisitions for "electronic typewriters" and "advanced calculators" in order to buy a personal computer.

Many people had to buy their own personal computers. One man wasn't even allowed to bring his computer to work. When a complex cost projection was needed, he'd call his wife. She would enter the information and give him the figures he needed.

The practicality of personal computers in big business grew with the introduction of more business and management programs. The introduction of the IBM Personal Computer was the final step in legitimizing the personal computer in big business. The personal computer went from hobbyist toy to corporate tool in

"Oh, come on, Boss. Just one <u>little</u> computer?"

only seven years. Today, the Fortunate 500 buy up personal computers like gummy bears.

Let's look at some of the uses of personal computers as they apply to big business.

Here is the disk for a stock market portfolio program.
(Be careful not to touch this disk with your fingers if you
plan to use it in your computer.)

• **Word processing.** Look around your office. Every place you see an electric typewriter, there, almost without exception, a personal computer would do the job of processing words better, faster, easier and more economically. (The exception is filling out one-of-a-kind forms and, occasionally, labels.)

Personal computers running word processing programs save money in two ways. First, the productivity of the operator is increased. (This is detailed in the next section on word processing.)

Secondly, personal computers are less expensive to purchase than "stand alone" or "dedicated" word processors. Until recently, personal computers cost about half as much to buy as dedicated machines that only did word processing. Most of the manufacturers of dedicated word processors have had to lower their prices—primarily because their own newly introduced personal computers were offering too much competition.

Further, personal computers offer greater flexibility. One is not tied to the original manufacturer for word processing programs, updates, and auxiliary programs (such as spelling, grammar and punctuation checkers). Also, personal computers can do all the other things personal computers do. Without the addition of an adapter (which may or may not be available), stand-alone word processors cannot.

• **Accounting.** In a large business, personal computers must take a back seat to their larger cybernetic relations. Personal computers simply do not have the power to handle the interactive accounting needs of a large corporation.

Certain modules of accounting run on personal computers, however, could prove more cost effective than programming and using a large computer. Direct mail order, for example, might account for only a small percentage of sales. Invoices, however, do have to be issued, inventories maintained, and records kept.

To do this, running an accounts receivable and inventory program on a small computer might be far more efficient than entering the same information into the large computer. The totals of these transactions can be added to the large computer daily, monthly, quarterly, or whenever advisable.

The sales department might want to run a mock accounting program to keep close track of sales patterns, sales personnel, and accounts. Information entered in a personal computer is often more accessible than information in a large computer.

• **Electronic spreadsheeting.** For the managers who need to project costs or analyze figures, a personal computer is as essential as an electronic calculator is to an accountant. If it takes an hour to manually "work up some figures," that's an hour of (expensive) managerial time wasted.

The false economy of not investing in a computer for an executive because the computer wouldn't be used "all the time," is the same as saying the sales manager should take the bus from appointment to appointment. "Why waste money on a company car if it's only going to be used an hour or two a day?"

The reason is that the car is cheaper than the sales manager's time, and if he or she didn't have a car, he or she would probably quit. And so it is, and will increasingly be, with personal computers.

• **Graphics.** Certain segments of big business seem to live on bar graphs and sales curves, with generous helpings of pie charts for dessert. If you've ever sat looking at a row of numbers thinking, "If there were only a way to *visually* present this information," then computer statistical graphics are for you. Desktop publishing would certainly make, at the very least, the company newsletter (A) less expensive to produce, (B) more timely, and (C) better looking.

• **Data bases.** In many areas of big business, the power of a computer to file information and selectively retrieve it is a major asset. Sales leads, customers, mailing lists, indexing, archival storage, in-

All these functions can now be combined in <u>one</u> machine.

formation management, employee records—the list goes on and on. Anywhere there *is* a list, in fact, the computer could probably manage it more efficiently and economically than by hand.

• **Information services.** In reviewing the hundreds of professional offerings available by many information services, one may find it hard to imagine a corporation not using at least a few of the data bases on a regular basis, and a great many others more infrequently.

For some, the ability to do research or check the current price of gold, stocks, hog futures—or any of a hundred other things—could, in itself, justify the cost of a personal computer.

Information that is available only after extensive research, or available hours after it is useful, or not available at all, is available on information services instantly—generally at less cost than might be expected.

• **Electronic mail and teleconferencing.** The ability to send information—from a letter to a report to a book—from place to place in a matter of minutes, not hours or days, can be of significant benefit. Naturally, FAXing it is the way of the nineties, just as FED-EXing it was the way of the eighties. Maybe electronic mail will be the way of the new millennium.

Teleconferencing can save thousands of dollars in travel expenses, not to mention precious days of executives' time. No need to hop on a plane and head for the office at each new emergency or new idea. Just turn on the computer, and there's J.B., and everyone else, anxiously awaiting your brilliant solution.

• **Networking.** In some large organizations, the need for personal computers to be in constant contact with each other is important, and for others, it's not. It will depend on what each computer is being used for, and the amount of information that must flow from machine to machine.

Department heads may want to be linked to everyone in their department, to other department heads and to their superior. Employees within a department might find it useful to be linked together, but it may not be necessary (or desirable) to have all employees linked to each other.

One major business publication, which shall remain nameless, installed a "serious" computer network. Almost from the first day, the editor of this publication began getting obscene messages in his electronic mailbox. He would be in the middle of a meeting in his office, and suddenly the explicatives that were deleted from the Watergate tapes were flashing on the video screen behind him.

The networking program this company used had no way of tracing where the "suggestions" were coming from. When I last heard, he was busily trying to trace it—somehow. File this under "The Risks of Networking" in your data base.

Another important networking feature for some corporations is the ability of the personal computer to tie into the large computer.

The "personal" in personal computers means that small computers are now inexpensive enough—when compared to the work they do—to be used and controlled by an individual, much as a "personal" office, desk, or telephone.

Personal computers free office personnel from mundane, repetitive tasks, and allow them to do what humans do best: create, innovate, inspire, stuff envelopes, and go to lunch.

When an operator tells you that she uses the

Remington

she stands up a little straighter.

She knows as well as you do that her choice of the Recognized Leader among Typewriters is a fine recommendation-- one which raises her in your estimation.

Remington Typewriter Company
(Incorporated)

New York and Everywhere

Chapter 15

Questions and Answers on Computers in Business

For our offices, we had a computer consultant set up our new computers. She recommended strongly that we get a disk optimizing program. She said something like it was good for our hard disks. What is disk optimizing?

MS DOS, the disk operating system on IBM and IBM compatibles, is a bit of a mad hatter when it comes to filing. As you create files and save them, MS DOS does not necessarily keep your work in one piece. It fits pieces here and there all over the hard disk. The letter you wrote your brother, for instance, will appear onscreen as one file, but it might be stored on the hard disk in five pieces. This is because after you erase things, you free up space here and there. When you write new material, the newly freed space may not hold your material completely, so DOS puts some here and some there.

Eventually, all those parts filed here and there slow the computer down. "Optimizing" puts all the fragmented files back together again, giving you faster computer operation. It is also supposed to save wear and tear on your hard disk because the head does not have to keep moving all the time to fit all your pieces together.

Computer magazines are laden with ads for optimizing programs, but I found two programs that are exceptional. Either one will do you well. Vopt ($49.95 from Golden Bow Systems, 2870 Fifth Avenue, Suite 201, San Diego, CA 92103; 619-298-9349) and OPTune ($99.95 from Gazelle Systems, 42 North University Avenue, Suite 10, Provo, UT 84601; 800-233-0383) work

187

so fast and efficiently, you can use them daily. Either can be set up so that when you turn on your computer, it will optimize. Such daily optimizing usually takes under 10 seconds, although the first time you do it will take longer.

OPTune has two extra features over Vopt. While both can lock out bad sectors, OPTune can "tune" your hard disk, too. That is, OPTune ensures that your hard disk is in synchronization with its controller and your computer's clock speed. If it is not in synch, OPTune will make adjustments to the hard disk.

There is some evidence to support the theory that hard disks were invented by the ancient Aztecs ...

*... although others claim it dates
back to Ancient Egypt ...*

*... while still others insist it all
started in Japan.*

OPTune can also correct or repair disk damage by rewriting sector identification marks and by moving data located in marginal sectors to better spots. One particular test OPTune makes, if you choose to use it, is so rigorous, it can take up to 14 hours to run on a 40MB hard disk. The test is to make sure the hard disk is performing well.

Golden Bow also has a program that will seek out possible problem areas on a hard disk and lock them out (that is, keep any information from being written on them). It's called Vmarkbad.

Why be so concerned about your hard disk? Hard disks have a finite life. It may take years for your hard disk to go out on you, but some day, when you least expect it—BIZZZZZZ. Out it goes. By using a disk optimizer, and a bad-sector checker like OPTune or Vmarkbad, you can extend the life of your hard disk and might get some warning as to when it might go.

(And, as I state again and again, make sure you *BACK UP YOUR DATA* onto floppy disks when you are using a hard disk.)

This leads me to a coda. If you are buying a computer for the first time, do look for one with a hard disk. Hard disks are so economical now, when purchasing a computer for business use, it makes no sense to buy a machine without one. Besides, fewer and fewer programs are fitting on a single floppy disk. You may have a difficult time using your computer if it does not have a hard disk.

If the difference in price between a 20MB hard disk and a 30MB hard disk is small, go for the larger disk. Programs are getting bigger, so it's nice to have plenty of space.

Can you explain macros, please?

I've received a couple of questions about macros just at the time I've been exploring macros—so macros are on my mind.

There are any number of "keyboard enhancer" programs on the market. The one I use is SmartKey. This allows any key on the computer to become *pages* of information, if I so choose. It could also be a series of instructions given to the computer or to a given computer program—sort of a mini-program. That all this can be accomplished by a single keystroke is a significant enlargement of the key's abilities, hence the word *macro* for "big."

I can hold down the ALT key and press the letter L (ALT-L), for instance, whenever I want my address and phone number inserted into what I'm writing. I had told SmartKey earlier that I wanted ALT-L to include the address and phone number, and each time I hit ALT-L, that information is dutifully added.

I have also created macros that perform a series of commands. If working on a screenplay, I can press ALT-D and my margins change for dialogue. Without the macro, I have to give seven separate commands to my word processor to reach the same goal. (The macro itself is a recording of those seven commands. When I press ALT-D, those seven commands are performed automatically, instantly.)

Macros are shortcuts. One can compute without them. If you use them, they save you time. In addition to special keyboard enhancers, most word processors these days have a macro feature, as do spreadsheets.

What's the difference between a personal computer and a business computer?

Not much, and sometimes nothing at all. A company that wants to sell computers to businesses calls its machine a business computer. A company that wants to sell to individuals calls its machine a personal computer. Some try to straddle both markets and advertise a "personal business computer."

The very same computer can be known as a personal computer, a business computer, a personal business computer, a microcomputer, a desktop computer, a small computer, an individual computer—and they'll invent a dozen more this year alone.

It's a case of the same thing described in several ways. What we might call "an all-expense-paid vacation," Congress calls a "junket" and the State Department calls "a fact-finding mission."

The author with his first word processor (Christmas, 1956).

PART III

Word Processing

A Short Course in Computer Literacy

Chapter 16

The History of Word Processing

Computers, alas, have not gathered the best of reputations in their first forty-or-so years of service to humanity. We once had the idea that we might lose our jobs to a box with a blinking light. We once feared that, as soon as "they" became smarter than "us," "they" would somehow take over the world. (Remember the movie *2001?* The villain was HAL, the computer. It did not take us long to figure out that the next letter in the alphabet after H was I, the next letter after A was B and the next letter after L was M. HAL = IBM. The first time I can recall a *friendly* computer in a movie was *Star Wars.)* And how often have we been treated to the brief end of the stick due to a "computer error"?

In the seventies and eighties, this changed. It began with baby computers known as hand-held calculators. Within a few years they went from $300 to $4.95 and could be found on watches, pens and refrigerators. We promptly forgot our multiplication tables. Long division? Isn't that a housing development on Long Island? Soon, with variations of these hand-held marvels, we could play football, count our calories, check our biorhythms and decide on which horse to bet. If these were computers, they weren't so bad.

By the late 1970's, the stage was set for the first full-scale personal home computers. With cute little names like PET and APPLE, they were free from the taint of evil; and how could anything truly menacing come from Radio Shack, that store in the shopping center next to the A&P that sold stereos and CB radios?

Those who did not yet make the plunge and acquire a Total Home Computer made do with ATARI video games or played PONG until the wee hours of the morning. Little computers, known as microprocessors, began doing wonderful things for microwaves and televisions. Digital readout became the norm for wristwatches. The family car had an onboard computer that told miles per gallon, temperature, and estimated time of arrival. The 21st Century had arrived, twenty years ahead of schedule.

Meanwhile, the brave pioneers, manning and womaning their PETS, APPLES and TRS (Tandy Radio Shack) computers in the late 1970's, were balancing the family budget, educating their children, educating themselves, and playing a variety of increasingly complicated games. They were the nucleus of a quiet revolution.

If the truth be told, they weren't so quiet about it. They began by telling their friends. America had witnessed nothing like it since the early 1950's, when people from up and down the block would pay a visitation to the neighborhood's only TV just to look at it, even if nothing were being broadcast at that moment; the set turned off, they would gather round this icon of the future. A test pattern was a thrill to behold. "That circle with the lines around it is all the way downtown, more than twenty miles away!" the proud owner would say.

With the same reverence, the owners of microcomputers (as they were called back in the late 1970's) invited their friends over to watch the family budget being balanced, or to take part in a game of video tic-tac-toe. Soon, though, the friends who were interested in computers got their own, and the friends who were not interested grew weary of watching another family's budget being balanced. A new way of sharing the wonders of modern technology was needed and was duly discovered: The Written Word.

You would have thought they had invented the English language. It began innocently enough with letters to friends, the ones to whom they couldn't talk in person.

These expanded into articles that filled the ever-increasing number of computer magazines. The articles spread to civilian magazines, newspapers, PTA dispatches, company newsletters and supermarket bulletin boards.

One day it had to happen, and it did: an actual *book* about computers. This was simply the first kernel in a very large pan of very hot popcorn. Almost at once there were dozens, then hundreds, then thousands of computer books. Then little publishing companies that

Here we have an early personal computer on the left and an early word processor on the right. It's hard to believe that no one thought of putting the two together until the last quarter of the 20th Century.

published nothing but computer books, and finally big publishing companies that published nothing but computer books. Not since Mr. Gideon began putting Bibles in hotel rooms has The Printed Word been spread with greater speed, volume and zeal.

And what, do you suppose, did these personal-computer-owners-turned-literary-giants use to write this cornucopia of prose? You guessed it: their personal computers, adapted to process not the family budget, but words.

Of course, word processing has been a part of Big Business for some time. Those giant room-filling computers of the early 1950's were there to process data. Numbers would go in one end, get sorted and re-sorted (processed) and come out the other. After a while someone said, "If we can process data, why can't we process words?" Well, they could and they did, and word processing was born.

We, as consumers, were first aware that computers were being used for more than payroll deductions when we started getting personalized impersonal letters in the mail. I'm sure we all got the one from *The Reader's Digest*. I must have received a dozen of these, proclaiming on the outside, "THE MCWILLIAM FAMILY HAS ALREADY WON $1,000,000 AND TWO SLAVES." Well, how can you throw such an envelope away without at least opening it?

The letter began, "Dear Mr. and Mrs. McWilliam and Children." They always seemed to leave the "s" off "McWilliams." There was no "Mrs. McWilliam," unless they meant my mother, in which case I would have been the "children."

The letter continued, "Imagine, Mr. and Mrs. McWilliam, what it would be like to live like a millionaire, complete with English butler and maid!" So much for the two slaves. Furthermore, the Grand Prize does not include $1,000,000, one discovers as one reads the increasingly smaller print, but simply "the life of a millionaire" for the duration of the actual Grand Prize: a glorious two-week vacation in beautiful downtown Pleasantville (home of *The Reader's Digest,* coincidentally).

Unfortunately, what a millionaire could spend his or her money on is rather limited in Pleasantville. The finest hotel is the Ramada Inn. The best restaurant is Howard Johnson's. The hottest night spots are the Cinema I & II. "All this and more is included in this Dream Vacation, Mr. and Mrs. McWilliam, but first, let us tell you about our special offer on the next 26 issues of *The Reader's Digest . . . ."* The Dream Vacation is not even ours, alas. We have a *chance* to win it. Our name has been automatically entered in the Grand Sweepstakes Drawing with 76 million other Americans, their children and their mythical Mrs.

PETER A MC WILLIAMS, I'll Personally Hand You Your One Million Dollar Prize If You Return The Winning Number ... In Time!

Dear Mr. Peter A Mc Williams,

You and I may be meeting for a very happy occasion. If your entry is the grand prize winner in American Family Publishers' Multi-Million Dollar Sweepstakes. I have an envelope which I'll be handing you in person. The outside of the envelope will be neatly and clearly addressed to: Mr. P. Mc Williams, PO Bx 19464A. And inside the envelope will be an irrevocable and binding guarantee of your ONE MILLION DOLLARS!

But that's not all, Mr. Peter A Mc Williams. You may be the winner of any of 20,000 guaranteed prizes.

The following nine numbers have been registered exclusively in the Mc Williams name: Nobody else has any of your numbers:

C4508443   OPY29128   IX280556   Z9W30270   RL008139

F1340018   XDX49509   LT188811   UHW99662

The MILLION DOLLAR grand-prize winning number has already been selected and sealed away. Here's hoping it's one of the exclusive Mc Williams numbers listed above.

After the excitement wore off, after the humor wore off, we learned to toss these missives aside. "Another computer letter," we'd sigh.

(A dear woman, who actually *lives* in Pleasantville, wrote to inform me: "(1) The Reader's Digest is in Chappaqua, N.Y. The mailing address is in Pleasantville. (2) The nearest Ramada Inn is in either Armonk or Elmsford, N.Y. (3) The nearest Howard Johnson's is either in Tarrytown or Elmsford, N.Y. We do, however, have two restaurants in Pleasantville that have been reviewed in *The New York Times* and have been given two stars. (4) Our movie theater is the Rome." Truth, it seems, *is* stranger than humor.)

But those were the dim, dark days of yore: back when computers cost hundreds of thousands of preinflation dollars; back when, if you wanted a personal computer to balance your household budget, you would have to buy an additional house just to put it in; back when the only companies that could afford computers were at least as big as IBM, and they used their computers *for* themselves, which certainly seemed as though they were being used *against* the rest of us.

That's all changed. Computers now cost but a few hundred to a few thousand post-inflation dollars. They sit on one side of a dining room table and leave enough room to eat dinner. They can be used *by* consumers *for* consumers.

Toward the end of the eighties, desktop publishing was invented and reached the masses. Desktop publishing simply meant one could process words one step further—print them using pictures, graphics, and elegant typefaces. Personal computers with laser printers and a new generation of software became Volkspublishers, the people's way to print.

So, after this rather rambling preamble, let's take a look at, of all things, word processing.

If you think of your mind as a sort-of computer, when you write even a simple sentence you have, in essence, processed words. The procedure goes something like this:

1. From your vocabulary, stored in your memory, you choose words that generally fit the subject about which you wish to write.

2. You select the best of these words.

3. You select words to connect the best words together.

4. You lay them out with a beginning, a middle, and an end based upon certain rules you have learned, again calling upon your memory.

There. You have successfully processed words into a sentence. You might then change and alter the words. That arrangement and rearrangement is a continuation of the word processing process.

There is a story told of Keats who, after looking out a window for a while, turned to his friend and said, "Something beautiful is forever a joy. What do you think of that?"

His friend looked up, considered it for a moment, said, "That's very nice," and returned to his writing.

Keats continued looking out the window. A while later he said, "A thing of beauty is a joy forever."

His friend put down his pen. "That," he said, "will live through eternity."

Keats, while looking out the window, was processing words. He knew what he wanted to say. He rearranged nouns, verbs, and adjectives until the beauty of his words matched the beauty of his thought.

Word processing computers are tools that serve the word processing that goes on in the *real* word processor, the human mind.

Word processing machines allow for maximum flexibility in alteration, change, correction, revision and expansion. After all this processing of words has taken place, the word processing computer will print out as many copies as you like, letter perfect.

Give me your students, your secretaries,
Your huddled writers
yearning to breathe free,
The wretched refuse of your Selectric III's.
Give these, the homeless, typist-tossed to me.
I lift my disk beside the processor.

Welcome to Word Processing!

Chapter 17

The Wonders of Word Processing

Discussing word processing is like discussing Beethoven's Fifth Symphony. There are a great many recordings of this symphony, all different. Some are less different than others. The several versions done by the New York Philharmonic are going to be more similar to each other than the one done by the Omaha All Kazoo Band.

(My favorite quote about the Beethoven symphonies comes from the Damark catalog. It tells us its collection of classics on cassettes includes: "Nine of the most famous Beethoven Symphonies.")

And so it is with word processing programs. There are about as many word processing programs as there are recordings of Beethoven's Fifth—maybe more. They're all different, but some are less different than others. The ones costing $400 are likely to be more similar to each other than are the ones costing $19.95.

All recordings of Beethoven's Fifth, from the Berlin Philharmonic to the Tijuana Symphony, will begin with (we hope) "DA DA DA DUM." So, too, (we hope) do all word processing programs have some things in common. Let's look at those similarities—the basic features you can expect from any word processing program. Then we'll discuss the many variations, additions, and refinements that ingenious programmers have added in the past few years.

In explaining a basic word processing program, I'll use the typewriter for comparison. When you type on a typewriter, the words are transferred directly to the paper. When you type on a computer, the words appear on screen. Rather than ink on paper, you have written

207

with electrons on phosphor. Ink on paper is hard to change; electrons on phosphor, easy.

*The machine has several virtues . . .
One may lean back in his chair and
work it. It piles an awful stack of words
on one page. It don't muss things or
scatter ink blots around.*

From MARK TWAIN'S first letter
written on a typewriter.

If you make a mistake on a typewriter and catch it before putting too many characters between you and the mistake, you have several correcting options. The first is an eraser. Not recommended. The next is paint; little jars of white paint. Similarly, there are little sheets of white carbon paper that will hide mistakes, in a fashion.

The ultimate solution to typing errors was the Wonder of the Age back in 1974: The IBM Correcting Selectric. On this machine you push a button, backspace to the mistake, retype the mistake, and a ribbon of flypaper comes out of the typewriter and magically *lifts the offending characters right off the page!* Why, this so thrilled typists throughout the country that there was a movement to give IBM Thursday of National Secretary's Week.

To make a correction on a word processor, you press the "delete" button and watch the blinking cursor erase all that went before it, letter by letter until you release the button. You then type in, or "keyboard in" as they sometimes say in Computerese, whatever you would prefer to have in that space.

Let's say you've finished typing a page, and it comes fresh and neat from the typewriter. You notice a sentence in the middle of the page that should not be there. Another sentence, that happens to be quite a bit longer than the sentence that should not be there, should be there. What do you have? A Moral Crisis.

A conundrum worthy of Aristotle arises: "Is making this change, which should be made, worth retyping the whole page?" And if it's a long document, several pages long, and the pages have already been typed, and the change would mean going onto another page, the question becomes, "Is making this change, which should be made, worth retyping the whole document?"

If you own a word processor, you need never face that crisis again. You will have to face other crises— such as how to pay for the word processor, perhaps—but you will never face the to-retype-or-not-to-retype crisis again.

Whatever you're working on in word processing, from a wedding invitation to the great American novel, is known as a **document** or a **file.** When you want to make a change in a document, you move the cursor to the point in the document where the change is to be made, and make it.

Taking words out, putting words in, correcting spelling, removing or adding whole pages of information can take place at any point in the document. The rest of the document adjusts accordingly, automatically, electronically. Change is easy because it's all done with electrons, and electrons *love* to change. You might say it is one of their primary characteristics.

This ability to change what you want to change, whenever you want to change it, is the key to the value and popularity of word processing computers. It is this that allows even the most basic word processing program to do more than the most expensive and sophisticated type-directly-onto-a-piece-of-paper typewriter.

After everything looks all right on the screen, it's time to print. Even the slowest printer types faster than all but the fastest typists, and printers can do it hour after hour after hour, 24 hours a day. The slower computer printers print at 15 characters per second (CPS).

Figuring an average word to be seven letters long (that's just my figuring; heaven knows the length of an average word), that comes to 128.57 words per minute (WPM). Moderate computer printers print at 25 CPS or about 215 WPM; the faster laser printers for computers travel at the remarkable rate of 300 CPS, which clocks in at around 2,570 words per minute. At this point in the world of computers, we abandon old systems of measurement and simply talk in the number of pages per minutes. (2,570 words per minute equals 8 to 10 pages a minute.)

As you might gather, even if changes are desired after the document has been printed, making changes on the computer and then printing a new document requires minimal time and effort. In fact, while doing word processing, you might print one version after another. The onus of retyping and re-retyping, and even re-re-retyping is gone. Push a few buttons and the printer clicks (or, with a laser printer, whooshes) out a new copy in a matter of minutes.

The implication this has on personalized form letters is obvious. You can send out hundreds of letters, all saying the same thing, each looking hand-typed, and the only thing you need to change each time is the name and address. And, fellow writers: freshly typed manuscripts are far more impressive than Xerox copies.

Those are the basics you can expect from any system that dares call itself a word processor. Although formidable, it's just the beginning.

Beyond the Basics of Word Processing

Some people require or desire a feature or two or twelve more than a basic word processing program provides. Who can blame them? After spending a thousand or more dollars on hardware, spending a hundred or so more on better quality software that will turn their Honda into a Prelude is certainly understandable.

What follows is a guide to some of the features designers of word processing software have created. Each description will begin with the Computerese name for the feature.

File lengths. File length determines how long a document is. Some less expensive word processing programs can handle only one or two pages of text at a time. (Of course, longer documents can be done a page at a time, just as on a typewriter.) The finest word processing software limits the size of the document to "disk capacity," meaning that, however many K the disk can hold, that is the maximum length of the document. As you go beyond, say, 100K, however, your computer may become uncomfortably sluggish because it has to keep track of all those tens of thousands of words. Novels, books and enthusiastic love letters are still best stored in several files.

Word wrap. This means that when you reach the end of the line (meaning right-hand margin, not major life crisis), the next word will begin the next line automatically.

This may take some getting used to. If you're accustomed to a manual typewriter, you may find your left hand moving suddenly upwards and slapping the side of the screen at the end of each line.

Once you've adjusted to word wrap, however, it's delightful. No more listening for the little bell. No more looking up to see how much room is left on a line. No more wondering if the next word will fit before the carriage stops dead. No more margin releases. Just type, type, type. The only time you'd use the carriage return is to begin a new paragraph or when you want the line to end before the right margin, such as in list making or poetry writing.

File insertion. Each disk can hold many files. A file can be anywhere from one letter in length to the maximum length permitted by the word processing program. If you were typing along on file A, and you wanted to add the contents of files B, C, and D to file A, with the push of a few buttons it would be done.

Using file insertion you could create files of frequently used paragraphs or phrases and have them added to the text in a matter of seconds. This is great for correspondence or contracts. I have my name and address in a file named AD. When I come to the end of a letter and want to add my name and address, I hold down my Control key (one of the extra keys on a computer keyboard) and press a letter. This is a code to let the computer know that I want to "read" a file into my text—and then I type AD, the name of my file. If I wanted to include my phone number, I would type ADP. Zip. There it is.

Block move. A block is a group of words that are all together in a bunch. If you've ever written a paragraph and then wished it were in another part of the document, you will appreciate block moves.

All you do is mark the beginning and end of the chosen text (this is the block), move the cursor to where you'd like the block to go, press another command, and zap! the block has moved into its new neighborhood feeling very much at home. There are other good things you can do with blocks:

Copy blocks, which lets you make a copy of the block, so that the original block stays where it is, but an identical copy can be written into another part of the document.

You can also write the block to a whole new file. Let's say you're typing along and discover you have written a paragraph that you will want to use again in other documents. You can mark it, name it whatever you like, copy it to a file, and move on. The next time you need that paragraph, you can use file insertion and read it into the text. All this moving around of blocks, by the way, is known as "text manipulation."

Global search. Although this sounds like something James Bond might request ("We'll find him, Sir. I'll have a global search run on him right away!"), global search in word processing is far less dramatic, although equally exciting. Global search will find anything, at any point in your document, in a matter of seconds.

Let's say you have a very long document, and you want to return to the section in which you were rhapsodizing on clouds. You would simply type the word "cloud" into global search, and the computer would find and display the first time you used the word. If that weren't the reference you wanted, the computer would find where "cloud" was used for the second time, and so on.

Search and replace. This not only finds any word or character in the document, it also changes that word or character to any other word or character. If you've written a letter to Michael, using his name throughout the letter, and now you want to send the same letter to Mary, all you do is have the computer find each occurrence of "Michael" and change it to "Mary." In a few seconds, the letter will be personalized to Mary.

Another use for search and replace is to save typing. Let's suppose you're doing a very long report on the heterobasidiomycetes (a subclass of fungi, for the two or three out there who didn't know). Now, writing as you would be on heterobasidiomycetes you would no doubt have to mention the word heterobasidiomycetes quite often. You might not want to type out heterobasidiomycetes as many times as you'd be using heterobasidiomycetes, and you may, in fact, after a while, find yourself avoiding the word heterobasidiomycetes altogether.

Now, rather than type the word heterobasidiomycetes each time, with search and replace all you would have to do is use an abbreviation, say "HH", each time you wanted to use heterobasidiomycetes. When finished, you would simply have search and replace find all occurrences of "HH" and replace them with "heterobasidiomycetes." Your report, fingers, and sanity would be saved by search and replace.

Macros. Macros are mini-programs you write to save you keystrokes. The word "program" may sound intimidating, but macros can be easy to create. In the above example of heterobasidiomycetes, another way around the problem is to create a macro for the word. Every time you want to use heterobasidiomycetes, you could, for example, hold down the ALT or Control key, press the letter H, say, and up comes heterobasidiomycetes. A macro might contain just one word, a few sentences, paragraphs, or pages of text. In other words, macros can also do the functions of file insertion.

The other great thing macros can do is turn a chain of commands into a few keystrokes. If resetting the margins, for instance, takes five separate commands to perform, you can turn those five commands into one macro. With the press of ALT-M—*voila!*— margin change.

Spell-check. This checks every word in your document against a list of correctly spelled words. This list of correctly spelled words ranges from 10,000 to 150,000. If a word in your document does not match a word in the word list, it means that either the word is misspelled, or the word is correctly spelled but not lo-

September 23, 1982

Prelude Press
Box 69773
Los Angeles, CA 90069
Attn: Peter McWilliams

Mr. McWilliams,

Thank-you for your request for the picture of the Lanier TypeMaster Word Processor.

Enclosed is a color photograph of the Lanier TypeMaster. My apologies for not having any black and whites in stock at this present time, but I hope the color photograph will be just as useful. You may take this to your photo dealer and have a black and white made from this.

If I may be of any furthr help to you, please let me know.

Regards,

LANIER BUSINESS PRODUCTS, INC.

Can you find the typo in this letter from Lanier?

215

cated in the program's list of words. (Your name, for instance, might not be in the list.)

The spell-check feature will stop at every instance of a word not in its dictionary. If a word is correctly spelled, you can tell the speller not to stop at it again, or you might add the word to the dictionary so it won't stop at the word in future checks.

If a word is incorrectly spelled, most spell-checkers produce a short list of correctly spelled possibilities. If you see the word you meant on the list, with one keystroke you can swap the right word for the wrong one. If the word you want is not on the list, you can manually correct it.

Incorrect spellings, by the way, include most typographical errors. This feature is great for ferreting out typing mistakes, the ones usually discovered *after* the letter is sent.

Often the spell-checker is part of a word processing program. If not, spell-checkers can be purchased as separate programs and used with whatever word processing software you own. (The next chapter, *The Curse of Noah Webster*, looks at spellers in greater detail.)

Thesaurus. This, too, is a feature appearing in more and more word processors. It helps you find synonyms for words. As William F. Buckley, Jr., once pointed out, "Sometimes you need a certain word to describe the precise longitude and latitude of a thought."

Not all writers like or use thesauri, but I am one who, although I almost never check a written thesaurus, like (and use) the electronic versions.

Sometimes I want a particular word, and I simply cannot remember it. (It's the kind of thing that comes to me on the road or in the shower, but one can drive or shower only so much per day.) I'll type a word that has a similar meaning to the one I want, press the thesaurus command, and get a list of synonyms. If the one for which I'm looking is not on the list, I can cursor down to a word that's close, press Enter, and get a whole new list.

When I find the word for which I'm looking, I put the cursor over it, hit Enter, and the thesaurus program replaces the imprecise word in my text with the precise one. If not, I hit the showers.

Centering. The computer will automatically center any word or group of words between the left and right margins. Great for headings, titles, addresses, invitations, poetry, and the like.

Page break display. This will display on screen where each page will break when printed. It helps to avoid the last three words of a paragraph beginning a new page, for instance. (Is that a widow or an orphan? I always get them confused.)

Automatic pagination. The page numbers will automatically be printed at the bottom, top, left, or right side of every page. Like most features, this one can be "switched off" so that no page numbers print.

Screen oriented. Programs that are screen oriented mean that what you see on screen is what you'll get on the printed page. (Also known as What You See Is What You Get, or WYSIWYG.) If you want justified right margins, they will be displayed that way on the screen. If you make a change, that change is reflected instantly on the screen in both the content of the words and the format of the words.

Word processing programs that are not screen oriented are known as **character oriented.** This means you see all the words displayed in the order, but not necessarily in the format, that they will be printed. Some people don't mind this. As long as one word follows another as written and the new paragraphs begin when requested, that's all that matters. Others will want to see what they're working on, in the form it will be printed, as they go.

Windows. All high-end word processing programs create windows. This means you can divide the screen into sections (windows) and edit more than one file at once. Your outline can be in window one, and the brilliant realization of that outline in window two. Two is the minimum number of windows—some programs have more.

The window concept, by the way, extends beyond word processing. There are window programs (the most popular are Microsoft Windows, DESQview and GEM) that allow you to run different programs in different windows. Your accounting program can be in window one, while word processing is in window two. Great for muse-struck accountants and/or bestselling romance writers.

Justification. No, this is not a list of good excuses for why you spent so much money on a fancy typewriter. This means the right margin is straight and even, just as the left. Most books, newspapers and magazines use justified right and left margins, also known as "flush right" and "flush left."

Studies have shown, however, that while perfectly justified right and left margins look more impressive on a printed page, unjustified ("ragged") right margins are easier to read. Moral: If you want to impress, turn the justification on. If you want to communicate, turn it off. *Time* Magazine justifies. *People* does not. (And you can see where *this* book stands!)

Justification is done by expanding shorter lines. This expansion is done by adding spaces. If little itsy-bitsy-teeny-tiny spaces are added between letters, this is known as **microspacing.**

Proportional spacing. Most typewriters allot the same amount of space for each letter, so that a capital "W" is the same width as a small "i." Proportional spacing prints the "W" wider than an "a" and an "a" wider than an "i." Most books and magazines print with proportional spacing. Proportional spacing produces printed copy that is as close as you can get to professional typesetting. This requires, of course, not only the appropriate software, but also one of the better printers.

While we're on the subject of printers, when the fanciest features of a top-quality word processing program combine with a laser or ink-jet printer, you have desktop publishing. This book was desktop published—I did it all in the comfort of my home. While discerning eyes can see that these pages don't have the quality of the machines that mint our dollar bills, it nonetheless looks as if it came from a big-name publishing house. We'll explore desktop publishing more fully in Part IV.

This chapter has exhausted only you and me. It has far from exhausted all the features currently available on word processing programs, and more are coming each day. Whatever your personal needs in the processing of words, the chances are good the program exists that will make your task a whole lot easier. If they can help me spell, they can do anything.

220

Chapter 18

The Curse of Noah Webster

I have always had a fondness for Thomas Jefferson. Anyone who could write the Declaration of Independence and say, "I have nothing but contempt for anyone who can spell a word only one way," can't be all bad. I will not be spending much time on the Declaration of Independence in this chapter, but I have a feeling that I will be discussing the subject of spelling a great deal.

I am an awful speller. I am so bad that I don't even know when a word is spelled correctly. Ninety percent of the words I take the time to look up (and I do mean time: I'm lousy at alphabetical order, too) are right in the first place. It's discouraging. Hence, one of the deciding factors in my purchase of a computer with word processing capabilities was the flurry of programs promising to forever end the Curse of Noah Webster. (He's the one who started it all, you know. He's the one who came along over 200 years ago and gave Americans only one way to spell a word. The *right* way. *His* way.)

Once upon a time, spell-check programs needed to be purchased separately from word processing programs, just as headlights were once considered an option on automobiles. Today, both are considered pretty much "built in."

For example, in the WordPerfect program, one only needs to hold down the control key and press the F2 key. The bottom of the screen then offers the following:

CHECK: 1 WORD; 2 PAGE; 3 DOCUMENT; 4 NEW SUP. DICTIONARY; 5 LOOKUP; 6 COUNT

If you press 1, the word that the cursor is on will be checked; pressing 2 examines the whole page, and 3, the entire document.

When WordPerfect has finished checking, it will tell you how many words it examined. If you want to know how many words are in a document without spell-checking first, press 6. You can create a new supplemental dictionary (that has all your legal words in it, for instance) by pressing 4.

Using WordStar, another popular word processing program, ALT-3 will check the entire document, while ALT-4 checks only the current word. There are many ways to skin a gerund.

Another great feature many word processing programs have these days is an online thesaurus. At the press of another set of keys, you can get a list of synonyms for whatever word your cursor rests. Many people avoid thesauri for the simple reason that they take too long to use. To find synonyms for "sharp," for instance, means pulling out the *Roget's,* thumbing through the "S" section until you find "sharp," and then scanning down a list until you find the shade of meaning you want—say it's "alert." Then there's a number next to alert, such as "531.14."

You now have to flip through more pages until you get to the "531" section headed by the word "care." Fourteen subsections down, you get to the list that you may want: "alert, awake, ready, smart, bright, etc."

If the word you want is not there, then it means flipping to the back again and finding another meaning—and another number—for "sharp." Back and forth until you have it. All this work can certainly draw a person out of a creative state of mind.

WordPerfect's thesaurus works by holding down the ALT key and pressing the F1 key. For "sharp," I get a list of 31 synonyms, including "piercing, cunning, bright, clever, intelligent." Each synonym has a letter next to it. If none of the words is quite right, I press the corresponding letter for a word that's close, and I get another list of synonyms. When I find a word I like, with the press of a key, I can swap it for "sharp" in my text.

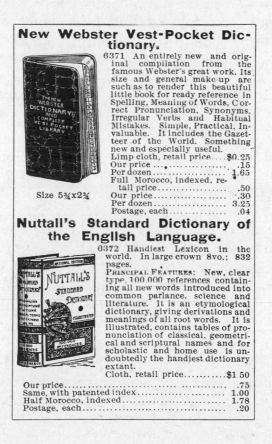

Using the WordStar thesaurus (which they license from Microlytics and is available as a separate program), I get an even 150 synonyms for "sharp." Pretty sharp, huh?

The thesaurus is so fast and easy, I actually use it.

The WordStar/Microlytics thesaurus includes brief dictionary definitions for many of its words. ("Sharp" is defined as "keen." A microscope is an "optical image-magnifying device.")

Another program is Proximity Technology's Choice Words. The dictionary and thesaurus reside in memory, available at a moment's notice. Say you are typing along, your mind in a distant pond. You think of using the word "aquatic." You want to check the meaning to see if it's the word you want. Move the cursor to the word "aquatic," hold down the left shift key, the ALT key and the letter "D" for "dictionary." Up pops a concise definition: "ADJECTIVE—of or relating to water."

Say you are learning English as a second language and the word "water" doesn't plunk a bell. Within the definition above, move the cursor to the word water and press the enter key. Up comes: "NOUN – WATER 1) liquid that descends as rain and forms rivers, lakes and seas 2) liquid containing or resembling water; VERB – WATERED, WATERING, WATERS – 1) supply with or get water 2) dilute with or as if with water 3) form or secrete watery matter." The WordStar/Microlytics definition is more to the point: "Water: the most essential liquid (H20)."

If a word you are looking up happens to be misspelled, the dictionary will first offer a list of possible spellings based on phonetics and typos. For instance, you might be writing about bedroom furniture and you describe an item with drawers. How do you spell that item? Is it "burow"? Press the ALT-Shift-D keys. Up comes a list of 12 spellings including the words "burrow," "barrow" and "bureau." Is it the last one you want? Bureau? Now press the three special keys again. Up comes the meaning: "NOUN – 1) chest of drawers, 2) administrative unit, 3) business office." Yep, that's the word.

For Choice Words you need at least 100K of free memory. The program uses its own data compression routine, allowing for the storage of 7 megabytes' worth of data in less than one and a half megabytes of disk space—fabulous! (Which, it turns out, means "1) like, told in, or based on fable, 2) incredible or marvelous" and the synonyms offered are "mythical, mythological, legendary.")

(Choice Words is also sold as Language Master. List price: $99. Proximity, 3511 N.E. 22nd Avenue, Fort Lauderdale, FL 33308; 800-323-0023.)

(Microlytics Thesaurus and Dictionary: 800-828-6293.)

The newest rage in word processing is grammar checking. Like spell-checkers, grammar checkers can zoom through a document and highlight suspected problems. Grammar, however, is not as exact a science as spelling.

The rules for grammar are ofttimes complex or subjective. One person's error is another person's style.

The early grammar checkers were great for beginning writers. They offered a solid foundation to grammar and style. For experienced writers, they were too slow and strict. I found they made bad writers better and good writers worse.

That is no longer true. Grammatik IV, for instance, can be tailored to one's needs and style. If you don't want the program to flag long sentences, for instance, you can turn that flag off.

Grammatik IV can operate inside or outside your word processor. It highlights words and phrases of

225

dubious quality, offers what it thinks may be wrong and advice on how to correct it. If you want to correct anything, you just pop into Grammatik's editor.

Within the space of a single chapter, the program caught: a lack of punctuation (a missing period); verb disagreement ("It find..."); improper infinitive ("to chose"); a gender specific word ("chairman" instead of "chair" or "chairperson"); improper article usage ("an file"); a typo ("form" instead of "from"); a question that ended in a period instead of a question mark; and more.

Some of the "more" was not always correct. The program does not claim to be completely intelligent. It stopped at the name "James Lapine" (a fabulous writer and director) and said the word "James" may be a possessive and may need an apostrophe. Well, it's not a possessive, nor is "Angeles" when I wrote about a Los Angeles restaurant.

Grammatik IV also stopped at the split infinitive "to boldly go" and suggested I unsplit it. No way. Captain Kirk always boldly goes. The *Los Angeles Times Stylebook* agrees: "The traditional taboo against split infinitives is largely a superstition. In many cases, if not most, the logical place for an adverb is in the middle of the infinitive construction." (Bet you didn't know the *Los Angeles Times* had a style book.)

A major advance incorporated into Grammatik IV: you can tell it never to bother you with certain problem types again. Off goes the split-infinitive flag. Off goes the incomplete sentence flag. Whatever you want.

You can also set Grammatik to your writing style. Fiction has tended to play havoc with grammar checkers. Such dialogue as, "You what!? How!? Over my dead body!" would be flagged as incomplete sentences, and a single line of dialogue in a paragraph would be flagged as a one-sentence paragraph. No more. (Advertising

226

copywriters had better pretend they are writing fiction. I guess it doesn't take that much pretending after all.)

You can also set Grammatik to "general," "business," "technical," "informal" or "custom." (I'd better write something here so I'm not accused of having a one-sentence paragraph.)

At the end of the checking, the program presents you with a statistical summary of your file. You receive such information as the readability indexes of your work, number of words, prepositions, and more. It's all designed to show you how complex or simple your writing is. If you are writing a vacuum cleaner manual, for instance, and the indexes show that you have to be in graduate school to understand it, you might want to go back and simplify.

This is all fine as long as you remember: Grammatik IV is not a god, it is merely a computer program. Saying you like your prose (or poetry) as it is, is always your choice. (Grammatik IV is from Reference Software, 330 Townsend, Suite 123, San Francisco, CA 94107; 415-541-0222.)

With spell-checking, grammar checking, online dictionaries and thesauri, you can have more control over English than you might have thought possible. These features won't make you clever or witty, but they will help you avoid appearing silly—especially in Noah Webster's eyes.

This computer work station is also a self-contained Little People Center.™ The Little People grow their own crops and herd their own cattle. All you give them is twenty minutes of sun and two ounces of Coca-Cola per day. In exchange for this, they will keep your computer screen spotlessly clean. Comes complete with Little People™ and Little Cattle.™ Does not include computer. Little People and Little Cattle Breeding Stock™ available at extra cost.

Chapter 19

Word Processing in the Office

Over the past decade we've seen what happens when the large, expensive, electric typewriter—be it the only one in an office, or one of several hundred—is replaced by a slightly larger, electric, more expensive word processing computer.

What happens is miraculous.

Let's look at the various tasks for which a typewriter is most often used in an office, and see how a word processing computer would handle the same tasks.

Certainly one of the primary uses for a typewriter in the office is correspondence: letters, notes, memos and the like. It would seem, from superficial examination, that some kinds of correspondence would benefit from word processing and others would not. Form letters, or letters that might use boilerplate paragraphs, would obviously fall into the "it would benefit" category, whereas original correspondence in which a letter is dictated and typed only once would not. Let's see if the latter assumption is true.

To type an original letter on a typewriter, one puts a piece of paper in the typewriter, types, and takes the letter out of the typewriter. Simple. To type an original letter on a word processor, one must create a file, type the letter (which would be displayed on the monitor), put a piece of paper in a printer, instruct the computer to print the letter, watch while the letter is printed, and remove the letter. Not as simple.

It would seem, then, that if most of the work done by a given secretary consisted of original letters, a word processor could be a hindrance. But let's look a bit more closely at how an original letter is created.

Most original letters are dictated. The secretary types the letter from the notes she or he has taken, and submits the letter for a signature. If there's a single typo or misspelling (bosses seem to *enjoy* finding mistakes, don't they?) (and they're *good* at it, too) (is that how they got to be bosses?), then the entire letter must be retyped. If typos are found in the retyped letter, it must be typed again, etc., etc. If the letter is free from secretarial error, the boss, seeing his or her thoughts immortalized on paper for the first time, will no doubt begin making changes. Even a simple "add this" or "take that out" means only one thing to the secretary: "retype the whole thing."

The word "retype" is seldom mentioned in a word-processed office, just as the phrase "crank it up" has fallen into disuse in automobile circles since the advent of the electric starter. Some phrases linger for nostalgia's sake more than anything else: car batteries are rated for their "cold cranking" abilities, and a boss in a word-processed office will occasionally say, "Would you retype this?" But what he or she means, and what the secretary hears, is, "Would you make these changes and print a new copy?"

Making changes is fast and easy. Simply call the file up on screen, remove what is unwanted, add what is wanted, and print the results. Fast laser printers turn out freshly printed documents at the rate of eight pages per minute.

Even if no changes are made, the speed at which a spell-check program can ferret out spelling and typing errors makes a word processor more than earn its keep.

Then we come into the areas of correspondence where word processors truly shine: boilerplate paragraphs and form letters.

Most businesses have paragraphs, even whole letters, that repeat themselves day after day after day. "Thank you for inquiring about our new Wonder

Widget . . . . " "We certainly hope you will enjoy your new Wonder Widget . . . . " "All of us are prostrate with grief that your new Wonder Widget did not live up to your expectations . . . . " And so on. With a word processor, these boilerplate paragraphs can be stored on a disk and added to the letter whenever necessary. Once added, they can be altered, added to, or shortened.

I have a boilerplate paragraph I use whenever I write a letter of complaint. I attempt to shame the company into *not* sending me a form-letter response. I do this with a form paragraph. It reads:

> *I am reminded of the man who wrote a letter to the Pullman Company back in the 1940's complaining of bedbugs in his sleeping car. He received a very apologetic letter saying that this was the first they had ever heard of such a thing, and that all the cars were being fumigated as a response to his letter. Along with this letter was enclosed, by mistake, the original letter of complaint the man had sent. Written by hand at the bottom of the letter was: "Send this SOB the bedbug letter." I certainly hope that I will not receive a "bedbug" letter from you.*

I have this paragraph in a file named "PULLMAN." It takes but a few seconds to add it to the text of any letter or, in this case, book. To type it would take several minutes, and to find the original from which to type it would no doubt take longer.

Names and addresses are typed and retyped in the course of a business day. A name and address is first found on the Rolodex, then typed at the top of the letter. Later, the same information will be typed once again on an envelope. With a word processor, a mailing list can be kept on a disk. In less than the time it takes to find a card on a Rolodex, the computer has not only found, but also added to your letter, the name and address in question. When it is time to print the envelope, a command or two from the keyboard takes care of it.

Form letters are well known to us all. The same thing needs to be said to fifty people, but each person must receive the information personally typed. A task of this kind in a Selectric office would sentence a normally cheerful, productive secretary to a day of drudgery and depression.

In a business I once ran, we would hire various sales organizations to sell our wares, each organization having a dozen or so salespeople. These were the people who would be selling our product for, in some cases, an entire state. I felt that a personalized letter welcoming them and telling them about the company was in order. This began as a two-page letter, but soon grew to five. Each time I hired a new sales organization my secretary would, understandably, grow pale and bored. About the time I thought it would be a good idea to thank every buyer who ordered from us with a personalized letter, she quit. Although I failed to realize it then, the two events were, no doubt, related.

On a word processor, fifty personalized, one-page letters would take less than an hour. With a laser printer, the operation would require minimal supervision.

Most programs permit the automatic insertion of the name and other information within the letter, so that, "I know you'll find Minnesota to be Wonder Widget Country, Jim!" in one letter automatically becomes, "I know you'll find Hawaii to be Wonder Widget Country, Carol!" in the next. In addition, each of the fifty letters would not require individual proofreading. Only the name and address would need verification; the balance would be letter-perfect.

Most of the other office tasks requiring a typewriter are extensions of the letter, and the contributions made by a word processing computer would be very much the same.

Reports, for example, are subject to many revisions before the final draft is approved. The same report may be retyped a dozen times before it is deemed suitable for circulation. The reduction of retyping that word processing brings to letters, it brings with an even greater sigh of relief to reports.

"Take a letter, Miss Jones: 'My dear George.' No, make that, 'Dear George, I don't see . . . .' No, make that, 'I see no reason why I should learn to process words.' Um, no, make that last part, '. . . why I should learn word processing.' And start the sentence, 'As an executive . . . .' Could you read that back to me after you answer the phone?"

On larger documents, some of word processing's other features are useful: the freedom to move a paragraph from one part of the document to another in a matter of seconds, for example, or the ability to find all occurrences of a word or phrase and change it to a different word or phrase. Using right-justified margins adds a professional look, and if you use proportional spacing, they'll think you sent it out to be typeset.

On long documents, the computer's ability to find typos and misspellings is particularly valuable. The longer the document, the harder it becomes to find mistakes. As the operating manual for The WORD (a spell-check program) points out, "Studies have shown that in documents longer than 20 pages, most people fail to find more than 50% of the misspelled words." A good spell-check program won't miss a one.

Once perfect, in what form should the report be circulated? Who gets original typed copies and who gets photocopies? With a word processor, nearly everyone can receive a personally typed copy.

Having the report on a disk can be valuable. You may wish to quote from it; it could form the backbone of a great many well-written letters. With only minor changes, a report to the president can become a report to the board of directors and, with a few more changes, a newsletter for the sales force.

Speaking of newsletters, we might as well speak about newsletters. Newsletters are the responsibility of some secretaries, and word processors make organizing them relatively easy. To put together, for example, an inspirational message from "the boss," one need only go through some recent correspondence (all neatly stored on disks), select a few timeless phrases, arrange them in a logical order and there you have it. No need to retype any of these gems. Just copy them from the files on which they are stored.

Some word processing programs let you set the type with right- and left-justified margins around spaces for photographs or drawings. Print a copy, add photos and drawings, and it's ready for the professional printer or the copy machine. (For even more good news about newsletters, see the upcoming section on desktop publishing.)

And now for the bad news (or, if you have a deep emotional attachment to your Selectric, the good news): what typewriters do better than word processors. The list is small. Come to think of it, it's not even a list; it's just one thing. What Selectrics do better than word processors is fill in blanks. When you type on a word processor, the text is displayed on a screen first and printed on paper later. Therefore, it's difficult to tell precisely on which line the typing will fall. With a Selectric, you position the ball above the line in question and type away.

It is not impossible to fill out forms with most word processors. Most have a simple command that turns the keyboard/printer into a mock-Selectric (which is great for all except laser printers). Position the form in the printer, then use the keyboard to type the information. One must be careful, though: unlike a correcting Selectric, there is no ribbon of fly paper to magically lift your mistakes from the paper. If you make a mistake, it's back to Correctype.

It is because of forms, and one-time labels, that people keep a Selectric or small electric typewriter around the word-processed office. It depends on the number and kind of forms and labels needed.

Usually standard company forms can be filled out faster on the word processor once the operator knows the spatial relationship between the form and the screen. Sometimes a special program can be run that duplicates the forms of a company, and sometimes it's simply a matter of knowing that question 23 should be answered on line 42, column 12. Line and column information is usually displayed somewhere on the screen, and getting to a certain line and column is easy.

So much for what a Selectric can do better than a word processor.

Let's look at a few of the random benefits gained by having a word processing computer around the office.

> Computers are becoming more familiar and easier to use. Businesses are no longer necessarily dependnt on large cneral sysms; individutteals wihin organizations no longer necessionels to interpret their needs in language which the computer can understand.
> —*London Times.*

Earlier in this book, I mentioned the ability to run programs other than word processing programs on the computer. The only difference between a word processing computer and an accounting computer is the software.

In an office in which one person is responsible for not only correspondence and reports but also invoicing and bookkeeping, a personal computer equipped with both word processing and accounting programs could easily double the effectiveness of this person.

In slightly larger offices, where billing and such is done by one person and correspondence is handled by another (the classic "this is the bookkeeper and this is the secretary" situation), it is sometimes possible for two people to share one computer. The bookkeeper gets it in the morning, the secretary in the afternoon.

If the need is so great that two terminals are required, my suggestion: buy two computers. Accounting will probably be happier with a dot-matrix printer anyway, so that saves $1,000. (Only in America do you have so many opportunities to save money by spending. I've saved so much recently, I'm approaching bankruptcy.)

The installation of a network can be done for two or more computers, but I still have reservations about networks (see the chapter on networks). While I admire the concept and the ability to share printers, networks can be sluggish. Besides, if the accounting computer is down and the checks must go out, it's comforting to know that the secretary's word processing computer can be converted to an accounting computer in a matter of minutes—assuming you bought two similar computers, which is a very good idea.

In a larger office, one that has its own "DP" (data processing) department with its own computers, the ability to run the literally thousands of programs avail-

237

able for a personal computer system can be valuable. To list them would (and does) fill a book. Suffice it to say that whatever your business is, there are, no doubt, programs—from figuring the amortization of a mortgage to balancing the boss's personal checkbook—that will make the secretary's work not only easier, but more effective.

One benefit of word processing in the office is that word processors are so quiet. The movement of fingers on a keyboard and the appearance of characters on a screen is very close to absolute silence. Some people find this annoying after many years of "click-click-click," so some keyboards have an electronic "click." After a weaning process, most people turn this feature off. If you buy a computer that clicks, beeps or boops, make sure the noises can be turned off.

There is no denying that some printers can be noisy sons-of-guns. They are about as loud as a Selectric being used full-tilt. However, the printer is usually not used as often as a Selectric. This is because many of the corrections that would normally require retyping have been discovered and corrected on screen. Laser printers, which are fast and efficient, are whisper quiet. Most offices have these, and I recommend them for most offices.

When asked by business people, "Should we buy now or should we wait? After all, new and better computers are coming out every day." I reply, "Yes, they are, and buy now."

Although personal computers will undoubtedly be less expensive in months and years to come, the money saved by increased efficiency and productivity will be far greater than whatever one might save by waiting.

Typewriter Cabinets.

In these cabinets the machine is always on a level, thus saving it from the bad effect of being constantly tipped over and so getting out of order. The cabinet will accomodate any size machine, and protect it from dust. When the machine is not in use it can be dropped out of sight, thus the cabinet serves the double purpose of a typewriter cabinet and an office desk. We show a larger assortment of cabinets in our new special Furniture Catalogue, which we mail on receipt er 8 cents to pay postage.

73134 Typewriter Cabinet. This cabinet is well made of solid oak, and highly *hand-polished*. Height, 31 ins., size of top, 30x36 inches; width of drawers, 10 inches. Has one extension slide and combination lock. Weight, about 150 pounds: finished antique. Price, complete... ....$16.25

Letter Writers and Etiquette.

7935 Dick's Common Sense Letter Writer. Containing 300 Sensible, Social and Business Letters, with appropriate answers on all possible subjects, etc. By William B. Dick. 16mo., bound in boards, cloth back...$0.35

7936 Dick's Commercial Letter Writer and Book of Business Forms. Containing entirely original Models of Letters on business subjects, with appropriate replies; also several specimens of Continuous Correspondence, exhibiting by a series of letters the progress and completion of Mercantile Transactions. By William B. Dick. 200 pages, 16mo., bound in boards...$0.35

7937 Worcester's Letter Writer and Book of Business forms for ladies and gentlemen. Containing accurate directions for conducting correspondence, with 276 specimen letters adapted to every age and situation in life. 216 pages. Bound in boards. $0.35

7938 North's Book of Love Letters. With directions how to write and when to use them, and 120 specimen letters, suitable for lovers of any age and conditio , and under all circumstances. By Ingoldsby North. 16mo. bound in boards.........................$0.35

7939 Chesterfield's Letter Writer and Complete Book of Etiquette. 16mo., bound in boards.....$0.35

7940 Martine's Hand-Book of Etiquette. A most valuable book. 16mo., bound in boards.........$0.35

7941 How to Behave in Society. A hand-book of etiquette for ladies and gentlemen, with rules for correct deportment, correspondence and forms of invitations, etc., with valuable hints in regard to engagements, weddings, balls and other occasions..$0.18

Chapter 20

Word Processing for Students

At first, personal computers became the greatest preppy status symbol since the alligator shirt. Lacoste, in fact, planned on marketing a personal computer available in twelve designer colors with a little alligator in the corner of the screen.

Now, personal computers are what typewriters were in my day—a tool to get the work done. Computers have become so generic, in fact, that many come without a name on the machine at all.

This chapter will examine what a personal computer, programmed for word processing, can do for students, be they high school, college, graduate students or "students of Life." The chapter will not deal so much with the educational possibilities of personal computers, although some of them will be mentioned later. The question answered in this chapter is, "What would happen if I sold my Smith-Corona portable typewriter to my little brother and got my parents to buy me a word processing computer?"

You may have noticed that this chapter is sandwiched neatly between a chapter on word processing in the office and word processing for the professional writer. This is no accident. As a student, you are expected to record, organize and regurgitate material with the efficiency and accuracy of an executive secretary, while maintaining a vast creative output and a literary style that ranges from the clarity of journalism to the imaginativeness of poetry.

While this goal of student life, like absolute zero, can never quite be obtained, a word processor can offer certain tools that might prove valuable in the quest.

Reports. The bane of academic life. And a report by any other name—essay, thesis, term paper, biography, rhapsody, investigation—is still a report: take the information in, mix gently, put the information out. Original thought is generally not welcome, and creativity is limited to rearranging the professor's thoughts and comparing them favorably with the greatest minds of all time. On the whole it's a dull world, but welcome to life.

There are good study habits (GSH) that have been passed down through the eons of academia. A student with GSH on his or her way to a term paper would do something like this. (Let's see, shall I make this student a male or a female? I'll flip a coin: heads, male; tails, female. It was tails. This will be a female student with GSH.)

During class she takes copious notes. She does not go to the sock hop after class, she does not even pause for a cherry Coke. She goes directly to her room and types her notes while the lecture is still fresh in her mind. While she types, she elaborates upon the notes, remembering other information the professor gave in class and adding references to similar material from past classes. She highlights the areas she does not understand and makes it a point to either ask the professor the next day in class or one of her classmates for clarification, or research the unknown variable in the library. After researching it, of course, she checks with her mentor to make sure that Spinoza and the professor were saying the same thing. As term paper time rolls around, she collates her notes, puts them in a comprehensible order, and writes her paper.

Like Sherlock Holmes, I doubt if this ideal student ever existed. I think she was created from all the "shoulds" that educators throughout time have laid upon themselves while *they* were in school but never bothered to follow either. Using this as our ideal, however, let's see how a word processing computer might fit into this cycle of GSH.

The student would go home after class and type her notes. These would be her version, in her style, of what the professor had said. These would be stored on disk, and a copy printed for review. If there was a question, she could ask the professor in class, ask a classmate, or research it. Or, she could write the professor a *letter*. Selecting passages from her notes on disk from past classes, she could put together—in just a few minutes—a thoughtful, courteous, detailed, perfectly spelled and typed letter from a student who obviously must be very special. The answer to this letter is not nearly as important as the impression it would make. (Don't do this more than three times a semester, however; you don't want to cross the fine line between intellectual curiosity and stupidity.)

At term paper time, her report is essentially written. All she does is pull from her disks the paragraphs she likes best, tie them together with a transitional sentence or two, and print a letter-perfect paper. While her fellow students are struggling to find (A) a topic and (B) a typist, our student with GSH (and a word processor) is at the student union enjoying a cherry Coke and looking forward to an uncrowded sock hop.

The key to good writing is editing. Most people include too much. With a word processor, you can remove the verbiage without the penalty of retyping. You can be freer in your expression, knowing that you can tighten later.

After a paper is written, printed, graded and returned, it is easy to pull the paper up on screen, make the changes and corrections recommended by the teacher, print a revised copy, and resubmit it. This takes little time and, although it may not alter your grade for that paper, it will gain you brownie points galore. When was the last time you heard of anyone *voluntarily* rewriting a paper?

At times in school—not often, but at times—you will be asked to create some original prose or poetry. A major mistake nonwriters (and a great many writers, myself at the head of the line) make is to think that before our sentences ever meet paper, they must be perfect. This is the cause of writer's block. It's not that the writer cannot think of anything to write; it's that the writer cannot think of anything *perfect* to write.

There is a theory that the first step in creative writing is to write down anything and everything that comes to mind. The next step is to edit, emphasizing what is good and removing what is not.

Once one becomes accustomed to the ease with which changes are made on word processors, it becomes easier to write more, take more risks, and go for ideas first and perfection later. It is not a magic wand, and we do not overnight become James Joyce, or even Jack Kerouac; but, given time, a freeing of expression does take place.

Teachers for some time now have ingrained in us the concept that an inability to spell automatically equals an inability to think. The only person who could not spell but who *could* think, in the opinion of most English professors, was Chaucer. You can write a paper that may contain some of the best prose and finest new ideas of the Western world and, if you misspell 10 percent of the words, you'll be hard pressed to find an educator who will take any of it seriously. Poor spelling, they feel, equals dumb.

This, of course, is not true. At least, I hope it's not true. Spelling requires an ability to inhale and exhale information verbatim, like being able to remember that 6 times 8 equals, um, uh, let's see . . . 5 times 8 is 40, plus 8, okay . . . rather like being able to remember that 6 times 8 equals 48. I'm sure we all know people who can rattle off the times tables, can spell any word, and are, in fact, creative wastelands.

Although it's not true that poor spelling equals dumb, it's still a belief. A widely held belief that is not true is known by a difficult word to spell: prejudice. So, either you wage a one-person campaign against this prejudice (and if you do, you can count on me for a small but heartfelt contribution), or you conform.

Alas, one of the most painful portions of the educational process is deciding against which bits of cultural nonsense we're going to take a stand, and to those which we're going to conform. If we take a stand against *all* of them, we are ignored, or locked up, or both. We must, it seems, pick our top six or seven dozen causes, flail against them with great vigor, and let the rest go.

If spelling is one you've decided to let go, the computer can help. As mentioned in the chapter, *The Curse of Noah Webster,* a word processor with a spell-check program can help you find the socially acceptable spellings. For the student who has spent hours over a dictionary looking up almost every word, knowing that the teacher was a Noah Webster devotee—and who has still missed a word or two—this feature of word processing will fall into his or her life like manna.

An interesting thing has happened since using my word processor to check for spelling errors. Rather than becoming a crutch, the word processor has actually *improved* my spelling. This surprised me. I thought I was a hopeless case. I had tried everything—flash cards, *Reader's Digest's* "Toward a More Powerful Vocabulary,"

Misspellers Anonymous ("I am helpless against my inability to spell . . ."), everything. I had given up.

I was great at finding synonyms. Whenever the word I wanted to use was too difficult to spell, I would find one that was easier. I would never, for example, tackle the word "synonyms." I would write "similar words" or "words that mean the same thing," "similar" being a tough one, too. I also found that after looking up all the words that I *thought* were misspelled, they were usually spelled correctly in the first place. This was very disheartening.

I found that after getting a list of misspelled words—and misspelled words *only*—from the computer, and choosing the correct spellings for these words, somehow the acceptable-to-Mr. Webster versions began to sink in. I would notice patterns. I would put too many M's in "coming" and too few N's in "beginning." I tended to drop the final *E* before adding "ly." Things like that.

The fact is that I, like most "poor spellers," *do* know how to spell most words. It's the ones we *don't* know how to spell that give us trouble. The pattern of these words tends to be as individual as our fingerprints. Knowing which words are our individual troublemakers, and then discovering the correct spelling for them, is the best way I have found for spelling improvement.

A personal computer can do more than a word processor, just as a cassette recorder can play more than biology lectures. Many other programs available for personal computers can be of value to students.

Personal finance, for example, can do everything from helping you create a budget to balancing your checkbook. A math program can turn your computer into an electronic slide rule and beyond. You can chart your biorhythms or cast your horoscope. The programs offered for personal computers are endless. As with prerecorded cassette tapes, some are valuable, many are not.

Then there are the programs that will actually teach you something. Computers are the perfect teachers. They will take you as far as you want as fast as you want, while providing limitless judgment-free tutorials in subjects you may find particularly difficult. If a student were a whiz at English Lit but found math incomprehensible, the computer would take this student quickly on beyond Beowulf, while patiently letting him or her know that 2 plus 2 does not equal 5.

There are programs that will teach you a skill necessary to operate a word processor: typing. If you don't know how to type now, don't worry. It's not hard to learn (speaking as one who has yet to learn), and you'll be glad you did. (Try *Mavis Beacon Teaches Typing*, a program from Software Toolworks, 818-907-6789.)

As described elsewhere in this book, a personal computer can be connected via telephone to very large computers with massive data banks. These not only provide access to what is going on in the world (UPI newswire, the electronic editions of various newspapers, etc.), but permit detailed research on what has already taken place. If you were researching, say, medieval French tapestry, you could enter the word "TAPESTRY" in the computer and receive a great deal of information on tapestry. Any time the word was used in *The New York Times,* for example, the article using that word would be instantly available. If the information were useful, you could store it on disk for later reference; if not, you could go on to the next article.

While we're discussing "other uses" for a computer, may I suggest that you *not* buy the flashy, full-color, complete-with-sound-effects games? These are addictive, it seems, and your room will become an arcade rather than a temple of Higher Learning. Enough said. A word to the wise is sufficient. Flight Simulator and electronic Monopoly are my favorites.

Beyond all this, a personal computer will give the student a skill that is valuable today, invaluable in five years and necessary in ten: computer literacy. Computer literacy is simply knowing how to use a computer: how to add information to it and take information from it. Most importantly, computer literacy is being comfortable with computers, treating them as tools and not gods—with respect for, and not in fear of, their power.

The best way to learn is by doing, and the best way to do is by owning a computer of one's own. It's the greatest investment parents can make in their child's future.

STUDENTS

Remove this page and send the rest of this book to your parents, along with your report card and a list of upcoming holidays, including your birthday. Highlight the part about not playing games; they'll like that.

It might help if you misspell a few words in the note and make the handwriting occasionally illegible.

Good luck!

Chapter 21

Word Processing for Writers

The past forty years have not been kind to those of us homesteading on the printed page. Flashy technological innovations—from television to transistor radios to long-playing-stereophonic-high-fidelity-compact-digital-records to six-track-Dolby-stereo-seventy-millimeter-Technicolor-Panavision-THX-Plus-motion pictures—have led people farther and farther from the written word.

One hundred years ago, the Home Entertainment Center consisted of a bookcase. For a handful of highly sophisticated individuals, home entertainment meant listening to the gramophone by gaslight; but for most, reading a book by candlelight was the way to spend an evening. The major outside-the-home entertainment of the early 1890's was concerts, musicals, plays and expositions. Parties were popular, from the rural quilting bees and barn raisings to the urban balls and socials. People also seemed to *enjoy* each other, and published recollections of the day refer to something known as **conversation** as being "stimulating" and "amusing."

These few distractions aside, it was a great time for the written word.

Sixty years ago, an occasional player piano or phonograph was beginning to take some readers away from reading, but the real competition books faced was from radio, which was about to enter its Golden Age. Outside from home in the early 1930's, the talkies learned how to sing and Busby Berkeley taught them how to dance. Tickets were cheap and vaudeville was dying, so "a night out" almost always included a movie and maybe a little dancing. References to that form of entertainment known as "conversation" were growing fewer and farther between.

Reading was still popular, however. Thanks to mass education, the literacy rate had risen; thanks to mass production, the retail cost of a book had dropped (hardcover bestsellers could be had for "one dollar the copy"); and thanks to mass greed, the number of publishers publishing had increased dramatically. Some say this was the Golden Age of the American Novel.

Today the Home Entertainment Center features a six-foot color television which can show videotapes, digital laser discs, 99 channels of cable, 276 channels of satellite programming, and thousands of video games; and a stereo that plays digitally-recorded compact discs, DAT tapes, and two-dozen stations of FM Multiplex radio; all this connected to a master remote control that allows you to manipulate everything from the comfort of your redwood hot tub.

Clearly, there is no reason to leave the home, much less read anything more significant than the operator's manual for the latest technological goodie. If one ever does leave the house to purchase a new videotape or buy chlorine for the hot tub, one need not leave this Audio-Visual Disneyland behind. Car stereos, portable CD players, Walkmen and Watchmen make it unnecessary to read even a *National Enquirer* while waiting in line at the supermarket.

Yes, technology has robbed us of a generation of readers. Not only are there far more dazzling alternatives to cracking a book, but, thanks to these modern marvels, the literacy rate in this country is on the decline.

What has technology given writers in return? Well, let's see. In 1780, steel-point pens were invented— light years ahead of the quill, which had plagued writers and various feathered birds since 600 B.C. In 1884 came the fountain pen: no more dipping (but lots

JOHN B. KREYMBORG,

QUILL
Manufacturer

95 South Second street,

(Opposite the Merchants' Coffee-House, Philad.)

MANUFACTURES ALL KIND OF QUILLS,

Dutch, English, German,
and Opaque,

FROM $2 50 TO 30 $ PER 1000.

SWAN AND CROW QUILLS,

at various prices.

He also offers for sale, and keeps constantly on hand, at Manufacturers prices, a large stock of

GRENVILLE'S CHEMICAL INK POWDER,

Warranted superior for immediate production of Jet Black Ink.

ALSO, SUPERIOR SEALING WAX,

Warranted to burn free and stick well, of various colours, viz. Light and Dark Blue, Light and Dark Green, Yellow, Brown, Gold, Rose, Flesh, Orange, &c.

more dripping). Ballpoints rolled along (sorry) around 1944. (Remember the PaperMate PiggyBack pen that Art Linkletter claimed "writes through butter"? A great boon to writers moonlighting as short order cooks.) Today, we have such marvels as the felt tip pen (even with nylon points, they're still called "felt tip pens"), the erasable ballpoint—and a hybrid of the felt tip and the ballpoint, the uni-ball micro.

Typewriters were introduced a bit before fountain pens, in 1874. They were produced by a manufacturer of firearms, E. Remington and Sons. (The Remington typewriter and the Remington rifle share the same birthplace—one of those quirks of history, like Pulitzer, who made his fortune from yellow journalism, presenting certificates for excellence in writing; or Nobel, the inventor of dynamite, awarding Peace Prizes.) Electric typewriters came along in 1920, the IBM ball made its debut in 1961, and the correcting Selectric in the mid-1970's.

*"Rejoice! Rejoice!
The steel tip pen has been invented!"*

THE PERSONAL COMPUTER BOOK

Looking back on this 2,500 year history of writing technology, one would have to answer our original question, "What has technology given writers in return?" with a conditional, "Not much."

Not much, that is, until the personal computer.

Word processing computers are sufficiently wonderful to forgive Science for its two-and-a-half millennia of foot dragging. Granted, word processors were not invented for creative writers. They were invented—like the steel point, the fountain pen, the typewriter and all the rest—for businesses. So, even if Science did not set out *intentionally* to rectify centuries of injustice to writers, the end result is so glorious that we can grant them general amnesty just the same.

It all started with journalists. Journalists used to be called "newspapermen," then women's lib came along and changed it to "newspaperpersons." This sounded silly, so the Federated Newswriter's Union (FNU) hired Image Consultants, Inc., a public relations firm, to create a new handle for those working in the newspaper industry. Image Consultants (IC) first gained notoriety when they changed the term "janitor" to "Sanitation Engineer."

IC, after months of deliberation and research, settled on the term "Journalist." It was dignified, historical, nonsexist, and more than 70 percent of the newspaperpersons polled knew how to spell it. It was a natural. The FNU approved, changed its name to the FJU, and embarked on a multi-hundred-dollar campaign to etch the word "journalist" upon the soul of every literate human. (IC has since been hired by the graduate students of Montana State University, where they are working on an alternative name for the major, "Meat Science.")

Journalists work for big newspapers that have big computers to do payroll and accounts receivable and financial stuff like that. About twenty years ago someone said, "If this computer can help the accounting department write checks, maybe it can help the reporters write stories." It could and it did.

Computer terminals replaced typewriters in newsrooms across the land. Clark Kent was transformed into—not Superman, but Captain Video. Journalists kept quiet about it, though. The idea that the paper was being written by "a computer" would not have gone over very well twenty years ago, and the male of the journalist species preferred to maintain his former image: cigar in mouth, Scotch in hand, pounding out a story on his trusty Remington Upright.

THE REMINGTON
Perfected Type-Writer.

Employment for Girls! Easy, genteel, profitable.
Copying at home, or *writing in Business Offices.* Hundreds in such positions, in all parts of the country are earning from 8 to 20 dollars per week. See article on page 467, issue of Dec. 8, of this paper. Send for circular. **E. REMINGTON & SONS,** 281 & 283 Broadway, New York.

[1882]

As some journalists moved onto the greener pastures of academic professorship, they discovered that they missed the ease and convenience of computer writing. They also discovered that Big Universities, like Big Newspapers, had Big Computers. Soon dissertations, theses, letters to mothers, and occasional term papers were rolling off university computers.

By the early 1970's, the sum total of computer-assisted creative writing in this country produced, on one hand, stories about lost dogs and lost innocence, and, on the other, scholarly tomes on the effect of 16th Century chivalry upon the mercantile industry of the late 1700's. Plus a few letters to mothers. And so it remained for the next several years.

Then, something happened in the mid-1970's to change all that: the personal computer. No doubt science fiction writers had them first; it's their job to be on the cutting edge of things. Then graduates of universities who missed the computer more than spring break got them. Then former-journalists-turned-novelists who wanted to gaze again at a TV screen with words on it. Then the friends of these pioneers, then the Sons of the Pioneers, then Roy Rogers, Dale Evans and, well, just about every writer or would-be writer around. It was pandemic. (I've been waiting for *years* to use that word in print.)

If you're a writer and you've read this far, I'm sure you're well aware of the ways in which word processors can enhance and assist the writing process. To review a few:

1. **Change is effortless.** Adding to, taking from, and moving around text is simple. The changes are displayed at once, neatly "typed" on the monitor, with no cross-outs, "^" marks or scribbles in the margin.

2. **Retyping is unnecessary.** Even after a manuscript is printed and an error or area of improvement is discovered, all one need do is: bring up the original document on screen, make the change, and print a new page. Simple changes take but a few minutes, and most of that time is spent waiting for the printer. Only the changes need to be typed. No more agonizing over whether the replacement of one word is worth retyping a whole page. Manuscripts are neat and free from penciled-in changes.

3. Spelling is perfect. Spelling and typing errors are detected by the computer. My mother feels that she must clean house before she can call a cleaning person. Many writers feel that way about copy editors: the copy editor is there to verify the perfection of the piece, not to correct it. The spell-check will let you know that every word in your text is a genuine, properly spelled word. Whether those words are used correctly or creatively is another story. There are, however, programs that will help with grammar and punctuation. Used with caution, such grammar-checkers are not without value.

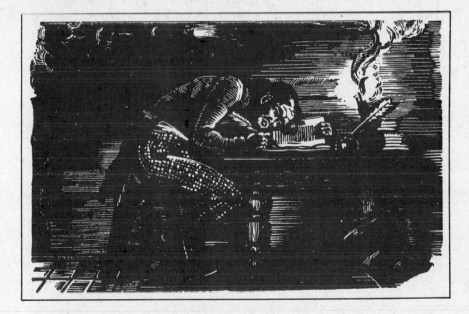

4. Word processors are quiet. I remember advertisements for Exercycle in the 1960's. A man was Exercycling away next to a bed, and on the bed was a woman smilingly asleep. (Back in the 1960's, of course, one automatically assumed this was his wife.) Under the photograph was the headline: "Exercycle: So Quiet He Can Exercise while She Sleeps."

I think the same marketing can be used to sell word processors. At the word processor sits a Barbara Cartland type, writing away, and in bed lies a 19-year-old hunk, smilingly asleep. The headline reads, "Word Processors: So Quiet She Can Write while He Sleeps."

I think, too, it would be fun to record a version of LeRoy Anderson's "The Typewriter Song" entitled "The Word Processor Song." The portions of the song devoted to typewriter clicking would be silent.

Until it's time to print something, word processors are blessedly quiet. If neighbors, roommates, lovers, or spouses have narrowed your hours of typewriter writing, word processing will provide you with a lengthened creative day. In a pinch you can even write in the dark. (Just to see if that last sentence were true, I have turned off the lights and am now writing this in total darkness. The keyboard is illuminated only by the light of the monitor.) If you can watch TV with earphones and not disturb the slumber of another, you can write with a word processor as well.

5. You are not chained to a typewriter table. The detachable keyboard, available on almost every personal computer, is wonderful. As I write this, the keyboard lies on my lap. If I had a keyboard extension cord, I could lie down and write, take the keyboard out to the patio (if I had a patio), or even use it in the bathroom. The long hours of sitting in the one position necessary to operate a stationary typewriter, with the cramps and tensions caused by that position, are no more.

6. No more carriage returns. Most word processing programs automatically place the next word on the next line when the right-hand margin is reached. In this way the words can flow, and you need only hit the carriage return when you want to start a new paragraph. No more little bells telling you that in eight more keystrokes your typewriter will stop dead.

7. Correspondence is easier. How often have you wanted to write essentially the same thing to five friends? You might get off a letter or two before boredom ("I have to type that *again?*") or guilt ("I should be writing my book and not these letters!") encourage you to abandon the project. With a word processor, all you have to write is one letter and print out five copies, changing only the recipient's name each time. *I* know this is a form letter, and *you* know this is a form letter, but *they* won't know it's a form letter—unless, of course, they also have a word processor, in which case they are probably sending you form letters already.

Some writers maintain their correspondence, but feel that they should be keeping a journal as well; others keep a journal, but fall behind in their correspondence. With a word processor, you can do both. If you enjoy correspondence, you can write about your life in letters to your friends, then choose the best paragraphs and copy them into your electronic journal. If journal-keeping is your preference, write your electronic journal, then send excerpts in the form of letters to your friends. In this way, both literary traditions are maintained.

There are other form letters you may want to send. In selling or promoting your works, it will probably be necessary to circulate a series of letters, each saying the same thing, to a variety of people: editors, publishers, agents, mothers. These must be individually typed and personalized to the recipient; a Xerox copy simply won't do. In the same way that personalized form letters can help a businessperson make a sale, personalized form letters can help you make a sale, too.

8. Research is easier. Using information services, discussed earlier, researching a project that might have required many trips to the library and much correspondence, can often take place in the comfort of your own computer terminal. And wait till you read the next chapter, *A Research Library Etched by a Laser*.

9. Other programs are available. Writers seldom have one-track minds; their interests are broad, passionate, and varied. The many programs that can be run on personal computers when they're not being used for word processing may prove valuable in satisfying a writer's greatest passion: curiosity. (All right, a writer's *second* greatest passion.)

10. They're fun. Computers are great, semi-expensive, fascinating toys. As a writer, you can justify the purchase of such a toy to just about anyone—including the IRS. (In most cases. See your accountant or the tax people at H&R Block for full details. Located at larger Sears, J.C. Penney and Montgomery Ward stores coast to coast. Offer void where prohibited by law, subject to cancellation without notice.)

If you're a writer, and if you're like me, you turned to this chapter first. I encourage you to read that which came before it and that which follows to get a more complete picture of how word processors might serve you in the creation or your work.

I have made my living as a writer for more than twenty years, and nothing—not a correcting Selectric, not a personal secretary, not even a #1 *New York Times* best seller—has thrilled or inspired me to write more than my word processor. Before my word processor, writing was a chore, a job, work. It's still a job, it's still work, but, thanks to the word processor, more and more often, writing is a joy.

(Any advertising agency that would like to use that last paragraph as copy for the "Word Processors: So Quiet She Can Write while He Sleeps" ad, please be in touch. I work cheap and am not afraid of selling out if the price is right, which it almost always is.)

הקל ופרסין
תקל הוא

266

Chapter 22

A Research Library
Etched by a Laser

I am in love with my computer again.

There is a line from the movie, *All about Eve,* in which the character played by Celeste Holm says (and I paraphrase), "Everything my husband loved about me he grew accustomed to long ago."

That, alas, is how it's been with my computer. First, the computer itself—specifically the word processing features of the computer—was a joy of joys. Never retyping anything and having a machine correct my spelling—well, that was heaven.

It was a long honeymoon, but eventually I became accustomed to computers. Then I got a hard disk. Computing was exciting again. But, as the Hindus say, luxury comes as a guest and soon becomes the master. Or, as Abigail Adams said in her February 13, 1779, letter to John Adams, "Luxury, that baneful poison, has unstrung and enfeebled her sons." The luxury of a hard disk unstrung and enfeebled me. It was computing as usual.

Fortunately, every six months or so, I could count on something to renew the thrill of computing: a keyboard with a track ball built in, a color monitor, speed-up boards, laser printers, expanded memory, RAM disks.

But it's been almost two years since the last excitement. I had nothing to look forward to when I faced my computer but *writing,* and, as Gore Vidal once said, "Only bad writers enjoy writing." (The trouble is, any number of bad writers also dislike writing. I am painful proof of this.)

This tale does have a happy ending. No, I have not learned appreciation for the blessings I already have. (I

267

am told some writers, even bad ones, still use pen and paper—I'm not sure I believe this, but I am told.) I have found a new computer addendum that has made writing fun again.

It's CD-ROM.

I have four discs for my CD-ROM. They look just like the CD's I play in my CD player, but instead of Haydn, they are alive with the music of words.

One contains the entire *Oxford English Dictionary;* the second contains the whole of the *Grolier Electronic Encyclopedia* (the *American Academic Encyclopedia);* the third is Information Finder (based on the *World Book Encyclopedia);* and the fourth contains Microsoft Bookshelf.

Allow me to start with the fourth first.

Microsoft Bookshelf is a collection of ten reference books, all online and instantly accessible. They are:

The American Heritage Dictionary
Roget's Thesaurus
The World Almanac
Bartlett's Familiar Quotations
The Chicago Manual of Style
Houghton Mifflin Spelling Corrector
Forms and Letters
U.S. Zip Code Directory
Houghton Mifflin Usage Alert
and
Business Information Sources.

CD-ROM requires its own special player. A card plugs into your computer, and the CD-ROM player plugs into the card. The player sells for about $700. Microsoft Bookshelf sells for $295. The combined price of these is, perhaps, what you plan to spend for your whole computer, but please read on: be tempted.

CD-ROM drives and CD-ROM have been available for a few years. They haven't exactly set the computing world on fire because there's been very little software of general interest, and the software that might be of popular interest is, for the most part, outrageously expensive.

For example, Bookshelf is $295 (without a CD-ROM drive). It includes a five-digit zip code directory. A *Zip+4 Directory,* published by another firm, is $3,950. A year of *The New York Times,* as much fun as that might be, is $4,500. And Lotus markets CD-ROM disks with stock market information that cost as much as $30,000 a year. (There are some CD-ROM bargains. The *Toronto Globe and Mail* for the entire year of 1985 is only $500 Canadian, which I think is about $1.74 American.)

The most appealing CD-ROM disk until now has been *Grolier's Academic American Encyclopedia*. It's $299, and worth $299, but it hasn't sold in great quantities because it requires a CD-ROM drive, which sells in the $600-$800 neighborhood. (If CD-ROM takes off, prices for CD-ROM drives should drop, just as the price of audio CD players did. And, with a larger market, the price of software should also drop.)

Bookshelf is the first software that breaks the resistance to buying a CD-ROM drive. Most people who write will find it irresistible, useful, and well worth $1,000 all by itself. If a CD-ROM drive is thrown in for that price, fine.

Accessing Bookshelf is simplicity itself. Part of the program is memory resident, part of the program resides on the computer's disk drive, and the bulk of the program, including the reference material, is on the CD-ROM disk. Pushing ALT-Shift at any point during any program, takes you instantly into Bookshelf.

"Instantly" is perhaps an overstatement. If you store the Bookshelf programs on a floppy disk, the computer will churn and chug away before Bookshelf is loaded. If you store your programs on a hard disk, access time is reduced to about a second. If you store your programs on a RAM disk—highly recommended—the response is instantaneous. (A RAM disk is a portion of your memory set aside to act as an ordinary disk drive—except much, much faster.)

After you hit ALT-Shift, a bar appears at the top of your screen with the words: Thesaurus, Dictionary, Spell, Usage, Manual, Almanac, Quote, BIZ, ZIP, Forms, Options and Help. Let's look at each of these individually.

If you're plugging away at the old word processor, and want to find another word for, say, "old," all you have to do is place your cursor somewhere within the word "old," hit ALT-Shift and then ALT-T (for Thesaurus). You are then treated to 34 synonyms for "old," along with descriptions of the various shadings of meanings. If one takes your fancy, simply place the cursor over the selected synonym and press return. It automatically replaces the old "old" with, say, antediluvian, hoary, fusty, or vintage. (The thesaurus, I found, had no synonym for "synonym.")

Nothing special yet. Disk-based thesauri, even relatively large ones, have been available for years. Ah, but not complete dictionaries. For example, I wondered if the plural for "thesaurus" was "thesauruses" or "thesauri." A quick check of Bookshelf's dictionary *(The American Heritage)* told me this about the word thesaurus:

> *"the-sau-rus n., pl. -sau-ri or -sau-rus-es. 1.*
> *A book of selected words or concepts, as a*
> *specialized vocabulary of a particular field,*
> *as medicine or music. 2. A book of synonyms.*
> *[Lat., collection Gk. thesauros, treasure]"*

So, both were right. It took me all of five seconds to find out. It took me another five seconds to copy the complete entry into this chapter.

Not only is the Bookshelf Dictionary faster and easier to use than the one on my bookshelf, it's also easier to read. The text is large and, when using a color monitor, shows different sections of the definition in different colors.

There are also biographical and geographical dictionaries. Why these aren't incorporated into the main dictionary, I do not know. The manual reads, "The Biography's entries are brief descriptions of the lives of well-known people throughout history." Brief is right. Even *Reader's Digest* would feel the need to flesh them out:

> *Bee-tho-ven Ludwig van. 1770-1827. German composer.*

> *Ca-ru-so, Enrico. 1873-1921. Italian-born operatic tenor.*

> *Lin-coln Abraham. 1809-65. 16th U.S. President (1861-65); assassinated.*

The Geography section describes the United States in three lines, but, in all fairness, it does include a full line about my home town:

> *Al-len Park. City of SE Mich., near Detroit. Pop. 34,196.*

The Spell section of Bookshelf does indeed find misspelled words, suggest correct spellings, and change the correct for the incorrect in your text, but compared to the spelling checkers built into most modern word processors, it is awkward, slow and cumbersome. It's also imperious. Instead of saying, "Word not found," as most spelling checkers do, it says, "Word is spelled incorrectly." In red, no less.

Spell caught some amusing errors. It claims, for example, that "Microsoft" is spelled wrong. According to the spell feature, so is "CD-ROM," "Roget's," "Bartlett's," as well as "Houghton" and "Mifflin." The spell-check program is the Houghton Mifflin Spelling Verifier and Corrector.

"I've been in Who's Who, and I know what's what,
but this is the first time I ever made the dictionary."
(Mae West's comment upon being told that the life
preserver the Navy named after her was in Webster's.)

The Usage Alert I found not very helpful. When asked to check a whole screen for possible errors ("to" instead of "too," for example), a large window covers almost all the text and lists the word in question. You are then instructed in the proper usage for the word and its possible alternatives. ("Weather," we are told is "climate; to erode; to withstand adversity," whereas "wether" is a "sheep" and "whether" is "if.")

Alas, to see if your word is correct requires checking the word in the context of the sentence, and almost all of the sentences are covered by the box telling you which word is in question. There is no way to get rid of the box temporarily. It is, simply, not well designed.

"If God had meant man to have a computer,
He wouldn't have given him a brain.
That's what I say."

The Usage Alert also lets you check for single words of dubious use. It does not, however, give "usage alerts" for some of the most misused words. The most frequently misused word of the day, I think, is "hopefully." It is almost never used correctly. "Hopefully" is not one of the words for which one's usage is alerted.

What Usage Alert is, in fact, is a "homonym helper," giving brief definitions of words that sound the same but have different meanings. With the power of CD-ROM, a Usage Alert could be so much more. (Grammatik IV, for example, does much more on a single floppy disk.) I look hopefully to the day when this section of Bookshelf is expanded and improved.

Bookshelf also includes the complete text of *The Chicago Manual of Style*. You can look up information in several ways, using a combination of key words and/or phrases to locate precisely the information you want, or you can scroll through the table of contents until the desired section is found. Once located, the *Manual* will tell you in its crisp, no-nonsense, authoritative style (the "Chicago Style") the definite, the usually definite and the possibly definite rules of writing.

Bookshelf keeps the entire text of the *World Almanac and Book of Facts* online. Here, for example, we learn slightly more about Beethoven:

Ludwig Van Beethoven, 1770-1827, (G.) Concertos (Emperor); sonatas (Moonlight, Pastorale, Pathetique); symphonies (Eroica).

Still not an epic biography, but something. (Isn't the Pastorale the Sixth Symphony? Or did he write a Pastorale Sonata, too?) Part of the fun is looking up whatever you need to look up in several of the reference books included with Bookshelf.

Suffice it to say that the *World Almanac* has every water table, climate record, sports score and, well, we even discover more about Allen Park, Michigan. We find out, for example, that the mayor is Domenic Boccabella. He's a Democrat and his term began in November of 1987. Allen Park's zip code is 48101. The population in 1970 was 40,747. The population in 1980 was 34,196. (My shrinking home town.) (Come to think of it, I moved out in 1973. Maybe I started an exodus.) (Lily Tomlin, a native Detroiter, was once asked, "When did you leave Detroit?" She responded, "When I found out where I was.")

Now we come to one of Bookshelf's most enjoyable parts: *Bartlett's Familiar Quotations.* You can look up quotes by word, phrase, or combination of the two. I, for example, wanted to use the quote about marriage being the triumph of hope over experience. I thought Shaw had said it.

I electronically looked up the rules for quoting in *The Chicago Manual of Style.* It warned me soundly: "It is impossible to overemphasize the importance of meticulous accuracy in quoting from the works of others." (That was, by the way, a direct quote.)

So, I entered "marriage" and the list of first lines went on and on. (The program lists quotes by first lines or by author, so if you wanted to see everything Shakespeare said on marriage, you could.) Although interesting, there were too many to go through one by one (writing under a deadline as one does). (Later, I was happy this list was long when working on another book which included quotes, *I Marry You Because...*)

I added "hope" to "marriage" as the words to look up and found it:

> *"A gentleman who had been very unhappy in marriage, married immediately after his wife died; Johnson said, 'it was the triumph of hope over experience.'" Samuel Johnson*
>
> *[From James Boswell's Life of Johnson]*

So it wasn't Shaw after all.

You can mark and copy any block of text, up to fifty lines long, and add it to the text of your document. It works fine and is a godsend. (No more copying quotes "meticulously.") There are two problems with this feature:

1. The text in Bookshelf is stored in files 75 columns (characters) wide. Most people have their word processors set up for the text to occupy around 65 columns. Hence, when text is read into the word processor, it flows onto the next line. This is fine for straight text, but the credit lines usually break in odd places. If Bookshelf is for writers, slightly narrower—or even user-definable—margins would be much appreciated.

2. After every quote, dictionary definition, rainfall statistic, etc., the copyright information about the book from which it was taken is added to your text. For example, following the above Boswell/Johnson quote, the program automatically appended:

It's a lot of clutter to remove every time you add a quote to a letter. If you make a list of quotes, this information is given after *every quote*. Making the addition of the copyright information a switchable option would be likewise appreciated.

The Zip Code Finder is lots of fun. You put the cursor next to the address in your text, push a few buttons, and ZAP (or should I say ZIP?), the correct zip code is found and added to the text.

Bookshelf has a business directory with which I didn't spend much time, so I don't know how helpful it is. Bookshelf also has a large selection of business letters and business forms. These can be read into a word processed document and changed at will. If you start getting the same letter from several different companies, you'll know they're using Bookshelf.

In short, Microsoft's Bookshelf is a useful program now (invaluable to some), with the potential for being as important to the writer of the 1990's as word processors were to the writers of the 1980's.

Another program, on another disk, is *The Oxford English Dictionary*—the whole thing, all 2,347 volumes of it. This isn't the *compact* edition you buy from the book clubs that comes in microprint with a microscope. No, this is the whole enchilada . . . definitions, quotes and all.

The interface is not as elegant as Bookshelf: these people are obviously used to academia. With a little practice, however, you can look up words and quotes faster—but with less exercise—than the multivolume printed version. You will also save the lives of about 28 trees.

It's a temperamental, moody program, but for anyone who wants the definition of nearly every word in the English language only a few seconds away, it's a temperamental, moody guest you'll be glad to know.

The *OED* on CD is a little heavyweight for me. On the other hand, the *Grollier Electronic Encyclopedia* is a little lightweight. Although in print it's known as the *Academic American Encyclopedia,* it's not what I would call "academic." "American," sure, "academic," no.

I mentioned in the chapter on data bases using the *AAA* to discover things one might never discover from the book version. (I used the example of strokes: all the people who have the word "stroke" in their biographies are listed—a difficult list to compile by, say, skimming every biography in a printed encyclopedia.) It's a valuable tool for horizontal comparisons, but it lacks depth.

The same can be said of Information Finder, based on the *World Book Encyclopedia* (the one your junior high school teacher tried to sell your parents).

The Electronic Encyclopedia and Information Finder are good for a quick look, but I'm waiting for the *Britannica III* on CD before I get truly excited.

Chapter 23

The Great American Screenplay (Computer Style)

The Great American Novel has given way to The Great American Screenplay (or stageplay).

Esquire Magazine some years ago had a cover with a monkey at a typewriter. The headline read, "Who in America is *Not* Writing a Screenplay?" How behind the times could *Esquire* get? The monkey, of course, should be at a computer.

I wrote a novel once. I was told it was too fast; it read like a screenplay. So I turned it into a screenplay. It read too slow, I was told, more like a novel. Until a new literary hybrid is developed—the screen-vel, maybe, or the no-play (don't the Japanese already have that?)—they lie next to each other, on my shelf, gathering dust. (Or, as we writers like to say of our un-published/unproduced children, "Waiting until the audience is ready for it.")

What I learned from the experience was that writing a script can be demanding in more ways than one. Film, television, and stage scripts each have unique format requirements. They have to look a certain way on the page. Dialogue has to be indented so. Stage directions have to be elsewhere. One format requires dialogue to be double-spaced. One format has a line of space under a character's name, while another format doesn't. Pages have to end in a certain way.

With all the indenting and tabbing and such, my fingers had a heck of a workout. When I was done, I had to go through the script to make sure the pages did not end in the middle of a description or someone's dialogue. Each page has to be complete unto itself. Some people like to have the word "CONTINUED" at the bottom of each page if the scene will continue on the next page. That means even more work, especially when it is time to rewrite and all those CONTINUEDs have to be shuffled around.

In sum, the format requirements can take a lot of effort. While there are people clever enough to make their own macros for some of this, I happened to have found a program called SuperScript ($99; Inherit The Earth Technologies; 1800 South Robertson Boulevard, Suite 326, Los Angeles, CA 90035; 213-559-3814). SuperScript works with WordPerfect 5.0 and 5.1, and comes in separate versions for feature films, television sitcoms, and stage plays.

To use SuperScript, you bring up WordPerfect as you normally would and start writing. SuperScript's commands all use the Control key. For films, Control-S sets the page for a slug line. No, a slug line is not a line of

Screenwriting in the thirties required two adults and a small child. The keyboard is left, video screen in the center, printer on the right.

dialogue spoken by an unfortunately undergifted character, nor is it a line of direction during a fight scene. A slug line identifies interior (INT.) or exterior (EXT.) location, and the time of day. "INT. BAR – DAY" is a slug line, for example.

Control-C sets the page for a character name, and Control-T for a transition ("CUT TO:" "DISSOLVE TO:", etc.). Capitalization is automatically performed where appropriate. The words CUT TO, DISSOLVE TO and FADE OUT can each be inserted with one keystroke.

A simple menu lets you create character name macros so you can press one key to insert often-used names. Your number keys then become dedicated character keys.

If you press Page Down in WordPerfect, you move from page top to page top. It's good for scrolling page by page, but you don't see how the page actually breaks—a concern in scripts. With SuperScript, you can page down by pressing Control-P, and the page break will be in the middle of the screen. Quite handy.

SuperScript works with WordPerfect's style feature. If you decide to change dialogue or stage direction margin settings after you have been writing, the settings will automatically change throughout the whole script. Therefore, you can tinker with a script's length and look.

When you are finished writing, press Control-F, and the formatter menu appears. For film scripts, you can choose whether or not you want CONTINUED's, scene numbers, automatic dialogue breaking, and more. It will even format some scripts that were not written using SuperScript.

I find it quite clever that the program keeps the style codes to a minimum. Style codes can take up a lot of room. If you press Control-C after writing stage directions, the cursor moves down two lines, a dialogue margin code is inserted, and the margins changed for dialogue. If you press Control-C again after you write dialogue, the program does not insert another dialogue margin code because it sees the margins are already set.

Control-C does even more. After dealing with the style code, the cursor blinks at the character name position. Either type a name, which the program will automatically capitalize, or wait four seconds and a menu appears. With the menu, you can type up to eight character names, assigned to numbers 1 through 8. Press one of the numbers, and you're back to your script with the name inserted and capitalized. The cursor moves down a line, ready for you to type your scintillating dialogue.

Each time you want one of the names after you press Control-C, press the appropriate number. You do not have to wait for the menu each time. If you want to insert one of the names in the scene description, hold down the ALT key and press the appropriate number.

I'm a believer in the left brain/right brain theory of creativity. Your right side is the flighty, imaginative side, and the left is the practical, analytical side. When you create, you want to stay on the right side as much as possible. The left side is concerned with the computer and which keys to push. When you can get the left side working on autopilot as much as possible, then you can spend more time playing on the right. Each time you have to look in the software manual or otherwise pause and consider what to push, you are abruptly yanked from the Land of Oz and returned to Kansas. Programs like SuperScript soon become second nature, leaving you to your slug lines.

By the way, those of you who are looking for a great story told in an engaging way, remember what the playwright Robert E. Lee (*Inherit The Wind*) says: "There are no plots; there is only what interesting people do."

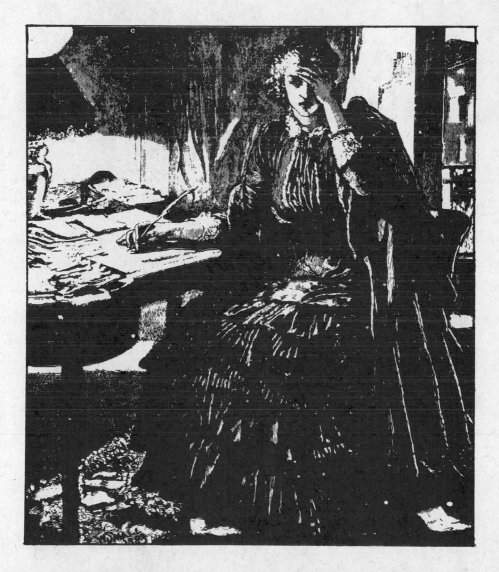

*"CUT TO: EXT. LAKE. No, DISSOLVE TO: INT. BEDROOM.
No, FADE TO: EXT. MAGIC MOUNTAIN. No . . . "*

Chapter 24

Poetry from a Computer?

This is a chapter about the only taboo in America that has not yet been the subject of a TV movie-of-the-week.

We all know about poets and we all know about computers. Poets and computers populate distant extremes on the continuum of existence. Poets are ephemeral, fey, ultrasensitive unicorns living on air and inspiration, usually consumed by consumption before the age of thirty. Computers are hard, exacting, unforgiving amalgams of steel and silicon, designed by scientists to serve Big Business and Big Government in exacting from us what little money and freedom we may have left.

Yes, we all know about poets and we all know about computers. The idea of a poet using a computer to create poetry is about as incoherent as a plumber designing the Taj Mahal. (Well, it *is* white and it *might* be made of porcelain.) Yet, it's happening every day, at great universities, in computer stores and in garrets worldwide: Poets are doing it on computers.

I have actually written poetry on a computer. There. I said it and I'm glad. I didn't set out to write a confessional. I thought I could objectively review this controversial subject from a detached point of view. But, in the end, I could not stoop to journalism. I had to tell you the truth—to reveal myself—and I'm willing to take the consequences.

I know, of course, this means no Pulitzer Prize, at least during my lifetime. (It wasn't until 1953 that the Pulitzer Committee even considered poetry written on a *typewriter.*) I know the sale of my next book of verse will be limited to a few computer enthusiasts who also happen to like poetry (twelve, in all). I know the poetry journals will invent cruel jibes and hurl them at me. They'll call me The Poet Laureate of Radio Shack, and snigger behind their quills.

As late as 1988, believe it or not, *The New York Times Book Review* allowed some poet to trash me for *an entire page,* all because of this very chapter in the original edition of *The Word Processing Book.* Imagine! My only regret, of course, was that the book wasn't in print at that time, so I had no way of cashing in on the publicity.

But I'm strong. I can take it. I don't want to take it, but I can take it. And, quite frankly, I'd rather take it than return to the land of pen and ink, of constant retyping, of watching cherished, beloved poems go in one end of a Xerox machine and not come out the other. ("Must like poetry," the copy center worker would chuckle.) No, I'll take it, and I'll be vindicated by the future, just as I am already vindicated by history.

The first poet to use a word processor was Milton. He was blinded in 1652 and, with the help of his daughter, wrote some of his finest works, including *Paradise Lost.* The actual processing of the words went on in Milton's mind. His daughter was there to record his thoughts; to read them back; to make whatever changes, deletions, or additions Milton deemed appropriate; and to recopy the final poem letter-perfect for later publication—all the things modern-day computerized word processors do so well.

Milton was probably not the first to write poetry using the word processing capabilities of another. Leisurely poets from antiquity on have dictated their opuses (opui? No. My online dictionary tells me it's either *opuses* or *opera)* to waiting scribes with better handwriting than they. Poets don't tend to admit this, however. The idea of struggling alone and forlorn for the ever-evasive couplet is an image we poets like to maintain.

Writers other than poets don't seem to have qualms concerning a little outside help. Socrates had a word processor. His name was Plato. Milton could not avoid giving credit where credit was due. He was, after all, blind, and the Braille typewriter was more than two hundred years in the future.

The first person to ever write a poem on a word processing *computer* is difficult to pinpoint. No doubt some scientist, back in the days when computers were larger than Marlon Brando, wrote a line or two immortalizing the delectability of his beloved. The computer, dutiful servant that it was, printed the whole thing on a Valentine's Day card without so much as a giggle.

By the time the computer-cum-word-processor got into the newsroom, closet Superpoets—posing as mild-mannered reporters—wrote verse after verse on screens of phosphor. Late at night, of course. Long after the mere mortals were at home and in bed.

Naturally, there were poets aplenty when computers-turned-word-processors eased onto the campus. Universities are, after all, the first and last refuge of poets; universities and Salvation Army Missions. Professorial types, pretending to be working on yet another dissertation, were in fact dashing off a few more stanzas of their epic, *An Ode on "Ode on a Grecian Urn."*

But all that's history. There is more poetry today being written on computers than graffiti on subways. (I once saw a young man colorfully expressing his considered opinion of a local law enforcement agency on a formerly blank wall. Ever curious about my fellow writers and their possible use of word processing in any form, I asked him if he had ever tried writing graffiti on a computer. "Yeah," he said. "I was working for this company in the mail room, and one night I was there late and I went into the computer room and tried writing some graffiti on one of the computers." How wonderful! I could see the title of my new book before me: *Graffiti in the Computer Age!* I could see the fan mail pouring in. I could see my royalty checks. "How did it turn out?" I asked, my eyes wide with interest. "Not too good," he said. "My spray can ran out of paint before I could finish.")

Why are poets turning to computers in record number?

Personal computers, outfitted with a quality word processing program, allow a writer maximum freedom to rearrange, take from, add to, alter, correct—in a word, change—the material being written. Of all writers, poets do more rearranging, taking from, adding to, altering, correcting—in a word, changing—than anyone else. Hence, the benefits of word processing accrue quickly for poets.

To demonstrate, let's take the work of that beloved poet, Isadora Goose, known affectionately to all as "Mother." Let's suppose that the well-known journal of poetics, *Humpty Dumpty,* asked me to update a few of Mrs. Goose's better-known poems. I would do it very much as Isadora herself might, if she were alive today with a word processor at her peck and call. Let's take the classic, *Little Miss Muffet.*

Now, I know that I would have to keep the basic structure of the piece, maintaining the natural rhythm and as many rhymes as possible. My job is to update, I must keep reminding myself, not to rewrite.

Little Miss Muffet
Sat on her tuffet
Eating her curds and whey.
Along came a spider
And sat down beside her
And frightened Miss Muffet away.

293

The first word that stands out is "tuffet." A tuffet is either a mound of grass or a stool. Mother's meaning is not certain here. She states that Miss Muffet *owned* the tuffet when she said, "Sat on *her* tuffet." However, the word "Little" seems to imply that Miss Muffet might be too young to be a landowner, hence "tuffet" may refer to stool or seat. Spiders, however, are more commonly found out-of-doors on grassy tuffets. It is a puzzlement, and great books have been written on this very subject by men and women far more learned than I.

The point is that you don't hear the word "tuffet" used very often in either context anymore. Real estate salespersons do not extol the wonders of a garden "with flower beds, beautiful shrubbery, and several very nice tuffets." And advertisements do not appear saying, "Dining Room Set, complete with breakfront, buffet, table, and six tuffets." No, "tuffet" will have to go.

But what to replace it with? I like the idea that Ma Goose meant "tuffet" to mean stool. Too many poems have been written "in nature," going on and on about the beauty of the out-of-doors. We need more poems about the beauty of the in-of-doors. The nearest two-syllable word that means stool, remembering that we must keep the Goose's meter, is "barstool." Everyone knows what a barstool is, even the readers of *Humpty Dumpty*.

With the press of a few buttons on my word processor, I find the first two lines have become . . .

Little Miss Muffet
Sat on her barstool . . .

The "Muffet" part must go. It no longer rhymes. The "Miss" will, of course, become "Ms." In that light, "Little" seems a bit condescending. This whole first line is in need of an overhaul.

What's a contemporary rhyme for "barstool"? Why, of course, "carpool." Wonderful. Teach the kids the importance of conservation from grade one. "Miss Muffet" is now "Ms. Carpool." We've lost an alliteration, though: the two "M's" in "Miss Muffet." And what about "Little"? What adjective describes this truly contemporary Ms. Carpool and begins with an "M"? Why, of course, "Modern."

> *Modern Ms. Carpool*
> *Sat on her barstool*
> *Eating her curds and whey.*

"Curds and whey" are the solid and liquid parts of whole milk when it curdles. This was very popular back when people sat around on tuffets, but has since lost its popularity. It is doubtful that our Modern Ms. Carpool would be sitting at a bar eating curdled milk. A banana daiquiri, maybe; curdled milk, no. We are, however, writing for a children's magazine, so we can't make this *too* contemporary. She'll have to be eating some healthy dairy product.

Further, whatever she's eating will have to rhyme with "whey" because we want to keep as many of the original rhymes as possible, and we already departed

from that in the first two lines: "Muffet" does not rhyme with "Carpool," no matter how far we stretch it.

What rhymes with "whey" and is a healthy dairy product? Simple: Yoplait, the brand name for a kind of yogurt. "Yoplait yogurt," unfortunately, does not rhyme with "curds and whey." We must invoke our poetic license and switch "Yoplait" and "yogurt," easy to do on a word processor.

Modern Ms. Carpool
Sat on her barstool
Eating her yogurt Yoplait.
Along came a spider
And sat down beside her . . .

The stuff about the spider is okay. I mean, it's traditional. Besides, "spider" and "beside her" make a great rhyme. Then we come to the last line:

And frightened Miss Muffet away.

The obvious thing to do is to change "Miss Muffet" to "Ms. Carpool" and collect one's box of Crayolas. But, no, there is something very wrong with this line. In the first place, would "Modern" Ms. Carpool really be frightened away by a spider? I doubt it. She might not appreciate his company as much as, say, Rob Lowe's, but to be frightened away? We could end the poem with, "Said she, 'Would you please go away?'" making Ms. Carpool the graduate of an assertiveness training group; but this, too, skirts the real issue.

Yes, the disparity is a deeper one. It goes to the very core of one of our primary cultural taboos: unjustified prejudice against spiders. Justified prejudice I can understand. People are prejudiced against mosquitoes. Who can blame them? It's justified. But where is the justification for the prejudice against spiders? Nowhere. A few black widows kill a few Sierra Club members every year, but so what? Cars kill 50,000 people every year, and we *love* cars. No, the prejudice against spiders is unjustified.

Beyond that, spiders actually do good. They eat mosquitoes and flies and all those other creepy-crawly things against which we have justifiable prejudices. It's time we changed, and change must come through education, and education begins at bedtime with nursery rhymes. Let's make the spider an ordinary sort of guy!

So, here we have our scenario: Ms. Carpool is sitting at a bar eating yogurt. A spider comes along, sits down next to her and, keeping in mind that he's a regular, normal spider, what does he do? Why, he orders something to eat, just like Ms. Carpool.

But what would a spider order? "I'll have a Yoplait Mosquito Yogurt, please." No. Spiders don't eat yogurt. People eat yogurt. No point in making this a Walt Disney movie. Spiders eat bugs. But going into a bar and ordering a plate of bugs is rather unappetizing, so how do we add a little class to the situation, and, locked into a rhyme pattern, rhyme his order with "Yoplait"?

Let's make this a gourmet spider. He would have to order bugs prepared in some French-sounding way, such as *saute* or *flambe*. Eating "bugs" is a bit weird, so we'll modify that just a bit, too. We add our last line to the Mother Goose Computerized Update, and, voila!

Modern Ms. Carpool
Sat on her barstool
Eating her yogurt Yoplait
Along came a spider
And sat down beside her
And ordered an insect souffle.

There were twenty-six words in the original poem. By changing only eleven of them, less than half, the entire poem was transformed into something quite different. Fifteen words remained the same. With a word processor there was no need to retype even one of them.

The nonsense above is a parody of what goes on in the creative mind as it refines, hones, and coaxes the English language into poetry. Yet, behind the fun is a portrait of the actual word processor at work—the human mind. For the poet, a word processing computer is a tool that remembers and displays the best of what has gone before; that makes experimental alterations quickly, silently, and with a minimum of effort; that waits patiently, alert and ever-ready for the next command, be it in five seconds or five days. A tool such as this might help free the mind of the poet, allowing true poetry to flow through.

The real news is not that word processing computers will do for poets everything typewriters do, only more and better and faster. The real news will come as poets apply the many joys and wonders of word processors to the creation of new and remarkable forms of human expression for the illumination of us all.

It seems as though eons have passed since *Publisher's Weekly* printed a letter from a senior editor at Random House stating emphatically that *no* genuine literature will *ever* be produced on a word processor. It seems like eons, but it was, in fact, 1983.

Gradually, almost everyone came around. George Plimpton, author (*The Paper Lion*) and editor (*The Paris Review*), swung from the former to the latter camp when a computer magazine commissioned him, in 1989, to write a piece on using a computer for the first time.

The first software he tried was the Poetry Processor written by Michael Newman. Besides never having used a computer before, Plimpton had never written poetry before. What follows is his first poem. It is a Shakespearean sonnet. The software freed him and let his mind do what it does best: think.

Penn Strokes

by George Plimpton

I wait: in stygian darkness of a can,
On either side of me a tennis ball;
Upon a clubhouse shelf we partners plan
A bouncing, history-laden protocol.
Green, fuzzy, hollow, are we, born to light
But locked inside a gloomy tomb of tin
But then a hiss of air . . . the sun! In flight
We slap against the gut of cats, and spin
Across the net to guts of other cats.
It hurts! We crave soft beds of grass or clay
To lie inert, not fly like acrobats
Twixt Becker-Lendl . . . Oh to hell with play!
Return us to that canister of dark
And leave us there, to never more embark.

Michael Newman's Poetry Processor specifically addresses the rules of poetry, and not only makes poetry writing on computers easier, but makes it more engaging (for anyone who's still reading this chapter) than most computer games.

Newman, a former protege of W.H. Auden and senior contributing editor of *The Paris Review,* has written and taught poetry for years. He became acquainted with computers and programming while involved in bio-research, and saw that computers would be perfect for poetry. Says Newman, "A sonnet is an algorithmic system of prompts. Each beat and rhyme can be measured. What better tool to keep track of such things than a computer?"

A word processing program will let a person change things easily enough, but it won't oversee meter; it won't count syllables; it won't watch for assonance, consonance, and alliteration; and it won't offer rhymes.

Michael Newman's Poetry Processor does. It also comes with a set of paradigms, offering such poetic forms as sonnet, sestina, villanelle, terzanelle, etc. Such strict forms may seem like straightjacketing to many people, but Newman sees it as freedom. "It is really classical poetry in its structured forms that is teaching you to write, and the Poetry Processor acts as a midwife," he says. "The forms stimulate you to write." If you prefer blank verse to metered, the Poetry Processor still helps you with what you want accented.

Newman hopes this program and two other related programs—a stand-alone rhyming dictionary called N.E.R.D.-in-Residence and a tutorial program dubbed Orpheus A-B-C—might instill a love of words in those who never thought that creative writing, especially poetry, could be enjoyable.

How does the program work? If you want a metered form, you choose from a list. Try a sonnet. The program brings up 14 numbered, blank lines and shows you both the meter and rhyme schemes. Meter is displayed in dots and dashes; a dot is a soft syllable while a dash is an accented syllable. (An **iamb,** by the way, is a two-syllable unit with the accent on the second syllable. **Iambic pentameter,** the heart of a sonnet, contains five iambs and appears thus: .-/.-/.-/.-/.-/) (And you thought we were only going to define *computer* terms.)

If you're stuck for a rhyme, highlight the word you want to rhyme and press a button. A handful of rhymes appears. If that isn't enough, you can leave the program and bring up N.E.R.D-in-Residence. (N.E.R.D stands for Newman's Electronic Rhyming Dictionary, by the way.) It provides not only dozens of rhymes, but also vowel-sound matches (assonance) and consonant-sound matches (consonance). With a dictionary of over 50,000 words, it's amazingly helpful. It will also fit into RAM and spring to life from within any program. (Your bookkeeper can write invoices in rhyme.)

Drawing on physiological research, Newman says, "The musical intonation of speech—prosody—

Some early word processors required one to write directly on the video screen...

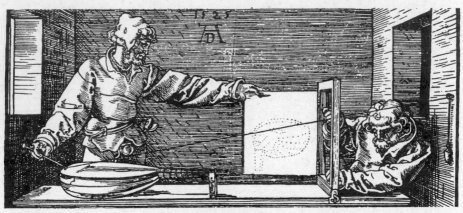

While others required the help of another person...

And many writers appreciated the help very, very much

causes blood to flow to right-brain cell circuits, engendering images. It also sends reward chemicals to the brain." Translation: it's fun. I quite agree. The manual is short and could use some clarification, but for the most part, quite workable. (Maybe it should have been written in iambic pentameter.)

His three programs can be bought as a package (around $150). For more information, write or call: Michael Newman, in care of The Paris Review, 541 East 72nd Street, New York, NY 10021; 201-525-2122.

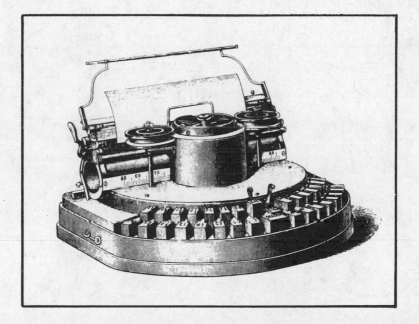

Chapter 25

Questions and Answers on Word Processing

I need a computer for word processing and basic small business tasks. My kids want to play games. Which computer should I get?

The best solution, I think, if you have a household with children and adults, is to get two computers. You can get an inexpensive game computer (a Nintendo, no doubt), and then a second computer for all your other needs. Games can take hours, and with two computers, you can avoid leaving a game to reconcile your check book—or fighting over who gets the computer now.

If there is only one computer user in your home, then a machine with EGA or VGA color graphics will satisfy both needs.

Is there any way a writer who is not freelancing, but is regularly employed, can deduct or write off his word processor on his income tax?

What are you employed as? If you're employed as a professional writer, I think you'll have less trouble than if you're employed as a dishwasher, although I don't know. For tax advice, see your tax consultant. This is a recording.

I am interested in finding a machine suitable for writing a novel.

Aren't we all?

What I need is a wonderful program to keep track of the many poems I've sent out to contests—where I sent them, and, if I get them back, the response. Have a recommendation?

For all of you who have specialized data base needs, such as keeping track of poems, you can make up your own data base with any of several good data base programs. A favorite is Nutshell from Iris Software (P.O. Box 57, Stoughton, MA 02072; 617-3431-1990; FAX: 617-344-4640). It sells for $189, and a relational version called Nutshell Plus sells for $295. Both versions offer clear and easy-to-use menus.

I also recommend Q&A from Breakthrough Software, a division of Symantec Corporation (10201 Torre Avenue, Cupertino, CA 95014; 408-253-9600). Q & A not only has clarity and power, but a good word processor and a system for obtaining information from the data base using plain English sentences.

I've heard that computers get in the way of the creative process. I am a writer, and I tried my friend's word processing computer for the better part of a day and never once felt creative. How can you then recommend word processors to writers?

When you're struggling to learn and remember the various technical commands necessary to operate a computer for the first time, you are using the rational/logical part of your brain.

Using the logical/rational part of the brain tends to inhibit the functioning of the creative/intuitive part (and vice versa).

After a while, the word processing program is learned and its operation becomes, as they say, *transparent*. At this point, when the operation of the computer becomes automatic, creativity can once again take the lead.

It's rather like a concert pianist who must first learn all the notes of a concerto before interpreting them, or a Jedi knight who must learn how to use a laser sword before turning his intuition over to The Force.

So give yourself more time—much longer than a day—before you decide that creativity cannot happen in front of a video screen.

THE TYRANTS FOE, THE PEOPLES FRIEND

308

PART IV

Desktop Publishing

310

Chapter 26

Desktop Publishing

I received a letter from a woman in Nutley, New Jersey, who asked for advice on a home desktop-publishing program. I've been meaning to write about desktop publishing for beginners, and what better time than for this chapter.

For those of you who have heard the term but do not know what it means, desktop publishing refers to page design and typographic control. Desktop publishing goes beyond word processing. It allows you to drop in graphics, headlines and captions, and to change typestyles. *Newsweek, Time* and most other magazines arrange their pages for visual interest. You, too, can design pages, whether it's for a fancy letter, or your own newsletter, magazine, book, menu, catalog, sermon— you name it.

Desktop publishing entered the mainstream in the late 1980's. Personal computers at last had the software to tackle complex needs; scanners, hard disks, printers and large amounts of computer memory had become relatively affordable.

The term "desktop publishing" is misleading. A *publisher* coordinates the activities of the writer, the printer, and the distributor. No computer program I know of can do *that*. (And very few human beings do it well.) (By "printer," I mean, of course, a professional *printer* who can print 100,000 copies of something—not the machine attached to your computer.)

What desktop "publishing" really is, is desktop *design* and *typesetting*. This allows one to more easily "publish" one's own work—that is, get the work to a printer in a format that, after printing, is more acceptable to the waiting world.

311

But the term "desktop publishing" has stuck, and there seems no going back. As with many other words—when applied to computers, it only marginally has to do with real life.

I am glad, however, the word "desktop" found a home. For a while there, it looked as though microcomputers (what personal computers were called in the early eighties) might be called desktop computers. It was a neck and neck (or should I say chip and chip) (no, I shouldn't) race between "desktop computer" and "personal computer." I agonized for weeks on what to call the first edition of this book. I flipped a coin, and a lot of other people must have flipped the same coin, because all of a sudden "personal" was indelibly linked to "computer" and "desktop" was out of a job.

"Desktop" began dating the word "publishing" back in the middle 1980's, and now, I am happy to report, they are happily married and the proud parents of more than one book.

This chapter, and the one that follows of my own personal experiences (and horror stories) with desktop publishing, is designed more as a primer than a textbook. For more detailed explanations, allow me to direct you to Daniel Will-Harris' *Desktop Publishing in Style* (from And Books). With humor and clarity, Will-Harris explains in detail just what desktop publishing can do. Terms are well defined and illustrated.

The first thing you need to do is write the text that you want to publish. (Many people who want to be published forget this first important step.) You do this with your word processing program. After you have the text, you prepare it for publishing, using either your word processing program if it has the extra features (as WordPerfect, Microsoft Word, WordStar and several others do), or "importing" the text into a desktop publishing program.

Preparing the text involves several design decisions. First, you need to choose a typeface. A **typeface,** sometimes called a **font,** is the character style. It can be classified in two categories: **serif** and **sans serif.** A serif font has the little lines on the end strokes of a letter. This book uses a serif font. Sans serif has no such extra lines. A sans serif typeface looks like this.

Within these two categories are a wide variety of styles, all with different names, such as Times, Helvetica, Century Schoolbook, Bell, Akzidenz Grotesk, Bodoni, Broadway, Palatino—the list is almost endless. Each typeface offers its own look, and the look you choose makes a statement almost as much as the words themselves. Many people don't give a moment's consideration to such matters, but to professionals in visual communications, a typeface speaks volumes.

Fonts come either as software, which tells your printer how to print, or fonts come on cartridges that plug into your printer (here I'm talking about your *computer* printer, of course) and these tell your printer how to print. In other words, you choose the font you want with your desktop publishing program, and then your font software or your font cartridge gives the printer the specifics.

Another thing to consider when desktop publishing is **leading.** Leading is the amount of space between each line of text. The term comes from the old days when type was set by hand. The spaces between lines were controlled by slivers of actual lead. If someone wanted more space between lines, they asked for more leading. If they wanted less space, they asked for less leading.

Too little leading can make the page look gray and dense; too much leading is hard to read. Programs measure leading either in millimeters, fractions of an inch, or in **points** and **picas.** There are six picas to the inch, and twelve points to a pica. Fonts are also measured in points. (This paragraph is set in 12 point New Century Schoolbook with leading of 13-1/2 points.)

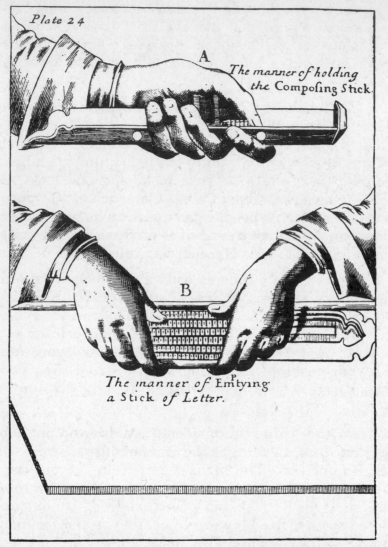

Plate 24

A

The manner of holding the Composing Stick.

B

The manner of Emtying a Stick of Letter.

As you prepare your pages, you also have to decide on such things as line length, where you are going to place headlines, the sizes of headlines, images and captions, whether or not you are going to use columns, whether or not you are going to leave blocks of "white space," and much more.

Page design is an art. With it, you can make reading your prose endearing or enduring.

Desktop publishing requires patience, and many people opt for having a professional do the work. (I do!) Fortunately, desktop publishing services are multiplying as quickly as tax preparation offices once did. (Remember when there *wasn't* an H&R Block on every block?)

In addition to type and all that is possible with the written word, desktop publishing opens the computer to the world of graphics—everything from a doodle to a representation of the Mona Lisa counts as "graphics" in desktop publishing.

Graphics are often manipulated in separate programs—called graphics programs or **paint** programs. (One "paints" on the computer screen using cursor keys, a mouse, joystick or track ball.) The graphics are then incorporated into the text. Text is most often manipulated within the desktop publishing program.

The two together—text and graphics—form *everything* you've ever seen in print.

If computers can reduce everything to two on/off bits, don't be surprised that they've reduced the known world of the printed page—5000 years' worth, stretching back to the ancient Egyptians—to two words: text and graphics.

So, while desktop publishing gives us less words to describe all we read and see, it gives us more attractive ways of presenting the words it leaves us with.

(Heavens! Ending not just a paragraph, but a whole *chapter,* with a preposition. And a chapter that ends with a discussion on the effect of computers on the written word. What am I thinking of?)

Chapter 27

A Few Words (Very Few) on Desktop Publishing Hardware and Software

We'll look at hardware in more detail in the chapters on selecting and purchasing a personal computer. If your eyes glaze over while reading this chapter, you might want to read those chapters first. I'll do what I can to keep it simple. Desktop publishing is, however, one of the most complicated demands one can place on a personal computer. (More on the ramifications of this in the next chapter.)

There is no such thing as the "right" computer for desktop publishing. Almost *any* computer will do *some* kind of desktop publishing.

A man from Vermont wrote to say he desktop publishes with a Commodore 64 (and emphasizes he and nine million others still use Commodore 64's). (The Commodore 64 once sold for around $64 at K-Mart.)

He connected his Commodore 64 to a laser printer using something called Quantum Link. I'm sorry to disappoint the nine million of you who might want one, but I have no further information on Quantum Link. Maybe Carl Sagan does, but I don't.

The people at Apple, of course, would have you believe that their Macintosh is the best for desktop publishing. Yes, the Mac did have a lot to do with the revolution in desktop publishing—the Mac combines graphics and text so easily—but a fully equipped Mac II, PageMaker 3.0 and an Apple LaserWriter will cost you in the neighborhood of $10,000. (The figure may or may not be accurate by the time you read this: it's a depreciating neighborhood.) (Please see the chapter, *Why You Should Probably Buy Neither an Apple Nor an IBM.*)

For less money, around $2,600, you can build a perfectly swell desktop publishing system. An IBM AT-compatible (that's the one with the 286 processor), a hard disk, 640K (or more) of memory, a monochrome screen—you know, the works—for, say, $1,200. Another $1,000 or so will buy you a laser printer, and for under $300 you can buy a desktop publishing program. Throw in a mouse and a year's worth of cheese ($90 for the mouse, $10 for the cheese), and there you have it.

The top-of-the-line desktop publishing programs for MS-DOS computers include Ventura Publisher and Pagemaker PC. These programs, however, have already blown our $300 budget. So, all right, make it a $3,000 package. (A $5,000 package if you want a Postscript printer—discussed in the next chapter.)

If that's all too dear, and a dot-matrix printer is what you can afford, there are several less expensive programs available. You do not need all the expensive hardware of a design artist to turn out pages with class.

A popular beginner's program for IBM's and compatibles is PFS: First Publisher. With it, you can have font sizes up to 36 points, up to 4 columns per page, and you get 150 pieces of free "clip art" (pictures) that you can drop into your text wherever you choose.

Another program that has many fans is Springboard Publisher. It offers everything First Publisher does and more. Your fonts can be as large as 72 points. You can work with up to 9 columns per page, and you get 500 pieces of clip art. Springboard Publisher also has a feature called Perspective, which allows you to alter an image to simulate three-dimensional space. (Glasses extra.)

Both First Publisher and Springboard Publisher are geared for beginners, with easy-to-read manuals. You do not, of course, have all the power of top-of-the-line programs. Such things as automatic hyphenation and global style changes are missing. Nonetheless, the programs are far less intimidating than those on the high end.

With a little more money, you might also consider Publish-It! from a company called Timeworks. Publish-It offers more control than the two previously mentioned programs, First or Springboard, and, although it's geared for novices, it has enough power to be used professionally. Small businesses might like it. A simplified version called Publish-It Lite—for dot-matrix printers only—costs just $89.

Of the Big Guys (Ventura and Pagemaker), the following broad generalization seems to apply: Ventura is used by people who want to do many-page publications, and work more with text than graphics. (Books are a perfect example. The text in this book was done with Ventura.) Pagemaker, as its name implies, is used most by people who do a few pages at a time, but have serious graphic needs. (Advertisements, say, or book covers—the cover of this book was done with Pagemaker.)

Although each is expanding into the other's turf with every new edition, the initial market they wanted seems to be the following they garnered, and—in terms of available support—following the following might not be a bad idea.

Chapter 28

The Joys and Disappointments of Desktop Publishing

Back in 1981, I tried to "desktop publish" *The Word Processing Book*. The term, desktop publishing, hadn't been coined yet, but what desktop publishing (almost) does today, I wanted to do then. I thought it would be great PR to say, "Written and typeset on a microcomputer." It was a fine idea. Alas, its time had not yet come.

The first challenge was proportional spacing. Probably every book you've ever read is proportionally spaced. It's something we take for granted when buying a book.

Back then, there was only one printer with a proportionally spaced type font, NEC. It was a good looking font, but there wasn't a program available to drive it. WordStar didn't believe in proportional fonts then. The only word processing program that did was called Magic Wand. Magic Wand didn't exactly proportionally space, but at least it got the right letters in the right places. The spacing was sometimes off.

But never fear—Magic Wand offered kerning. **Kerning** is the ability to move a single character to the right or to the left a microfraction of an inch.

I'd print out a test page. The "t" was too far to the right. I'd add a kern command in front of *every* "t" in my file. (With search and replace, of course, this was less work than it sounds.) The "m" was too far to the left. Kern it over a bit. On and on it went. Finally, it looked okay. The file, however, was so full of kern commands, it was unreadable.

Then it came time to print. Ordinary paper didn't give the sharpness I wanted, so I bought a special clay-coated paper IBM sold for use in their compositors (a fancy word for their typesetting typewriters). It gave a sharper image, but smudged easily. The pages had to be photostatted before they could be cut and pasted.

Finally, it was done. It looked terrible, *and* it cost more than typesetting (largely due to the photostatting charges). The next edition was professionally typeset.

Desktop publishing once required two people to operate it.

All the computer books I did in the early 1980's were prepared this way: I would send the word processing file to the typesetter by modem, and the typesetter would send back rolls of set type. (When they would arrive, I would be amused at how things often come full circle: thanks to computers, we were back in the days of scrolls.)

We would proofread the type, make changes, and send the scrolls back to the typesetter. (This was before FAX machines, too.) The typesetter would make the changes and send us the "final" type, again on a scroll.

A paste-up person and I would work together—she cutting and pasting, me pointing and asking, "Is there room for the mechanical rabbit here?"

The last of the computer books was written in 1984. By 1987, the time came, as time does, for me to write another book. I felt the need to be creative. I had something important to say. I had bills to pay. (One of those three reasons was my primary motivation. I'll let you guess which one.)

The book was to be called *Peter McWilliams' Personal Electronics Book*. The publisher insisted on my name in the title. (I am far too modest to put my name in the title, but I am clever enough to choose a publisher

who will insist that my name be in the title.) In exchange for my name in the title, I got to provide the publisher with what is known as camera-ready copy: type and graphics pasted up and ready to be photographed and printed by the publisher's book printer.

As you may have gathered, my books have more than a handful of graphics interspersed with text. Being my own publisher for the computer books had spoiled me. Each page looked exactly the way I wanted it to look. I told the paste-up person which absurd and incongruous graphic I wanted where. I was not at the mercy of someone with a title to defend, such as Art Director or Book Designer.

It was three years since my last book. In that time, desktop publishing had been born and had grown into graceful adolescence. (I'm aware that "graceful adolescence" is an oxymoron, like "military intelligence"; but then, to a certain degree, so is "desktop publishing.")

I was excited about the prospect of seeing graphics and text on a computer screen, moving them around until they looked marvelous together, and printing the results on a laser printer, ready to send to the publisher.

It was a dream only partially fulfilled.

I decided to put together a state-of-the-art desktop publishing system. I started with Ventura Publisher from Xerox. The two leaders in desktop publishing programs are Ventura and Pagemaker. Pagemaker, as I mentioned, is good for making a few pages. When making many pages, one after another, as in a book, it falters. Ventura was the better choice.

The computer was a 386 IBM clone—a fast machine. Desktop publishing, unlike, say, word processing, requires all the speed you can muster. "Requires" is perhaps too strong a word. Desktop publishing does not require the speed. Your sanity requires the speed.

For a screen, I chose a large monitor—19 inches—especially designed for desktop publishing. This provided a large, sharp image.

To add graphics, photographs and anything else not addable by a keyboard requires a **scanner.** This scans the image, converts it to a graphics file, and stores it in the computer.

To manipulate the scanned images in precise and intricate ways requires a second program. Being a fan of Z-Soft's PC Paintbrush, Z-Soft's PC Publisher was an obvious choice.

Naturally, a mouse was in order. I chose the Microsoft Mouse. Microsoft has done more to popularize mice on IBM compatibles than anyone else. Their mouse is easy to use, reliable, and supported by everyone who supports rodents in any form.

Then came the question of getting all this desktop-published brilliance out of the computer and onto paper. The best system for doing this is called PostScript. PostScript printers are absurdly more expensive than regular laser printers (roughly twice as much), but, what the hell?

In a fit of extravagance, I also looked at the $18,000 Varityper VT600. This is a PostScript printer that promises twice the resolution of other laser printers at only four times the price. I couldn't get the thing to work. *They* couldn't get the thing to work. I spent more time waiting for the Varityper technician than I've spent waiting for Godot. The few times the VT600 did work, the results were not overwhelmingly impressive. (This was 1987—maybe they've gotten the veri out and gotten the thing typing by now.)

So, there I was, Candide about to embark on the world of desktop publishing. It seemed, at that time, like the best of all possible worlds. It seems now, like any other world, full of its goods and its bads.

The first disappointment was the size of the pages on the screen. Having a 19-inch monitor, I figured, would allow me to see two facing pages, exactly as they would print. Not so. Ventura Publisher does not have infinitely variable screen sizes. The book page was either slightly smaller or considerably larger than what the finished pages would be. Even more frustrating, they were not proportionate. The page on the screen was narrower and taller than the page that issued from the laser printer. (This was the monitor's fault, not Ventura's.)

Also, the typeface on the screen was not the typeface that eventually printed. What you saw was what you got in that the words on the screen broke where they broke on the printed page and flowed around graphics as they would on the printed page, but the type style, the size of the page and the proportion of the page were different. (The type problem has now been solved. You can buy **screen fonts** for any of the PostScript type faces.)

That photographs would not print clearly using desktop publishing was not a surprise. The number of dots in a printed photograph are far greater than the dots (**pixels** they're called) available to desktop publishing. Scanning a photograph and printing it out worked. You could see what the image was, but it set back the mass reproduction of photography roughly 75 years.

The biggest disappointment came from graphics. As you can see, I use lots of turn-of-the-century etchings and woodcuts in my books. Surely, I thought, these would print just fine. They did not. They were OK and recognizable, but not as sharp as I would have liked.

There was another problem with graphics: they slowed the program to a crawl. Graphics are stored as large files, each pixel on the graphic precisely located. To load a graphic into the program takes time (much more than text). To manipulate a graphic takes more time than text. To print a graphic takes more time than text. We're talking about the difference between minutes and seconds here. At a certain point, when too many graphics were added, the program ground to a near-halt.

I made an editorial (read: cataclysmic) decision— drop the graphics. I would have the professional book printer add them later, along with the photographs.

That speeded things up considerably. We got down to what desktop publishing does best: text. Here it shone with a brilliance that has given desktop publishing its favorable reputation. Once a box defining a photograph or a graphic had been placed on the page, flowing text over, under and around it was a breeze.

The making and moving of boxes is wonderfully easy. In three seconds you can have a box that would take ten minutes to create by standard paste-up methods. Headers, footers, page numbers, indexing, tables of contents—the sorts of things that take seemingly forever at the end of a book project—all these were handled quickly, automatically and brilliantly by Ventura.

On the positive surprise side: the text in the printed books looks better than I thought it would. I was afraid I might have to apologize for it, saying it was an example of a desktop-published book, that it was a book about the cutting edge, that it was fair to experiment with new techniques of publishing—you know, excuses. (Actually, I was too cheap to send it to a professional print place for professional output that would be type-house quality—and cost anywhere from $3 to $10 per page.)

The way it turned out, I didn't have to explain anything to anyone. If someone didn't know the book was desktop published, I doubt if they would discover it by the quality of the type on the printed page.

The same is true of this book, the one you hold in your hands. The type was set entirely "in house" (my house, to be exact) on a 386 computer, using the text taken directly from my word processor files. The text— including headers, page numbers or anything else that looks like a letter or a number—as well as straight lines, boxes and dingbats (these things: • ▢ ✍ ↝) were printed on an "ordinary" PostScript laser printer (the Qume Scripten). (By ordinary, I mean it is the kind of laser printer you can buy at your local computer store.) The graphics and photos were "stripped in" by the professional book printer.

As it turned out, the printer actually *preferred* the "art" (as they call it) to be sent separately. They shoot (photograph) art at a different exposure than text, and would have to separate it anyway. It still would have been nice to see it on screen and printed out.

By the year-2000 edition of *The Personal Computer Book,* maybe my wish will come true.

Elephants have disabilities when it comes to, say, dancing.

PART V

Personal Computers and the Disabled

Chapter 29

Even If You're Not Disabled, Please Read This Chapter

This section, in book form, was one of the great publishing failures of 1984. Even though it got lots of publicity (Betty Furness, for example, was kind enough to have me on *The Today Show*), it ran up against what some people warned me it would run up against: a prejudice against books on disability.

It's a circular prejudice. Booksellers don't carry books about disability; therefore people with disabilities do not visit book stores to buy books about disabilities; therefore, bookstores do not carry books about disabilities.

Well, computers for the disabled is one of my pet passions, and this time I'm sneaking this information right into the middle of a book about personal computers for everybody. Consider *The Personal Computer Book,* then, a Trojan horse. Hidden between its benign exterior and generic chapters is information that's difficult to get into bookstores any other way.

Why did I ask you to read this chapter even if you aren't disabled? Because you might know people who are, and they may not know the information in this section. Passing it along to them (feel free to Xerox the whole section) would be of great service.

The hard fact is that someone you know who is not disabled now may become so in the future. The facts are these: at the age of 21, one in twenty people in this country is disabled; by the age of 65, the figure is one in four. The wear and tear of life—with its myriad of accidents and illness—takes its toll, and the older one becomes, the greater the chance for disability. (Many people believe that disability is something one is born with, and if they're not disabled now, "It will never

333

happen to me or anyone I know." Alas, such is not the case.)

Two people you should know about: Walt Woltosz and Ken Yankelevitz.

Walt Woltosz began his work with computers and the disabled in 1980 when his mother-in-law was diagnosed as having amyotrophic lateral sclerosis—ALS, or Lou Gerhig's Disease. She unfortunately died before the software and input devices could be fully developed, but the event had a profound effect on Walt Woltosz's life, and the work continued.

Walt left his job as an aerospace engineer for United Technologies Corporation and started Words+, Inc. (P.O. Box 1229, Lancaster, CA 93584; 800-869-8521.) Words+ has become the largest adaptor of personal computers for the disabled.

His add-on devices and entire computer packages come in a variety of designs and applications, depending on the disability. If the disabled person has the control of a *single muscle group* (the ability to twitch one eyelid, for example), Walt can provide a computer system that allows that person the ability to communicate again.

Walt's most famous client is Steven Hawkins. He wrote the bestseller *A Brief History of Time*, using one of Walt's systems.

Whatever your needs, I suggest giving Walt (or one of his able associates) a call. If they don't have a device that can help, they will refer you to someone who does.

Ken Yankelevitz is a flight simulation engineer for McDonnell Douglas. In his spare time he makes joysticks for the disabled. But aren't joysticks for playing *games*? Do disabled people want to use computers to play games? As Ken explains, "Disabled people are just like everybody else—especially kids."

And kids seem to be Ken's specialty. Although disabled adults appreciate the opportunity to play Pac-Man or chess or Decathlon, Ken seems to take special delight in helping disabled children control the hopping about of Qbert, or walking with Big Bird down Sesame Street.

"Some kids use the same type device as the game controller to operate their wheelchairs," Ken explains. "Playing games teaches them accuracy and coordination, which they can use in steering the chairs. It can also be good exercise." So, there are practical benefits to game playing. "Sure," says Ken, "but mostly it's just fun." It's also fun to watch disabled youngsters trounce able-bodied friends at video games.

Ken's controllers are designed for use with movements of either the hand, head, mouth, foot or tongue. They attach to most computers, including the "just" game-playing ones.

He formed KY (Ken Yankelevitz) Enterprises (213-433-5244). Yet to show a profit (Ken's special controllers are generally less expensive than regular mass-produced joysticks), Ken refers to the entire activity as, "An expensive hobby." His wife, Diane, takes part in the family hobby, too.

Were I writing this as a feature piece for a local newscast, I might end it with something syrupy like: "Ken Yankelevitz helps simulate flight for grown-ups during the day, so that he can stimulate flights of fancy for young people at night."

Fortunately for us all, this is not a TV news feature. I can close this piece by simply saying, "Good work, Ken (and Walt). Film at eleven."

An early hearing aid.

Chapter 30

The Deaf and Hearing Impaired

Personal computers are easily adapted for the deaf. All the necessary elements can be found in any computer store—or computer department of any K-Mart, for that matter.

And yet, although the implementation is easy, the results are profound. For the deaf, it is as though the telephone has just been invented. They can call anyone with a computer, and, for the first time, using screen and keyboard, *chat.*

It seems altogether fitting that the telephone should finally be available to the deaf. One hundred years ago, the telephone was invented by Alexander Graham Bell while researching hearing aids for the deaf. For the better part of a century, everyone *except* the deaf got to enjoy the fruits of Mr. Bell's labor. (Bell Labs invented the transistor, and other components which led to personal computers, so it seems that Mr. Bell's company did have something to do with getting the telephone to the deaf—in a painfully roundabout way.)

It's easy to see why computers are so usable for the deaf and hearing impaired. The primary output device is the screen (or printed text) and the primary input device is the keyboard. Both of these are *visual* and require no hearing.

The only time a computer uses sound to communicate is for the explosions, laser rocket fire and monster munching of video games, and an occasional beep some programs make when an error in entering is made. In neither case are the sounds essential to appreciating and using the program.

I "talked" with Henry Kisor, book editor for the *Chicago Sun-Times,* and once-rival syndicated computer columnist. We hooked our computers together over phone lines and I, a supposed expert, could not figure out how to save—either on disk or in print—what we were typing back and forth. After much fiddling, Henry kindly offered to save it on *his* end and mail me a copy. Although this is like asking someone for an interview, and then asking them to take notes for you, I gratefully accepted.

In it we discuss, among other things (including sex! Stay tuned.), telecommunication devices for the deaf, or TDDs. These are basic keyboards with one line of text display and, sometimes, a printer that prints on adding machine paper. Unfortunately, TDDs are not compatible with most computers, although translation programs for computers are becoming available. The problem is, most computer owners will not buy this program unless they have a deaf friend or relative.

Computers communicate using a code called ASCII (pronounced "ASK KEY"). TDDs communicate using Baudot code. Some TDDs come with both ASCII and Baudot capability. As the world of computers is clearly ASCII, this is a trend in TDDs that should be encouraged.

Here's a mildly edited transcript of our conversation. (I only took out the parts that made me look unbearably stupid.)

Please tell me about your own deafness. You were not always deaf, I understand. More like Beethoven.

I lost my hearing postlingually, at age 3. (That's shrink-speak for losing hearing after acquiring language.) Meningitis. Learned to read and print right away, so never lost the ability to use language.

In an interview in InfoWorld, you mentioned that deaf people have trouble acquiring reading and writing skills. Why?

Those are the deaf-born. Unlike hearing children, they aren't born into a world of language, experiencing it from the moment of birth. Deaf people can only see and feel things. Hearing babies learn simple abstractions quite early. Deaf people take a lot longer... Some never achieve enough language to score in the "normal" range of IQ tests, though they might be otherwise extremely bright.

This saddens me. For some time now, I've thought that all a deaf person would have to have is a computer, and they'd be able to communicate with anyone else who had a computer. But you are suggesting that there may be a greater problem of literacy here.

That's true. If you called the average deaf-born person on the computer, most likely you would be struck by the bare-bones grammar. It would be very like sign language... subject, verb, object, with few frills. Almost broken English. But I think the computer would add to the literacy of the deaf-born. After enough time passed, perhaps his general literacy level could be close to that of the hearing. It really depends on individual cases— general intelligence, residual hearing if any, and so on.

Do you think computers will help them with the learning of English?

Yes. A computer can be used as an interactive teaching tool with the deaf. A child presses a key; the computer reacts instantly. A computer is a lot easier to read than the lips of another person.

Doesn't reading increase the vocabulary and teach sentence structure, or is reading difficult for people born deaf?

I'd better be careful here; I don't know. Reading is a passive, not an interactive activity. Some people might get a lot out of it, some might get little. The inability to manipulate abstractions easily could make reading difficult.

Born-deaf people have trouble handling abstractions, more so than other people, that is?

Here again, I am speaking from hearsay. One, I think, needs language to deal with abstractions... not necessarily mathematical (those are easy to grasp), but linguistic ones.

Easy? I don't even know my multiplication tables. Thanks a lot.

Ho, ho. But I'll reiterate my conviction that computers, being an interactive tool, will help the deaf a great deal.

How have computers changed your life, if indeed they have?

1. For the first time, I am able to roll up as large a phone bill as my wife does.

2. For the first time, I am able to communicate with hearing people without having to look at their lips, or write them letters and wait days for them to be delivered.

3. I am able to interview writers on the phone, as you are doing.

Have you had much experience with TDDs?

I have three... one at home, one at work, and a portable. I call my wife every day for the domestic news. I have used it to make motel and train reservations. But it isn't as large a part of my life, since TDDs are generally limited to the world of the deaf. I don't mean to criticize them. They were the first big step out of the electronic isolation of the deaf; the microcomputer is the second.

What specific suggestions do you have for a deaf person exploring computers?

Get a modem! One can get a Commodore 64, a modem, a terminal program and a cassette recorder for under $300. That opens up an enormous new world one never knew existed.

What should the deaf look for in computers? Any special requirements?

I can't think of anything... beyond what it takes for a hearing person to go online.

Tell me about your experience with bulletin boards. What are they and what do you use them for?

I use them for three reasons:

1. To get my technical questions answered about certain name-brand computers, and to download free software.

2. To pass on questions my readers ask about their computers—in 24 hours you'll have answers from 50 hackers.

3. To communicate for the joy of it with electronic "pen pals."

Do you use the CB on CompuServe for chatting?

Yes... I've been on CB a lot lately. The slow turn-around time is a pain. Especially in the evenings when CompuServe is slow in general. But given the alternatives, I should not complain.

Is there any message about computers you'd like to give to the deaf readers...or friends of deaf readers... who will be reading my book?

Just to make a modem the first peripheral they buy, even before a printer. And I also suggest that they look into a lap computer, even an inexpensive one, whatever seems most affordable, as their first or even only computer. It can accompany them everywhere (I take mine in my briefcase most places).

In an emergency, they could call CB and ask someone to make a voice call for them (this is theoretical... it would take some convincing of other CBers that it was not a joke). More practically, I have heard of a new network of bulletin boards called Deaf-Net being set up in various cities as an experiment. It will bridge the gap between computers and TDDs and serve as a clearinghouse of information, as well as an emergency phone center.

I have heard of lap computers attached to speech synthesizers, but know very little about them. That's one possibility... especially if the synthesizer could be attached to a phone (but how's the deaf person going to know if anyone answers, and how to get a reply?)

Yes. We're into the chapter on the blind. Have I forgotten to ask you anything?

No...but I have an interesting observation. You are aware of CompuSex on CB, aren't you?

Yes, but my Bible prohibits me to explore anything but missionary electronics.

Har de har har... I was talking to a psychologist who is also a CBer and made horrifying noises about CompuSex to her. She replied that a lot of CBers are people with severe physical disabilities who have no means of finding sexual partners. She contends that a lot of them find sexual fulfillment with erotic conversation on CB. Makes sense, I guess....

Oh. I think I'll put that in the book. I think that people take to CompuSex (and PhoneSex for the hearing) who have the most basic sexual disability of all: they're not attractive enough for the "market" and can pretend to be anything they want. Funny, though: they're getting off with someone who is likewise saying, er... exaggerated things.

I guess so. Maybe most "normal" people would look askance at CompuSex, but I think it serves a good purpose for those who have no other outlet.

We should point out that people use CB for more than sex. I am told by a psychologist that CB has proven very useful to people recovering from disabling accidents. Some of the first reaching out they do has been to other CB users.

I enjoyed our "talk." There's only one problem with this form of communication: I still don't know how to pronounce "Kisor."

Kaiser! (As in "Frazer.")

Thank you. Over and out.

Right. Goodbye.

"You promise me a computer and what do I get? Nothing. Get off the cat. Nothing. That's what I get."

Because computers require skills that most deaf
people have (the ability to see) and can acquire (typing),
the job market for deaf people working with computers
is large, and growing larger every day. Jobs that require
inputting data (programming, data processing, word
processing) and no telephone interaction would be
ideally suited for a deaf or hearing impaired person.

The Day after Mother's Day

"*A flower?*
I wanted a PC."

Chapter 31

Speech Impaired

A great many people have speech impairments, for a great many reasons. People born deaf often have trouble speaking because they've never heard what understandable speech "should" sound like. Cerebral palsy sometimes causes speech that is difficult to understand. Strokes, tracheotomies, and laryngectomies frequently cause speech loss of varying duration. Cancer, MS, ALS and other diseases silence tens of thousands every year.

The causes are many, but the result is the same: no voice, or an inability to pronounce words that are easily understood.

Until now, those who were unable to speak communicated with written messages or a point board. A point board (or lap board) is a flat surface with the alphabet and a series of frequently used words, symbols and phrases on it. ("I'm hungry," "I love you," "I don't think Sartre had precisely that in mind," etc.) The user points to the words and letters, and the observer gets the message. Point boards are especially helpful to those who have insufficient motor control to write.

While written messages and point boards work, they have their limitations. Neither notes nor point boards are of any use on the telephone. Summoning aid in an emergency without the ability to speak is a considerable task. Point boards require someone to look over the pointer's shoulder, or to sit next to them, and do nothing else but watch while the message is constructed, letter by letter.

Voice synthesizers to the rescue!

Voice synthesizers are relatively inexpensive ($200 or so) and connect to almost any computer. Most plug into the printer port and, rather than printing what is said, it speaks it. The speed and pitch can usually be adjusted.

External audio speakers can be added for more volume or better fidelity.

The voice it synthesizes, alas, sounds unmistakably like a computer. Even the most expensive ones sound like no human from this planet. But voice synthesizers are nonetheless understandable, are quickly adjusted to, and many find them a valuable alternative to message writing and point boarding.

Disabled people who go from point board to voice output find the pressure is off to point quickly and accurately. The message can be worked on—while others are talking or reading or fixing dinner—and when it's ready, the synthesizer speaks it out. Interaction is slower, but is more casual and conversational than with a point board. Also, with a voice synthesizer, several people can hear at the same time. Very important when telling a joke.

Almost all the information in the chapter on computers for the deaf applies to those without a voice as well. Computers do not require that one either hear or speak to operate them. Any job using a computer can be held by a voice-impaired person. The only limitation would be the amount of verbal interaction necessary. (Word processing, data entry or computer programming would be easier than, say, phone reservations.) And the ability to call anyone with a computer and "chat" opens new worlds of communication.

Telephone communication with people and companies who do not have computers or any special equipment (such as TDDs) is possible with a voice synthesizer. For example, to find out if tickets are available for a given concert, you can type in the message, "Hello. I am not able to speak, but I can hear, and my computer is doing the talking for me. Could you please tell me if you have any tickets for the Beethoven (or Van Halen, or whomever) concert on Friday the 14th? If so, could you tell me in what locations and at what prices?"

You dial the ticket information number, wait until someone answers, and push the "speak" button (it's different for different computers), and the message goes out over the phone. The person on the other end gives the information, you write it down, push another button, and have your computer say, "Thank you. Goodbye."

If you want the tickets, you can program in the information, such as your credit card number, address, price of tickets, number of tickets, and so on. Another call, and the tickets are on the way.

The same system can be used for ordering groceries, sending telegrams, checking bank balances, getting phone numbers, and arranging with friends when to next have a genuine computer-to-computer chat.

Most computers have a way of programming in several frequently used sentences—whole paragraphs, sometimes. In this way, "Hello, I'm glad to see you. How have you been?" or "I bid hearts" or "This is just an ordinary personal computer with a speech synthesizer added" need not be typed each time.

Walt Woltosz's Words+ has several solutions. Please give him a call (or write him a letter, if you don't yet have a computer with speech synthesis. Words+, P.O. Box 1229, Lancaster, CA 93584; 800-869-8521.)

A librarian I talked to, who lost her speech due to ALS, continues her work as a children's librarian, and uses a computer to tell stories—complete with music, sound effects, different voices and even graphics. "If children can relate to Star Wars and computers," she said, "they certainly can relate to their librarian talking through a speech synthesizer."

350

Chapter 32

Learning Disabilities

Learning disabilities are often more difficult to pinpoint than physical disabilities, but they are just as real and can be just as limiting. In many cases, personal computers can help overcome these limitations.

Before we begin, let us explore for a moment a myth. The myth goes something like this: Computers are cold, impersonal, aloof, distant machines, devoid of a single positive human emotion. Believing this, one wonders what good computers could possibly be to anyone, let alone to people with learning disabilities.

This myth grew up in the black and white 1950's and flowered in the anti-establishment 1960's. During that time, the only "people" who could afford computers were Big Business and the government. Computers were *programmed* to be cold, impersonal, aloof and distant. Considering their owners, this is not surprising.

The only interaction the average person had with computers was the DO NOT FOLD SPINDLE OR MUTILATE card enclosed with every bill. (If a bill was past due, there were two cards.) Businesses started to blame everything that went wrong on "computer errors." Science fiction movies increasingly portrayed the computer as the villain. And if we ever met someone who actually knew something about computers, these people seemed cold, impersonal, aloof and distant, too. They must have gotten it, we thought, from too much contact with the computer.

In fact, the computer got it from too much contact with *them*. These were the Computer Programmers. They spoke a special language even the owners of the million-dollar computers couldn't understand. They had a closed club. They created the computer in their own

351

image. Not that all computer programmers were like that—just the ones hired by the people who owned the computers.

A computer, in fact, is neutral—like a phonograph. Just as you can play either Mahler or Midler on a phonograph, you can program a computer to be either cold and aloof or warm and cuddly.

The concept of warm and cuddly programming is new, but it's catching on. It's the next step after "user friendly." A warm and cuddly program would probably spoil a big businessperson's lunch, but it's just the thing for people with learning disabilities. (See? I got back to the subject. I don't know how, but I got back.)

When one imagines the ideal situation for teaching people with learning disabilities, a series of human qualities comes to mind: love, understanding, compassion, caring, forgiveness, support and encouragement. But there are some superhuman qualities that come to mind as well: infinite patience, inexhaustible energy and unlimited availability.

Given that the first seven can only be provided by another person, it's nice to know that the last three can be provided by personal computers.

Patience. If it takes a student 10,000 tries before learning that six times six is thirty-six, that's how many times the computer will present the problem. At no time will the computer get angry, upset, frustrated or in any way human. (Some programs offer encouragements such as, "That's closer! Let's try again.")

This infinite patience takes the pressure off the student. It is frequently this pressure that people with learning disabilities have difficulty with. In an effort to make fewer mistakes, they make more. This causes more pressure, leading to more mistakes. A thoroughly nonjudgmental "partner" in learning breaks this cycle of expectation and failed performance, allowing the student to learn at his or her own pace.

Energy. A computer will never say, "I'm too tired, we'll do it later." If it's on, it's ready to go; any time, all the time, 24 hours a day. Barring a power failure or a breakdown, the alertness of a computer never varies. The lesson is presented with the same "enthusiasm" at 8 a.m. as at 10:30 p.m. Answers are given or checked as quickly at noon as at midnight. Hyperactive children have finally found their match.

Availability. The best special education teachers in the world seldom have the time to give each student all the attention he or she may need. They have other responsibilities, other students, a family of their own, social and personal needs.

Computers, on the other hand, are simply *there,* to be used or not used, as the student desires. The computer adapts to the student's personal timetable. People with learning disabilities frequently respond poorly to the "We've done enough science; it's ten o'clock, time for geography" system of education. And who can blame them? Just as the light of cognition is about to glow, some idiot pulls the plug because "it's time."

Computers also make available the next lesson precisely when the student is ready for it. This is how computers could have helped me in elementary school. In half my subjects I was ahead of the class; in half my subjects, I was behind. I spent my days alternating between boredom ("Will these people *ever* catch up?") and frustration ("They got all that so soon? I don't get it at all.") I consequently became a "behavior problem," known in non-technical circles as the class clown.

Who says that one hour is the correct amount of time for each subject? And who says how much should be covered in that hour? That monster known as The Class Average decides. Never mind that the best students will be bored and check out, and that the worst students will fall hopelessly behind. The average student has been served, and what more can we hope for?

This problem in traditional classroom education is even a greater problem when working with the learning disabled. Special education classes frequently mix not only students with varying disabilities, but also various grade levels.

Computers provide personal instruction, at the speed the student is ready to learn, over the distance the student is ready to travel.

Unfortunately, this chapter is the most theoretical and speculative in the whole book. All I've been able to do is discuss the *potential* computers have in teaching people with learning disabilities. The computers are there, the software is becoming more and more abundant. Just about every major educational publisher is developing a line of educational software and they've got the money to do it, too.

There are good programs that teach the alphabet, spelling, or basic math, and these are a good start, but the *continuing* programs are missing. Until that vacuum is filled, computers will only be selectively useful in educating people with learning disabilities— being invaluable to some students, peripheral to others, intermittently helpful to most.

One of the most successful tools in teaching people with learning disabilities is Logo. Logo is a computer language that uses a turtle (cursor) to draw graphics designed by the student. Here's a report by educator Susan Jo Russell.

Logo in Special Education
By Susan Jo Russell

The word "slow," when used to describe children with special needs, is a literal description of how we teachers see them—it takes them longer to get where they are going. That is why the solution at first appears to be to pack more time into the school day. But the child with special needs, like all other children in our classrooms, is an individual who thinks, learns and communicates in an individual way. Instead of more time for learning, we need more worlds—more environments that allow individual styles and paces, that offer engaging content, and that provide new opportunities for teachers to observe and interact with children's thinking. That is where the computer can help us.

During the last two years, I have been working on a project using the Logo program with six-to-ten-year-olds who were physically handicapped and/or learning disabled. Two facts have impressed me: first, how readily many children, even those who have experienced much failure in school, make Logo their own; second, how much of their work with Logo tells us about their thinking.

Therese first came to school—a school for physically handicapped children—at age ten. She had a severe hearing loss but had never worn a hearing aid. She used few words, relying on sounds to express her feelings. She had a rare syndrome that resulted in immature growth and made her need braces on her legs and lower body. She looked as if she were five and communicated as if she were two. The school staff knew little about what Therese knew or how she learned.

We began using the turtle robot that functions with Logo, and a button box (a plastic box with widely spaced buttons used as a substitute for the keyboard). Therese showed immediate delight at the movement of the turtle on the floor. After a few sessions, she clearly distinguished the functions of the button labeled F (for forward) and T (for turn). Later we introduced her to the same commands using the computer keyboard and screen in a version of single-key Logo. She had difficulty coordinating the actions of watching the screen and finding the right key on the keyboard: moving her eyes to the screen, she would lose her place on the keys. Despite this difficulty, as well as the barriers of hearing and speaking, she persevered.

One day she outlined a large square on the screen with her finger. Then she outlined something in the bottom center of the square. "Open the door," she said. After making the door, she said, "and a window" and outlined several windows within the square. I imitated her movements: "A window here? A window here?" She pointed again and said, "One, two, three, four, five," showing me five positions for windows. This conversation was the longest and clearest I had ever had with her. It may not sound monumental, but to have shared an experience with Therese in which she was directing, in which words and ideas were understandable, was a rare experience.

Willie is almost nine years old. He repeated first grade and is now completing second in a public school classroom. His skills in mathematics and reading are well below what would be expected for his age. When he entered school, Willie cried for hours daily and almost never talked. Now, three years later, he still talks infrequently and often does not answer even when addressed directly. Despite a supportive classroom environment and popularity among his peers, tears come to his eyes when he is confronted by new material.

One of Willie's first Logo pictures was a car. While he made it he spoke little, but when he was ready to make the wheels, he asked me how to make a circle. It was the first time he had addressed me directly. In his fifth and sixth sessions he made a picture called "the plane in space." For this picture he chose his numbers unerringly, showing a strong sense of proportion and design. His working style was consistent: he worked silently and steadily on his own, asking me questions when he needed a new tool for what he wanted to do.

Willie's language skills are poor, but Logo provides a world in which he excels. Willie draws as well on paper as on the screen. But what is interesting about his work in Logo is that he can translate what he knows about shape and proportion into Logo commands, which require him to estimate, compare, sequence, visualize, plan and use numbers. He chooses his own problems and solves them, communicating his ideas in a mode that is comfortable for him. Although his schoolwork with two-digit numbers is shaky, in this context he uses them confidently.

For Therese and Willie, Logo provided compelling motivation in a world that is both structured and open—structured because the child has to work with particular commands that produce particular effects; open because an unlimited number of ideas can be implemented with it. Both Therese and Willie were limited in their spoken and written communication. The context of Logo encouraged the expression and sharing of ideas. Unlike drawing, for which they could guide the crayon directly, Logo required them to translate their intentions into a series of commands understood by the turtle. To do that they had to analyze and plan—in effect, to think about their own thought.

Therese can now handle only the simplest single-key commands. It is a manageable environment for her, yet one in which she can direct the action. Willie, who can use most of the regular Logo commands, manages a more complex environment. Because Logo is accessible yet powerful, both of these children can gradually expand their knowledge of the tools Logo offers them. If we do not limit children's access to new worlds because of our expectations about their abilities, then they will show us unexpected strengths.

"I don't know if I can take another <u>day</u> at school without a computer."

Some disabled people are finding leader birds helpful in getting around.

Chapter 33

Muscular, Motor, and Movement Disabilities

This is, understandably, the longest chapter in this section because it covers people with disabilities involving movement—the largest population of disabled people in the country. This includes severe arthritis, amputees, spinal cord injuries, degenerative nerve and muscle diseases, cerebral palsy, strokes, accidents and many other causes. Whatever the cause, the result is the same: impaired movement of some portion of the body.

When I was in the fourth grade, we received an insurance policy for young folks (of which I was one at the time). It had a list of what our parents would be paid for which injuries to our little bodies. "Loss of one arm, $5,000. Loss of one leg, $5,000. Loss of two arms, $10,000. Loss of two legs, $10,000. Loss of one arm and one leg, $10,000. Loss of one arm and two legs, $15,000. Loss of two arms and two legs, $20,000. Loss of one eye, $5,000. Loss of two eyes, $10,000. Loss of one arm and one eye, $10,000."

And so went the seemingly endless list, combining body parts at $5,000 per, until the "Maximum Payable Benefit" of $25,000 was reached.

I have a fear that this chapter might at times start sounding like that insurance list. I'm going to have to go through various combinations of motor disabilities—both partial and complete—in order to examine how computers might prove useful to people with those disabilities.

Those who have limited or no use of their legs might find themselves agreeing with Gary Figelski: "As far as computers go, my disability makes no difference whatsoever." Gary lost movement from the waist down in a military accident. "I used computers before the accident, and I use computers after the accident. The only difference is that now I sit in a wheelchair."

"I hate to type," he says. "I wish they'd perfect voice input—not because I need it, but because I'm lazy." He may work for his brother's computer store, "But first I'm going to learn how to drive my hand-operated van and travel around the country for a while." He plans to take his computer with him.

Because computers use the hands and eyes for input and output, those who have use of hands, arms, head, and eyes have no reason to read this section. ("Why did he wait this long to tell me?") Any computer book applies to you without alteration, as does any

People with no upper-body disabilities have few special needs when it comes to operating computers.

computer. No special software or input/output devices are required.

This is what makes people with full upper-body ability such good employees for companies who use computers. Disabled employees traditionally have far less turnover than able-bodied workers. (The turnover rate for able-bodied computer operators—data processors, programmers, word processors—is enormous.) Companies frequently get tax breaks for hiring the disabled, and, quite frankly, it's good PR.

All this bodes well for those with able upper bodies. Personal computers are turning up everywhere in business, both large and small. This is opening job opportunities for the disabled faster than anything before.

Wheelchairs built for two were very popular around the turn of the century.

In addition, at-home businesses—accounting services, word processing, writing, programming, desktop publishing, consulting, and dozens more—can be started with and supported by personal computers. As your business grows, soon you'll be giving able-bodied people what they say they really want in life—a chance.

Ed Loundey finds himself in precisely the reverse situation of Gary Figelski. Although he has full use of his legs, an illness left him without the use of his hands and arms. Ed, working with Scott Arnold, developed several methods of input for his computer.

All involve the use of that ancient art, Morse Code. The dots and dashes that make up the letters, numbers and computer commands are communicated to the computer through a series of devices.

The first is a foot switch. Operated by the big toe of each foot, one toe is dots and the other toe is dashes. Ed is quite proficient in this form of entry and could, no doubt, beat me in a typing contest.

A second method is the sip and puff switch. This is a tube, like a straw, that responds to slight changes in pressure as the operator sips in or puffs out small quantities of air. The computer translates the sips and puffs into dots and dashes. This method obviously requires no use of muscles below the neck, making it a valuable input device for quadriplegics.

The third device is a head switch. The rocking of the head left and right sends dots and dashes to the computer. This method requires the use of neck muscles alone.

Ed is able to change disks and turn his computer on and off with his feet. Other people with use of their legs and feet but limited use of their arms use computer keyboards and type with their toes. Ed feels the use of his foot switch with Morse Code is faster.

Walt Woltosz of Words+ has even more suggestions. Contact him at P.O. Box 1229, Lancaster, CA 93584; 800-869-8521.

David Geffen broke his neck in a diving accident two years ago. It left him with no use of his legs and only partial use of his hands and arms. He's attending law school, and uses his computer primarily for word processing.

Before getting his computer, he was using an electric typewriter. He had a device designed that attached to his wrist and held various objects. Strapping a pencil in the holder, he used the eraser end to hit the keys one at a time. Entering text on the typewriter was slow but tolerable; making changes and correcting mistakes he found exasperating.

Now, on his computer, he simply moves the cursor to the spot he wants to change, makes the change, and goes on. When the document is perfected to his satisfaction, he prints out a final copy. This ease of alteration is one of the primary reasons word processing is so beloved by writers, secretaries and students—disabled or not.

Money Luckett was born at the end of the Depression. "I was named Money because my parents said I was the only money they'd ever get," laughs Miss Luckett. ("'Ms.' is a manuscript," she says.) Polio at the age of twelve left her with the use of only her lower left arm. (She calls herself a Born Again Southpaw.) Money sleeps in an iron lung at night and must use a portable respirator during the day.

She "auditioned," as she puts it, for a special government program for "the severely disabled." "They did all these tests", Money says, "and they determined I was too severely disabled for the severely disabled program."

She finds this rather amusing, as do the hundreds of people she corresponds with regularly. She writes more than a thousand letters each year.

Professionally, she is an investor and military analyst, describing herself as "slightly to the right of William F. Buckley, Jr." ("Is there *room* to the right of William F. Buckley, Jr.?" I asked. "Oh, yes," she answered, "I can even take my wheelchair.") Does she mind her lack of mobility? "Oh, no. I've got too much to do to get around."

Having the use of only one hand presents a problem at times in computing. Computers have something called a **control key**. When pushed, it gives every key on the keyboard a different value. Holding down the control key while hitting the letter "G" would, in some programs, send a command to the computer. (In the word processing program Money uses, WordStar, "control-G" tells the computer, "Delete the letter under the cursor.")

Now all this control stuff is fine if you have two hands, or even the use of one finger on each hand. But with only one hand, hitting "control-P" can be impossible—unless you have awfully large hands. (The same is true for people using mouth sticks, which we'll discuss shortly.)

The solution is to have the keyboard adapted (by software or hardware, depending on the computer) so that the control key, when pressed, is activated and remains activated until it is pressed again. In this way, the control key works like a shift-lock on a typewriter: once you hit it, everything is typed in capitals until you hit it again. The method for hitting "control-P", for example, would be CONTROL KEY (turning it on), then "P", then CONTROL KEY (turning it off). "The computer company did this for me, and they never even cashed my check," says Money.

An additional aid is macro-making. A macro turns any key on a computer keyboard into any other key. With a macro, hitting a single key can add *pages* of text to your documents. Frequently used commands, such as "control-KSQP" ("save to disk what I've written thus far, and return the cursor to the spot I'm at now"), can be assigned to any unused key. (How often would you use the "{" key for example?) (Newer versions of WordStar have placed that entire command in the F9 key—to the enjoyment of us all.)

Most computers come with numeric keypads. This gives two sets of numbers on each keyboard—the set above the letter keys and the set on the keypad. One set of numbers could be turned into macros, and, with a single keystroke, you could add your name and address, or today's date, or character names in a story, or the formal name of your condition (it's usually long and Latin), or frequently used words, phrases, sentences or paragraphs.

Also, all IBM-compatible computers have at least ten function keys, which are labeled F1, F2, etc. Although most programs use them "to the max," some don't use them all. These, too, are "macro available."

People with the use of neither arms nor legs—but who have full use of head and neck—have several options for computer input. One is the sip and puff straw or the head switch discussed earlier in this chapter. Another is the spoken input from Words+ (800-869-8521). Still others are the joysticks that operate by tongue or head movement. (Please contact KY Enterprises, 213-433-5244.)

Some people with only head movement can use a mouth stick. As its name describes, this is a mouthpiece with a pointer attached, used for hitting keys on a regular computer keyboard.

Special plates are available that fit over regular keyboards. These provide a hole for each key, and a physical separation between keys. These plates are valuable if the movement of the head is shaky or uncertain. A plate makes it more difficult to hit the wrong key. These plates are also good for people with cerebral palsy or other disabilities in which the hands are available for use, but control over the hands is trembling or erratic.

The more severely disabled who have use of enough groups to make two distinct movements—no matter where on the body these movements take place—can communicate with the computer using Morse Code. If someone has use, say, of his right toe and left thumb, devices would be connected to toe and thumb that sensed motion. The motion of one would be dots; the movement of the other dashes.

The most severely disabled, who have use of only one muscle group, can use products from Words+ (800-869-8521). The late Dr. David Rabin was a professor of obstetrics and gynecology at Vanderbilt University's School of Medicine. Several months before his death, he used a system from Words+ to write the following article for *The Wall Street Journal*.

Trapped in My Body, I Electronically Escape
By David Rabin, M.D.

Among the catalog of terrifying diseases one learns of at medical school, none frightened me more than amyotrophic lateral sclerosis. I have often asked myself why during the four years since I developed the illness.

Was it the picture of that first patient etched indelibly in my memory? We had gathered in one of those awful, gloomy basement lecture rooms that used to be an indispensable part of the architecture of teaching hospitals—rows of stark benches rising steeply from the "well", more appropriately the pit, which sported a blackboard, a lectern and one medieval chair. That chair was occupied by a seemingly elderly man stripped to the waist. Perhaps it would be more accurate to say that the chair occupied the man, so small, so cachectic, so vulnerable, so insignificant. He was reduced to flesh and bone, and what remained of his muscle was engaged in a macabre dance of death—the dreaded fasciculations of ALS.

His voice was all but gone, and to this day, I wonder what private hell he silently endured during that hour as the neurologist detailed the myriad physical signs on his broken body. The booming voice of the neurologist rendered the prognosis: "Hopeless! This is creeping paralysis! He will be demeaned, isolated, frustrated, unable to communicate, and probably will be dead in six months."

Today, I am the man in the wheelchair. However, I do not feel demeaned. I have combated isolation by speaking out to those of my colleagues who still retain the obsolete views of my neurologist "teacher," and as a family we have tried to divert our frustrations into creative energy—all of which require the ability to communicate. I lost the use of my hands more than two years ago, and as I faced a tracheotomy, my worst nightmare was whether this would finally turn me into a nonperson—every sensory perception intact but strictly one-way traffic.

Fortunately, miraculously, none of this would prove correct. On the day after my tracheotomy, I received a letter from a fellow physician who also has ALS telling me what countless prior inquiries had failed to elicit, that a computer was available that could be operated with a single switch. Not "on the drawing board," not "just around the corner," but with specifications on hardware and software, a purchase price and a delivery date.

The significance of the single switch is that it can be operated by anyone, however physically handicapped, who retains the function of one muscle group. For me, my eyebrow muscle is strong enough to depress a light switch and thereby gives me access to the full power of the computer. Other patients have a functioning finger or toe. The first person to use a similar computer program had a switch fitted to her mouth and bit down.

The screen presents the alphabet to me. A pointer ("cursor") moves at a speed that I select, and I press the switch when the pointer is next to the letter I want. This opens an electronic dictionary to a page of words beginning with the desired letter. The process is repeated, and with the aid of the pointer, a word is selected. It takes longer to explain than to do!

What has the computer, in conjunction with a printer and voice synthesizer, afforded me? I talk to my family—that is most wonderful. I can make conversation with friends—the jokes take a little longer, but they don't seem to mind. I can work independently again—write papers, review manuscripts, cooperate by mail with other scientists—and I am able to interact with the persons in my laboratory. I write out my ideas before we meet and sum them up afterward. Because of the loyalty and devotion of this group—and for me the indispensable ability to communicate—our research continues to be original and productive.

After 27 years of marriage and total sharing, Pauline and I have discovered the joy and satisfaction of writing together. Topics come from the news, from books we read, from our own experiences and from the human comedy all around. Ideas seem to be generated simultaneously, one of us prepares a draft—I, of course, use the computer—and then we enjoy a dialogue whereby we attempt without haste to use the rich textures of the English language.

A computer program such as mine, operating from a diskette no bigger than a 45-rpm record, can change the lives of hundreds of patients who retain cognitive function but are unable to communicate. While it was originally developed for a patient with ALS, its application in selected patients with stroke and other neurologic syndromes, and in individuals who have lost their vocal cords, should be equally helpful. The main problem appears to be a dearth of information among health-care professionals about the medical applications of the computer.

Coping with ALS is a grim ordeal—but it is not hopeless. Every patient needs an infrastructure of love and support. Now, for those of us who could no longer communicate, the computer provides ALS patients with an Alternative Life Style.

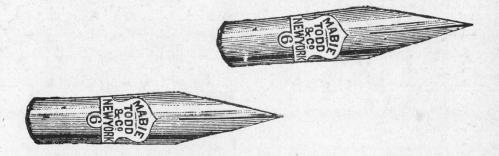

That thoughtful and beautifully composed piece was written with the movement of a *single* eyebrow, using a system from Words+. Dr. Rabin illustrated that courage and determination are the driving force behind the use of personal computers for the disabled, the force that will ultimately decide how practical and useful personal computers will be for each individual disabled person.

"No, this isn't a computer store,
but you just won $10,000."

Chapter 34

Blind and Visually Impaired

As the advertisement reads, "Close your eyes. Now have someone read you this page." That explains as well as anything the difficulty blind people have using computers. So much of computing is visual— monitors, printouts, instruction manuals, computer books and magazines. Adapting personal computers for the blind can prove to be one of the greatest challenges in computing.

(Autobiographical aside: My grandfather rented Ivy Green, Helen Keller's birthplace, from Captain Keller after the Keller family moved on. My father was raised there, and while I was growing up, I was told stories about Helen Keller. When we watched *The Miracle Worker* on television, my father gave us a running commentary on which bits of architecture were accurate and which were not. Later, when we went to visit Ivy Green, now a national shrine, my father said, "I never thought I'd pay two dollars to get back into *this* place." End of autobiographical aside.)

Fortunately, many blind people know touch typing and numeric keypads. Putting information into a computer is not much of a problem. (Have you noticed, by the way, that the arrangement of numbers on a computer or adding machine keypad is different from the arrangement on a telephone keypad? We seem to have a national disability when it comes to creating and accepting standards for things.)

Input being no problem, the question for blind people is, How do I get the information out? There are basically two methods, speech synthesizers and Braille.

Programs are available that instruct speech synthesizers to read all or selected parts of the computer screen. Capitals are indicated by either a beep or a higher pitch. Commas are indicated by a pause, periods by a longer pause. In the proofreading mode, words are spelled out letter by letter, commas become "comma" and periods become "period," and so on.

This system is obviously more useful with some programs than with others. It seems to work well with word processing and writing programs. Both involve a fairly linear progression of ideas and numbers.

Electronic spreadsheeting and accounting are more difficult. Spreadsheets have rows and columns of numbers that are identifiable to sighted people by quickly checking the top and sides of the screen. Blind users must travel to the top, side, and back to where they were to find out the value of a single number.

Accounting programs tend to change screen formats frequently. Sighted people can quickly scan the screen and find the desired figures. Blind people must frequently have the entire screen read out (taking several minutes) to find the one piece of information a sighted person could have found almost at once.

These scenarios are of blind people using off-the-shelf software. Adapting popular and powerful programs for the blind is not a high priority for most software houses. It's one of those vicious circles: because the market for blind computer software isn't there, blind people do not buy computers. Because blind people do not buy computers, the market for blind computer software isn't there. Neither, for that matter, are there many instruction manuals on cassette tape or in Braille.

Another problem with some off-the-shelf software is that it imbeds control codes in the text. These codes tell the programs what to do with certain words or numbers. They are never displayed on the screen, but *are* sent out to voice synthesizers. These codes can send synthesizers into a tizzy. Beyond that, programs that rely heavily on graphics are obviously of little use.

As time goes on, more and more blind people will discover the value of computers, and more software will be written for the blind user. As it stands, good programs are available for the blind, especially for word processing.

Using a computer, a voice synthesizer and available software, the blind person can create, edit, review and print text without an expensive Braille reader or the help of a sighted person. Some programs will even print out in Grade II Braille using a standard letter quality printer. (The platen is replaced by a softer rubber one and the "period" prints the text, backwards, in Braille. When removed from the printer, the reverse side of the sheet is in Grade II Braille.) This allows for written communication to both blind and sighted friends and associates.

Computers with voice synthesizers also allow for access to the thousands of services available on information services. These range from at-home shopping to daily newspapers and online encyclopedias. A modem added to the computer, and a subscription to the service, are all that's needed.

(Whenever possible, put the information from the service on disk, exit the service, and then "read" the information. This saves the hook-up charge to the data bank, which is usually billed by the hour.)

CD-ROM versions of encyclopedias, dictionaries and other reference works are fully available to a blind person with a speech-synthesizing computer.

For the visually impaired who are not completely blind, the above uses of computers can be valuable, as well as a few others.

Many visually impaired people find that reading from a video screen is easier than reading from paper.

The light is coming *from* the letters on the screen, not reflected *off* them, as is the case with type on paper. The contrast and brightness can be adjusted for maximum ease of reading. One program is available that enlarges the type on the screen several times. Another idea is to use a larger video monitor. This gives a full-sized screen display in larger letters.

Prior to computers, the blind had basically two forms of written communication: Braille typewriters and regular typewriters. Braille typewriters allowed for no editing, correcting or inserting. Once the paper was punched, that was it. (Some blind people, I understand, got good at flattening down unwanted dots with their fingernails and adding desired dots with a pin.) Regular typewriters allowed for input, but no way to check what was written without sighted assistance.

Computerized word processing for the blind is as wonderful as it is for everyone else—if not more so. In our excitement about what personal computers can do, however, we should remember that there is a lot of work to do in making available other computer programs to the blind and visually impaired.

Words+ has some wonderful ways of making computers available to blind people. Please give them a call at 800-869-8521.

"If I had a computer,
I'd com-pute in the morning,
I'd com-pute in the evening,
All over this land..."

As *T.K. Atherton's drawing illustrates, a personal computer may or may not speed up scientific research.*

PART VI

Other Uses for Personal Computers

Chapter 35

Personal Computers in Education

Because personal computers are infinitely patient, they make excellent tutors.

Because almost everyone under thirty living in this country was raised with—and perhaps on—television, many young people feel more comfortable looking at a monitor than being with another human.

Because personal computers are interactive, a student may get more individual attention per day from a computer than per month from a teacher.

These reasons, and many more, make personal computers an inevitable part of education's future. For the present, however, the average schoolteacher need not fear being replaced.

Personal computers do not teach. *Programs* teach, and programs—like textbooks or film strips or video tapes—must be written, created, and compiled by people. There will be effective programs and there will be ineffective programs, but for the moment there are not enough of either to make a major impact on education as we know it.

Not that there are not plenty of things to learn today from personal computer programs—everything from multiplication tables to spelling to grammar to touch-typing. The point is that the vast potential personal computers offer in the area of education is just starting to be tapped.

One CD-ROM disk can hold the entire *Encyclopedia Britannica,* including photographs. You could theoretically store, in the same space currently occupied by an average teenager's record collection, all the information necessary for a four-year college education. Not only would that information be there, as books in a library, but the information could be elaborately cross-referenced.

The problem is that the market for educational software has not been as great as for, say, business programs or games. In this supply and demand economy, the supply meets the demand, and the demand for educational software has not been overwhelming. Interest in educational software has been steadily increasing, but it's not at the Demand level yet; it's more a Request.

There are still too few computers in classrooms to spend the money necessary to develop elaborate educational software. One plan gave a tax break to computer companies that donated computers to schools. The plan limited the donation to one computer per school. One computer per school is about as useful as one Selectric per typing class. But it's a start.

Most software houses who want to sell educational programs must rely on concerned parents for sales rather than progressive school boards.

Although educational programs do not begin to approach—either in quality or quantity—what they will be ten years from now, a personal computer's other abilities could benefit almost any student today: word processing for homework and reports, information services for research and current events, programming for science projects, games for mind-body coordination (and fun), and the list goes on. (For example, please see the chapter *Word Processing and the Student.*)

The most valuable computer-assisted education a parent can offer a child today is how to be comfortable with computers. These television-typewriters will be around for some time. Their numbers will be increasing yearly. By the beginning of the next century, the computer will be almost as common as the television in the home or the typewriter in the office.

Familiarity with computers is generally known as computer literacy. Computer literacy doesn't require speaking a computer language, nor does it require programming skills, nor does it even require extensive knowledge of already-written programs. All it requires is a sense of ease around computers, and the knowledge that personal computers are powerful tools, not menacing characters out of science fiction.

The one toy that holds fun for years

How many parents weary of buying toys that the children soon become tired of, or that are easily broken?

This Christmas, give them a gift that they will have lots of fun with for months, *and years*—a toy that they will not tire of and that will not break—that will teach them to think and to be accurate; that will train the eye and hand.

All the family will enjoy Anchor Blocks, fathers and mothers as well as the youngsters.

RICHTER'S ANCHOR BLOCKS

REG. U.S. PAT. OFF.

Build Forts, Armories, Bridges, Churches

All kinds of buildings can be built with Anchor Blocks, from the very simple ones for beginners to large and elaborate designs. These buildings are like *the real things* in miniature—not mere skeletons.

Complete instructions and books of designs are furnished with every set, which make building very simple and easy enough for any boy or girl. The play is not confined to set designs, however. Famous buildings can be reproduced in miniature, just like the real buildings—or original designs can be worked out by the youthful architect.

And in less than a minute the finished structure can be dismantled and another started. Just push it over. No tiresome delay; no tedious labor to take the model apart. This advantage the Anchor Blocks possess over all other construction toys.

Many blocks and metal pieces are included in the various sets, in different shapes and sizes, and in three colors—red, buff and blue. Anchor Blocks are made of *stone* and will not chip or break, but will last "forever."

ORDER NOW — Stocks are Limited

Go to your toy dealer's and ask to see these sets of Anchor Blocks. If he cannot supply you with the set you want, order direct from us.

We will fill your order through a reliable dealer near you or send direct by Parcel Post. If the Blocks are not even better than we have stated, return them at our expense and your money will be *promptly refunded*.

You cannot give your boy a better Christmas gift. Be sure to get the set you want, by ordering now. *Do not wait* as stocks this year are limited and may be exhausted early.

← MAIL THIS COUPON FOR FREE PICTURES

Chapter 36

Personal Computers in the Home

The American home comes in such wonderfully varied forms.

There are the mama-papa-kiddie households of the Norman Rockwell paintings. There are bachelor pads. There are eight flight attendants sharing two-bedroom apartments in four different cities with time-tables and work schedules more intricately calculated than a space shuttle launch. There are crash pads. There are senior citizens "living together" because, if they got married, one or the other might lose his or her Social Security. Teenagers in their first apartment. Widows and widowers living alone, or with their children, or with their parents. Divorced singles. Unmarried parents. Recluses. Communes. Farms. Cities. Small towns. Big towns. Apartments. Co-ops. Frame houses with white picket fences.

I am not for one moment going to pretend that there's a "typical" American home, any more than I'm going to explore how a personal computer would "fit right in."

A personal computer either will fit right in, or it won't, and that will depend on the needs, the interests, the curiosities, and the budget of the people in each home. It's in the home, more than anywhere else, that the "personal" aspects of the personal computers can best be seen.

The household that buys a personal computer today is still on the pioneering edge of this much-touted computer age. While some find it fun being a pioneer, others find it unsettling being even a settler. They will wait until there are towns and Holiday Inns and a McDonald's on every other corner. And, sooner or later, computerdom will have all that. Sooner or later is not yet here.

Of course, business is still the most popular use of computers in the home: either people running a small business out of their home, or work taken home from the office. I'm including writers in this category, whether published or not. Every writer *wants* to get published, just as every businessperson *wants* business to be successful. Alas, that's not always what happens, but—successful or not—you're still in business.

With no business uses whatever, most households, I think, buy a personal computer for the games. Once in the home, however, they experiment with a few of the other things personal computers can do—maybe a little word processing, maybe a little CompuServe dating—and expand in that household the horizons of personal computing.

A modem added here, a printer there, more programs—and soon one could almost run a small business. Add a few business programs, and you can remove the "almost" from that last sentence.

Personal computers encourage not just children, but the child in all of us—that bubbling mass of curiosity and love of adventure—to explore not only the outer world, but also the inner world of our own potential.

Think you have a story worth telling? A poem worth writing? An idea worth expressing? Get a word processing program and tell it, write it, express it. With some computer programs you can even set it to music.

Think you could write a better program than the one you just paid $29.95 for? Give it a try. Fortunes have been made sitting up late, peering into a flickering screen. (Nights have been lost that way, too; but let's remain optimistic.)

Feeling artistically inclined? You might try your hand at computer graphics.

Want to know what's going on in Philadelphia tonight? Find out who's "online" at CompuServe and "chat" with them. There are no strangers in the world of personal computers—a lot of strange people, but no genuine strangers. There are certain advantages to frontier life, and the friendliness of fellow pioneers is one of them.

Or you could have your biorhythms charted, your I-Ching thrown, or your astrology read.

And don't forget the games. Games have been a central part of hearth and home for centuries. Getting together over a game of Snafu or Adventure or Star Trek can be as rewarding as gathering together to play Monopoly or Parcheesi or Mahjongg.

But, ultimately, to discuss the typical uses of a computer in the home is as hopeless as trying to define the typical home.

RUN! LITTLE COCKROACH RUN!
A New Craze Hits America
COCKROACH RACING

**A NATURAL FOR
CONCESSIONAIRES
SIDESHOWS-MUSEUMS
PARKS-FAIRS-CLUBS
ANYWHERE**

**A RIOT OF FUN
SEE THEM RUN
HOLDS the CROWD
GETS THE
MONEY**

DIRECT FROM EUROPE—FIRST TIME IN AMERICA

NEW YORK SUN Says: "It was a historic occasion, this first official introduction of Cockroach Racing in America. The crowd screamed with delight as the favorite crept from behind and nosed its way among the leaders."

REX BILLINGS, Gen. Mgr. Luna Park, said: "Positively a sensation. A swell number for a free act."

WM. F. SCHORK, Manager of Hubert's Museum, New York, says: "The greatest hit since the Flea Circus. Come and see it at Hubert's Museum, 228 W. 42d St., New York."

AN ACTUAL RACETRACK — 10 LIVE COCKROACHES running hell for leather from starting post to finishing line. Over HURDLES or any kind of HAZARDS. The most unique attraction ever offered the Public.

All you need is the track with its PATENTED STARTING DEVICE and a supply of SPECIAL RACING ROACHES, only obtainable through us. ANYONE CAN OPERATE IT. Life of average roach is 5 months. New roaches can be supplied promptly.

WRITE, WIRE OR PHONE
INTERNATIONAL MUTOSCOPE REEL COMPANY
Manufacturers and Distributors for
ARTHUR PHILLIPS, EXCLUSIVE AMERICAN REPRESENTATIVE
451 West 31st Street, New York
Telephone: Longacre 5-4793

Chapter 37

Games People Play

Computer games. Is there a living, breathing human in this country who has not heard of Pac-Man? Only Johnny Carson has a higher recognition factor than this hungry circle with a pie-shaped mouth. (Pac-Man, by the way, is a Japanese invention. It comes from the Japanese word, *pak,* meaning to open your mouth and shove food in.)

Not since the smile button (a distant cousin of the Pac-Man) have a few simple lines, drawable by any first-grader, grossed so much money.

The young do not need a chapter detailing the endless fascination of computer games. Do you think the younger generation is unmotivated? Do you think they have no interests, no direction, no passions in life? Drop by the local video arcade sometime. You will see riveted attention, focused concentration, and rock-steady reflexes that would spark the envy of a concert violinist.

If you want an education in video games, bring along a roll of quarters. The Masters will be happy to teach you, as long as your quarters hold out.

As with Ping-Pong or tennis, video games look easier from the sidelines. Before you sigh that these kids are wasting their time, try a few sets. You'll see that the coordination and split-second timing required to play—and acquired by playing—these games is nothing short of spectacular.

The Army, realizing this, has made the aiming mechanisms on their newest multi-million dollar tanks the same as the ones found on the most popular computer games. The generation that grew up with Missile Command can go to war with…Missile Command.

No, the young don't need to know about the wonders of video games. It's us old folks who read *books* about computers and wonder what all the fuss is about who need chapters on computer games. (The young figure that, for the price of this book, they could play Donkey Kong—or Konkey Dong, or whatever that game is—eighty times.)

So, I will turn the balance of this chapter over to Mr. Michael Evans, who will describe what video games are like for us non-enthusiastic—but nonetheless open-minded—non-teenagers.

From the video game, "Shoot the Bird."

Me and My Computer
A Classic Love/Hate Relationship

by Michael Evans

Recently I bought a computer—a friendly, attractive little home computer. Along with it, I purchased a series of programs that some humorist chose to call "games." If you detect a hint of bitterness in my remark, you're close: in short, I was not ready for the "fun and challenge" of computer games.

It all began one fine Saturday when I sat down to while away some time in computerized amusement. The game disk was labeled Penny Arcade. It contained various pinball, tennis, Ping-Pong, and lemonade-stand games, all of which looked harmless enough to the untrained observer, so I loaded it and selected a game called Little Brick Out.

Little Brick Out consists of a paddle, a ball, and several rows of multicolored bricks. On command, the computer will toss you the ball, and you must keep it from getting past the paddle. If you hit it, it will bounce off, strike a brick, and make that particular brick disappear. Each brick that vanishes adds a few points to your score, and the object is to get rid of all the bricks. Sounds easy, right? Try it sometime.

The first thing you will notice is that the screen is very bright, which makes it hard to distinguish between the multicolored bricks and the brightly colored spots that don't go away when you close your eyes. In addition, every time the ball hits an object it makes a little "bip" that sounds like a malfunctioning smoke alarm. While you are distracted, the computer lobs the remainder of the balls past your paddle, leaving you with something resembling a baseball score.

Perhaps the most disconcerting aspect of Little Brick Out is the sound it makes when it sneaks a ball past you. The buzzer makes you feel not unlike a hockey goalie who has lost the rest of his team and must face the enemy alone.

Abandoning Little Brick Out, I moved on to Star Trek, a game that evokes both excitement and a sense of personal failure.

You play the part of Captain Kirk and are responsible for the utter elimination of all Klingons from the universe. All of them. By yourself. I don't mean to complain, but somehow the odds just don't seem fair. There are 40 of them and one of you. You have a time limit; they have all day. You try to behave like a gentleman; they shoot at you while you're trying to open communications. You have to refuel and get more weapons every so often; they are somehow able to wander through space without expending any energy whatsoever. As if all this weren't enough, you can chase a slippery little Klingon clear across the Galaxy only to discover that he has borrowed a "cloaking device" from the Romulans (arch-enemies for years), and while he can still shoot at you and break vital parts of your life-support systems, you can't even see him! Why couldn't the Romulans give us the cloaking device? Why do the Klingons get all the breaks?

I decided to "beam out" of Star Trek and try my hand at something a little closer to home—Blackjack. First of all, the computer said that *we* cut the cards and I lost. Wait a minute. At no time did I even *see* a deck of cards, electronic or otherwise.

Before long, a message appeared on the screen saying, "I'm shuffling now!" Again, I had nothing to go on but the computer's word, which may or may not have had any basis in truth. Finally, it dealt the cards. It dealt both of mine face up, and one of its face up and one face down. At this point, I was convinced I was being taken for a ride. Here it was, displaying my cards for all the world (and itself) to see, while I was denied the same access. And if that weren't enough, it wanted me to bet money on the game! I tried to bet a nickel, but it came back with a message informing me that the house minimum was $5. I wondered why it felt entitled to set the house minimum in my house, but since I had gone this far, I figured it was worth $5 to continue. I typed in "5" and hit the Return key.

I had a Queen and a Six. Sixteen points. The borderline. The computer had a King showing, but no amount of persuasion would get it to let me peek at the other card. I figured it had probably "dealt" itself 21 points, so I asked for another card. It gave me a 10. Needless to say, I busted. And my opponent had 13 points, but it won anyway. (I never paid, though. I don't think it would have paid me if I won.)

I decided to try another selection. Then another. And another.

At this point, I began to wonder about the effects of computer games on my overall health. Aside from the fact that every minute spent playing games is a minute not spent playing tennis or otherwise toning my body, I began trying to guess exactly how much radiation the human body absorbs when it spends five hours a day in front of a television screen trying to destroy little space creatures with a laser turret. And why would I continue to play with a machine that obviously had the utter degradation of my sense of well-being as its primary goal?

I have a theory. I call it the Cycle of Unrequited Punishment. It goes like this. Suppose I do shut the thing off and turn to some other wholesome activity. How does the computer respond? Does it feel rejected and unwanted, or drop into a funk? Does it promise never to be unsportsmanlike if only I'll turn it on again?

No. It sits there, smug in the knowledge that I'm not playing with it because I know I can't win. The machine simply refuses to recognize that it's being punished.

Smashing it won't do any good. Its brains are etched onto silicon and encased in plastic. They, and every other part, are replaceable. And the repaired unit won't acknowledge that it's been properly rebuked. So who's punishing whom?

Now we've reached the critical stage in the cycle. Faced with all of this unrequited punishment, the weary computer owner tends to grasp at one last hope: the way to put that machine in its place is to beat it at its own game.

That's when the cycle starts all over...

Don't get the idea that you can't win. Of course you can. The computer knows that even laboratory rats need occasional positive reinforcement. Let me describe my first victory.

I decided to select a game that left nothing to chance—no dice, no cards—something based on sheer mental manipulation. Knowing better than to play chess with a machine that understands Bobby Fischer's psyche better than his own mother, I chose to play Othello, a checker-like game that requires some crafty thinking.

It began well. One of the first things the program did was ask me if I would give it an advantage. I resisted the temptation to become snide: "What's the matter, afraid you'll lose?" Instead, I just laughed and said "NO."

It set up the board and the game began. We both played well, but before long it fell for one of my traps and let me capture one of the coveted corner squares. I pushed mercilessly, taking men and replacing them with my own. I felt an almost inhuman glee. When the last chip was played, the machine beeped once to signal the end of the game, and printed.

ME: 25

YOU: 39

WANT TO PLAY AGAIN?

That was it. No fanfare, no congratulations. I beat the computer, fair and square, and all I got was a printout of the score and a question whose tone implied that my victory was of no consequence. I bitterly typed in "NO," and unplugged the machine.

In retrospect, perhaps the computer was just being game—a willing combatant. Or maybe it'll take a whole string of defeats for the computer to begin showing signs of desperation. I might even have to bring home another game disk—and win those, too—just to drive the point home.

But right now, my computer sits on the bottom of my closet. I've got to have time to think.

Thank you, Michael.

While Michael's thinking, let's take a look at a few new video games from INTELATARITENDO—"Games as Original as their Name."

Here we have some from INTELATARTENDO's new series, "Life is a Video Game."

THE TROJAN WOMEN

You are a male in a culture in which 98% of all top governmental and military positions are held by women. Your goal: Get an amendment giving equal rights to men added to the Constitution while raising two children.

SHOOT THE SHEEP

You are a farmer who tries to protect his sheep from a deranged stranger. Little do you know that the stranger is playing a video game in which he is trying to shoot as many sheep as he can before being stopped by a deranged farmer. Fun for all.

SCHOOL DAYS

You are a schoolteacher in the days before computerized education. Good luck!

THE YOUNG THE REST OF US

You play one half of a young couple who have an uncontrollable passion for each other in Victorian England. Many surprises.

CURIOSITY

You are one of several curious monkeys, and you are put into a series of interesting situations. Educational as well as fun.

LVXVRIA

WHAT THE HELL'S GOING ON HERE?

You are shown a picture on the video screen. You have 30 seconds to offer a plausible explanation. (The Grand National Playoff of this game is held every year in Washington, D.C. Winners are frequently offered high-level positions in the White House Press Corps, the State Department, and the CIA.)

"Oh, who <u>cares</u> about the dog, Auntie Em, she wants to take my computer, too!"

Chapter 38

Computers and Kids

Kids *love* computers. Not only do computers embody something kids are completely familiar with—the television screen—but computers *respond*. The California Raisins don't respond. Captain Kangaroo doesn't respond. Even *Sesame Street* doesn't respond.

Computers respond.

It's funny: To an entire generation, computers represented the very personification of distance, aloofness, unfeeling, and uncaring. To the current generation (no pun intended), computers are friendly, cuddly, personal, and fun. How quickly things change.

Kids don't seem to mind learning a new language, if that's what it takes to talk with their new friend. To children, a keyboard is a new avenue of communication, not the appendage of some lowly office machine.

Not only can computers respond, but they can be programmed to respond in certain ways. Kids thus take to programming—not because they have a business to run or a deadline to meet or a letter to write—but for the best reason of all: it's fun.

Computers hold an additional fascination to young people for an almost irresistible reason: grown-ups, for the most part, don't know what the hell is going on. To adults, computers are the things that remind them that payments are past due. Computers are neither interesting nor fun. They are, in fact, intimidating.

Like a boy showing his mother a snake, or a girl turning a cartwheel in front of her father who can barely cart it into the house, kids delight in feeling affection for things their parents find impossible.

Music has often been the battleground in this war of tastes. The John Philip Sousa generation couldn't understand the younger generation's fascination for George Gershwin. The Gershwin generation couldn't comprehend the young Frank Sinatra. The Sinatra generation didn't know what to make of rock and roll. The rock generation thinks rap is odd.

But, somehow, it's the parents who bought the phonographs and who bought the records, even if they couldn't "understand a word of it." And so it is with computers.

Do you love your children?

A few years ago, the *National Lampoon* had a cover photo of a dog with a gun to its head. The headline read, "Buy This Magazine or We Will Kill This Dog." The dog looked worried. It was the largest newsstand sale in *National Lampoon* history.

That cover struck a familiar two-note chord within us, fear and guilt. Fear and guilt. Guilt and fear. Those primary manipulators have been used to sell us everything from religion to war to soap for generations.

Which brings us to the point of this story.

Do you love your children? *Really* love them? How much do you love them? $100 worth? $300? $1,995? Remember, we're talking about love, not money. You say your love for your children is unlimited. Is it? Is it really? When put to the test, do you find your love has certain, uh, limitations?

We're talking about your children's future here. Their education. Their careers. What can you give your little ones that's more important than the ability to compete in the technological age of tomorrow? We're talking about jobs. We're talking about your babies' ability to put food on the table. We're talking about their survival.

Buy this computer or you'll kill your kids' future.

It was easier back in the old days. Kids wanted roller skates and bicycles. Eventually, they got them. Today, kids can quote statistics from the President's Council on Physical Fitness on the importance of physical exercise to little bodies. Loving parents must now supply their offspring with bicycles, roller skates, running shoes (not inexpensive tennis shoes, mind you; they don't provide adequate arch support), and whatever else Vic Tanny might have provided for the Little Tannys.

All this is fair, of course; almost karmic. Parents have been raising kids with guilt and fear for generations. Thoughts such as, "Wait until your father gets home," or "Eat your vegetables, there are children starving in China," were never designed to appeal to a child's sense of reason. That kids are now using the age-old child-raising techniques on their parents is a justice that seems, well, poetic.

Child psychology has convinced us that if kids go wrong, *it's the parents' fault*. Naturally, parents don't want to be responsible for creating incomplete human beings, so kids now couch their requests in terms of growth and development, not fun and games.

Disneyland is not amusement, it's education—especially now that there's EPCOT. Television must be watched for school (*The Cosby Show* will be discussed in sociology on Thursday). Science projects are no longer hobbies, but preparations for Tomorrowland.

Which brings us to personal computers.

Aren't personal computers the most *wonderful tools* for creating whole human beings? They're educational and recreational and technological all at the same time, and as we all know, technology *is* the future.

How could you *not* buy one for your kid? Don't you love your children?

If personal computers had come out when I was growing up, they would have been lumped in the general category of Erector sets, chemistry kits, and microscopes. Educational? Sure. Invaluable? Nah. I don't think my life would be significantly diminished if I had never built a model of the Brooklyn Bridge or burned sulfur or watched brine shrimp hatch.

Although I'm grateful to Mom and Dad for these memories, my parents did not go out and buy me all these educational goodies on one day, or even one year— although I'm sure I devoutly wished they would have back when I was eight or so. I did my best to make them feel guilty, but I don't think they read enough child psychology. No matter how hard I tried, I could not convince them that if I didn't win a Nobel Prize, it would be their fault.

The only people better than kids at stirring the cauldron of guilt and fear in parents' hearts are advertisers. Heavens, they're ruthless. First, they convince the kids that, "If you don't have a computer, you will not grow up to be a human being." Then, they have compassionate pitch persons sell the virtues of various computers to parents, as though buying a computer for a child was a given, like shoes or vaccinations.

Yes, computers are the wave of the future. Computers are marvelous tools. They are also marvelous toys. At some point in a child's childhood, a computer would be a fun way to learn about, well, computers.

But relax, parents. It need not be this year. It need not even be next year. There. You have a self-proclaimed computer expert (God does not make experts; experts make experts) telling you it's OK to wait. You can buy a computer for your child on the same schedule as you would any other exciting but expensive toy. Relax. No need to feel guilt, fear, or to keep up with the Jones' kids or their computers.

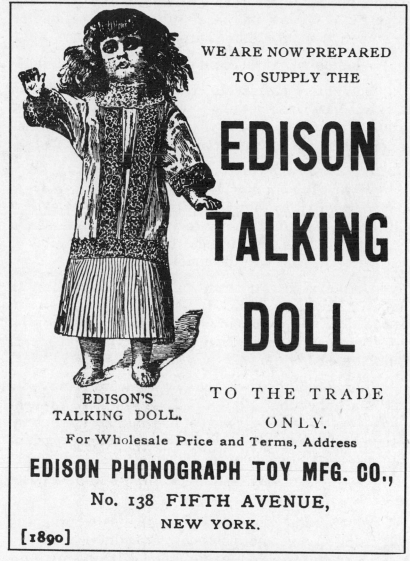

WE ARE NOW PREPARED
TO SUPPLY THE

EDISON

TALKING

DOLL

TO THE TRADE
ONLY.

For Wholesale Price and Terms, Address

EDISON PHONOGRAPH TOY MFG. CO.,
No. 138 FIFTH AVENUE,
NEW YORK.

EDISON'S
TALKING DOLL.

[1890]

Doesn't look a *bit* like Edison to me.

Buying a computer, for a child or an adult, should not be an impulsive act. Imagine buying an automobile without knowing the difference between an engine and a transmission. It will take research, study and work. (Buying a computer is one of the most intricate and educational computer games around.)

What, for example, could a kid use a computer for?

Computers are excellent educators. They do not judge and they never get angry. A computer will respond, "That is incorrect, try again," ten thousand times without once getting upset or calling the child a hopeless idiot. Of how many saints could you say the same?

While the computer does not judge a slow-moving student, it will also take a fast-moving student as fast as he or she can go. If there are 100 steps in a lesson, a computer will take you through them in five minutes or five years. The computer does not care.

Do not expect, however, a personal computer to turn your child into Plato. My above comments refer to the *potential* of the computer in education, not its current standing. The selection of educational programs available today, while vast, has a limited scope.

Computers are good today at teaching things by rote—multiplication tables, spelling, alphabets, touch-typing—but are not very good at conceptual instruction. In time, as mass storage devices and better programming are used, the computer will play an increasingly important role in education. But that's a few years down the road.

We all know computers play games exceptionally well. This activity is not as easy to discount as it seems. Adventure games do develop quick thinking and rational response; action games increase hand-eye coordination. While not measurable on later SAT scores, the cumulative effect of computer games tends to be more positive than negative.

But the best reason, I think, for having a computer in the home is simply to get kids used to computers. The keyboard and screen will be a part of their future—at work, at school, and in their homes. The earlier a computer is part of their daily environment—like cars, electric lights, telephones, or any of the other newfangled gadgets we have come to depend upon—the more comfortably they will integrate computers into their daily lives.

As the kids of today grow into tomorrow's adults, the computer will become just another tool, nothing special, a machine, taken for granted. The sooner we reach that point, the better off we will be.

So, eventually, you will probably buy your kid a computer. (If you can, do it before they're fifteen. At fifteen, if you'll recall, they start shopping for cars.)

Selecting the right computer takes time, and pressure to buy *now* is strong. You have Madison Avenue, sales people, educators, newspapers, magazines, books, television, and your very own guerrilla warriors doing their best to convince you that time is running out.

Finding the time and resisting the pressure is important. It's not easy, but loving children seldom is.

In the delightful piece that follows, Carolyn Benson Cohen details not only the enthusiasm of youth, but also the befuddlement of parents when it comes time for a family to confront one of the burning questions of the nineties: "Should we get our kid a computer?"

The Kid, the Computer, and Me

by Carolyn Benson Cohen

Computers represented the wave of the future, and who wants their kid to be late for the future?

Let me begin with a parent's true confession: all my kid knows about computers was learned in the gutter. We didn't discuss such things at home. When my boy began to get curious, he had to go to the streets for answers to his questions. It wasn't that we didn't care; we just didn't know a darn thing!

The first indication I had that his tastes were maturing was when he asked for a $20 subscription to a computer magazine. It was a big jump from the five bucks we'd doled out from time to time for the cheery periodicals of childhood.

"You're only 12 years old—what do you want that magazine for?"

"I like to read it, Mom."

"Read it? Are you crazy? It's all full of numbers and symbols..." Then I remembered the little notebooks he'd been leaving around the apartment lately, little notebooks filled with—you guessed it—numbers and symbols. I turned the pages of the magazine, one eye on my blue-jeaned, T-shirted, dirty-sneakered son, one eye on the fat, glossy publication. It boasted a lot of words, as well as those mysterious numbers and symbols, and a few of the words made sense to me. I was very much in favor of his reading words. And his birthday was coming up. "O.K., but you're going to have to explain this one to your father."

The very next day the boy started asking if the magazine had come yet. When it finally arrived, they both disappeared until dinner. The evening was spent on the phone mumbling unintelligible numbers and words to unnamed friends.

We had further indications that his interests were expanding when he began to drop hints about his computer savvy. This was a child who usually kept us starved for information about his life, so, while trying to ignore his egotism, we perked up our ears. In fact, as parents sometimes do, we tried to take advantage of his conversational mood to serve our own needs:

"That's good. How are you doing in history?"

With great aplomb he vaulted over more sensitive areas and kept to his topic: "You should have seen the program Kenny and I made up after school today!"

"Kenny who?" When he was younger we knew all his friends.

"Oh, I don't know. He's one of the kids."

Computer Science, with the aid of three small computers hooked up to the big computer of a nearby university, was taught in the seventh and eighth grades of our son's private school. He was a sixth grader, but, I gathered, he spent his leisure time hanging over the shoulders of those more qualified to use the equipment. Such was the beginning of his computer experience: "Over against the wall, kid. I'm an authorized user!"

Soon he was disappearing after school to the homes of several of those boys, particularly to that of one known only as "Adams." Phoning the assorted numbers he left on the kitchen table, I discovered a network of adolescent computer junkies all over the city. My kid was hanging around with some of the local high-tech addicts.

One of the boys had a mother who taught at the school, and after a P.T.A. meeting I cornered her with some questions. She bragged that she had just bought a computer for her family. I was astounded—we had reached a whole new plateau in keeping up with the Joneses! She told me about the clever and unusual programs her darlings were writing and offered advice about what to buy when the time was right. "Your son should have at least 512K," she warned, and for the first time I learned that my child had needs that could be measured in K's. K's of what, I had no idea.

For several months my husband and I mulled and mused. Could we justify such an expense? And yet, from all we had been told by the school and by our son himself, he clearly had ability. Computers represented the wave of the future. Who wants their kid to be late for the future?

Meanwhile, somebody's mother was teaching my child FORTRAN. He had gotten wind of the faint possibility that we might buy a computer and had jumped into the fray with no subtlety whatsoever. He talked about it all day. Every night before he went to sleep he lay in bed like an angel, whispering another reason why we should have a home computer. We kissed him good night and tiptoed away as he quoted memory capacities and lists of available software.

To make a long story short, we reviewed the bank account, reappraised the budget, rethought the issue, and relented.

Now, imagine that you have $1,000 or more and are going to spend it on your child. You talk to all the experts, confer, make a decision, and inform the boy of your beneficence, right? Wrong. In our case, what we knew about buying a computer could fit into a salt shaker. My husband's business associates were either blank when it came to home computers or suggested something simple "so the kid can play games." So where did we go for advice on how to spend this large sum of money? To our son. His largest purchase to date had been a $40 electronics kit on which he spent an entire summer's earnings and with which he got a much-needed "A" on a science project.

The responsibility didn't faze him. For several weeks he phoned and visited the pubescent underground of computer junkies, debated the respective qualities of various machines with curious names and numbers, and stopped in to see his buddies at Radio Shack (where he had become well known by programming their demo). Finally, one emerged triumphant, and we ordered it from a company in California.

One day, not long afterward, the kid was home with a cold. He lay limply across the sofa, the huskiness of his unpredictable voice exaggerated and thickened with congestion. With a television set propped at his feet he was a docile patient, although I found his lethargy disconcerting.

When the doorbell rang I rushed to answer, thinking my son was fast asleep. There was the United Parcel Service delivery man holding a big box. "Mom," I said to myself, "you're going to see a real show." I called softly to the boy, who drew himself up from some inane rerun. "Come here a minute."

When he saw the box, his lassitude fell away like the afghan he had been clutching about his neck. He began to leap about like someone on a pogo stick. "It's the computer! It's the computer!" his poor voice cracked and bellowed. The UPS man stood with his mouth open looking at the two of us. When the pogo stick settled down to earth, he helped us tear open the box.

"Save the instructions!" I shouted as the boy triumphantly lifted out the carefully packed pieces. But he knew what everything was. I was the dangerous one, almost discarding an extra 128K bytes of uninstalled memory we had ordered. Spotting something that looked like a row of staples, I thought it was part of the packing. "Mom! Don't!" the kid screamed, just in time.

We quickly moved some furniture and I set up a card table for the computer, leaving the boy to figure it all out. Frankly, I was on the retreat to a room where I knew how everything worked. When school was out, he placed an emergency call to Kenny.

"Who's Kenny?"

"He's a kid who knows how to install extra memory."

Across town faster than a speeding bullet, Kenny banged on the door. "Mom, this is Kenny Adams," my boy said. A swarthy child with a Kellogg's smile stood poised on the threshold.

"You mean, this is Kenny *and* Adams? I thought they were two separate persons!"

Kenny walked in with an air of authority befitting his superior knowledge. He grabbed the computer from its perch on the card table and trotted with it under his arm to the kitchen. "Gotta have a room with no rugs," he explained, as I rushed to move things out of the way. With a flick of Kenny's wrist, the top sprang off the computer and we all peered inside. It was practically empty! On the bottom I saw a shallow layer of what looked like black Lego blocks. Kenny stuck his head, hands, and the extra K's inside the computer, and soon declared that all was well.

The day the computer arrived, the parade of boys began. Soon I had met all the unknown kids whose computers my son had visited. Most had first and last names by now. Some came bearing extra disk drives, some with game programs, some just to test, play, and program the latest computer. They were nice children, of various ages and even more various sizes. They didn't ask for food, but if it was offered, they cleaned me out. They were clever and funny and polite and thoroughly wrapped up in the world of computers. I've felt much better about the gutter and my guttersnipe ever since!

As for me, I sat down at the computer with the manual one day when the kid was in school. "Push the switch into an upward position," I read. "You will be rewarded by the 'POWER' light at the bottom of the keyboard coming on." I pushed the switch. The POWER light came on. A smile spread over my face.

417

418

PART VII

Selecting, Purchasing, and Learning a Personal Computer

Chapter 39

Of Fear and Computers

I was seated in the cavernous Radio City Music Hall, listening to Bette Midler's opening monologue. ("I must look like an angel dancing on the head of a pin," she told the balcony.) The subject of personal computers arose.

This surprised me. I had been to essentially the same concert not three months before in Los Angeles (I am happily addicted to Ms. Midler), and personal computers were not mentioned. (The San Fernando Valley, home of Valley Girls, was: "Ah, The Valley, The Valley. One million people. One hundred stories.")

Bette asked the New York audience, "How many of you have one of those computer things at home?" The applause, while not as great as that following "Boogie Woogie Bugle Boy," was nonetheless strong. Bette seemed chagrined. She could not understand why people, especially *her* people, would want to sit in front of a monitor and tap data onto disks.

"I got into show business so I wouldn't *have* to do data processing," she explained.

A fair number of people are afraid of computers. Understandably, these people find themselves uncomfortable in the presence of a machine that thinks. What if it gets smarter and smarter and one day just *takes over*, like HAL in the movie *2001?*

Well, computers no more think than phonographs sing or tape recorders talk. Like most machines, computers simply use electrical impulses to do things faster, easier and more efficiently than humans can.

We have difficulty seeing the computer for the machine that it is, I think, because personal computers are such an original invention. We have very little to compare them with.

We've known about the existence of computers for years: Big Business had them and IBM made them. But few of us have come face-to-screen with the operation of computers themselves; hence mystery, myths, and anxiety.

The computer is the most original invention since the phonograph. When Edison invented the phonograph, almost by accident, a little more than 100 years ago, there was nothing like it. A machine that captured *sound?!* Cameras captured images, but artists had been doing that for years. But sound? No one had ever done it. No one had even tried.

Mr. Edison's Talking Machine thrilled, amazed, enthralled—and frightened. It was the work of the devil, some said. It was unnatural. It was hazardous to your health. It would corrupt the young. (That last concern is still under debate.) But before a decade had passed, a gramophone was in almost every home, and people treated it as the machine that it was.

Of Fear and Computers

The telephone was an interesting but impractical device. One had to *YELL* into it, and, even at that, the listener on the other end could barely hear what was being said. Some critics said a string with two tin cans was more effective. For a while, they were right. Telephones were first installed as emergency devices, like fire-alarm boxes for the home. Chats with the neighbors still took place over the back fence.

Then came the automobile, and with it, the cry that disguised no small degree of anxiety: "Get a horse!" Horseless carriages were, after all, noisy devices that polluted the air. (At least we got the noise under control.) Scientists somberly declared that the human body could not withstand speeds of one mile per minute.

Early movies were of people kissing or sneezing or of traffic going by. These exciting vignettes were projected onto a sheet in a rented storefront. Seating was on benches with no backs. The film base was nitrate—highly flammable. The projector's source of illumination was a kerosene lamp. The show at the rear of the "theater" was frequently more interesting than the one up front. One hoped a telephone would be available to summon the fire department, and that a camera would be available to record the blaze for future nickelodeon presentations.

The first radios were crystal sets. Home-built, they permitted one listener, using headphones. Reception was spotty, but it didn't matter as there was not much to listen to anyway.

The resolution of early television was so poor that actresses had to wear black lipstick. A few lucky households back in 1939 got to see the premiere of *Gone With the Wind*—not the movie, just the premiere.

Then there was that disagreement with Germany and Japan, from which came, among other things, computers. Well, people were so afraid of these monoliths that every science fiction movie made between 1952 and 1976 had to feature either (A) insects with glandular deficiencies, causing them to become large and assertive; (B) spaceships, full of alien creatures, bent on taking over some small town in California; (C) computers that get smarter and smarter and decide that the superior race on earth is no longer humans and something nasty must be done about it; or (D) all of the above.

Which reminds me of a joke.

A group of scientists and a group of theologians decide to ask the most powerful computer in the world, "Is there a God?" The computer responds by saying, "I am sorry, I do not have enough memory to answer that question."

The scientists and theologians, intrigued, arrange to hook together the 1,000 largest computers in the world, and ask once again, "Is there a God?" The computer answers, "I am closer to an answer, but I am sorry that I still do not have enough memory."

That an answer to such an important question is close at hand excites the business community. Every computer in every business all over the world is connected. Again, the computer is asked, "Is there a God?" The computer answers, "I am very close to an answer, but I am sorry to report that I still do not have enough memory."

The entire population of the world, in a frenzy, hooks together every device that has any sort of computer memory: microwave oven timers, automotive electronic fuel injection systems, arcade games, digital television tuners, pocket calculators, cash machines, typesetting computers, satellites, Speak 'n Spells, dishwashers, everything.

A world-wide television audience, larger even than the day Oprah revealed how she lost all the weight, watches as the theologians and scientists ask once again, "Is there a God?"

The computer answers, "There is now."

All the popular inventions since the phonograph have grown out of things familiar. The automobile was a buggy with a motor instead of a horse ("the horseless carriage"). The telephone was a talking telegraph. Airplanes flew, like birds and balloons. A movie was a photograph that moved ("a moving picture"). Radio was a talking wireless telegraph. Talkies were the movies plus a phonograph. Television was radio with moving pictures.

But computers... what do computers resemble? They look like television-typewriters. But that's just what they look like. They don't *act* like anything familiar because, like the phonograph, they do something that machines have never done before.

In the past, machines have helped mankind with *physical* tasks: building, moving, listening, watching. Computers help mankind with *mental* tasks: sorting, remembering, filing, retrieving. They don't think, but they help humans with thinking.

With computers, things happen quickly, almost instantly. As movies that appear to move (but are really 24 individual still pictures per second), so too computers, because they sort and resort information so rapidly, give the *appearance* of thought.

Computers sort and re-sort things quickly, very quickly—much more quickly than any human can begin to approach. But *what* is sorted and the *way* it is sorted is entirely up to the human in charge.

If a saint is at the controls, then we can all be thankful, for the computer will be sorting good. If a despot is in charge, then we have every right to fear, for that computer will be resorting to evil. Like any other tool, its use depends on the user. The more powerful the tool, the more devastating—for good or for ill—the result.

The computer itself is just a machine. It may not be a familiar machine, because it's a machine that does things an electrical household gadget has never done before. But we will, I am sure, grow accustomed to it. We've quickly grown accustomed to the many technological wonders (telephones, phonographs, electric lights, automobiles, movies, airplanes, radio, television, food processors, E.T. bicycle baskets) that have changed our lives these past 100 years.

Human beings are, after all, very adaptable machines.

Chapter 40

The Drawbacks of Personal Computers

Yes, there are drawbacks to personal computers, and I'll tell you what they are. You won't have to hear it first from Geraldo.

There are drawbacks to everything, of course, and drawbacks must be weighed in proportion to benefits. Further, most drawbacks can be reduced or eliminated if approached creatively. So, in this chapter, we will be looking not only at problems, but also at solutions.

Here they are then, the several drawbacks (and suggested remedies) to personal computers I have encountered.

1. Computers are expensive. Personal computers cost a lot—in both time and money. Some people I know have enough money, but they don't have much time. Some people I know have enough time, but don't have much money. Most people I know have neither enough time nor enough money. Personal computers require a sizable investment of both.

Will this investment pay off? Will it be worth it? As with installing a swimming pool, it's hard to know until you take the plunge.

A personal computer is something that you will buy, use a few times, and then abandon, a monument to your impulsiveness and lack of determination—like a Cuisinart. Or, you will buy a personal computer, wonder how you ever got along without it, and use it daily for a variety of tasks you would never dream of doing again by hand, a living example of your good taste and practical nature—like a Cuisinart.

Recommending that you "start small" doesn't help much. As those who bought a discounted version of a Cuisinart will tell you, most of the knock-offs were no bargain—they butchered meat rather than slicing it, and mangled vegetables rather than chopping them. The very people who might have been happy with a *genuine* Cuisinart found the imitator unacceptable, assumed the praise heaped upon food processors was grossly overstated, and returned to the processing of food by more traditional methods.

If you want, for example, to do word processing, and attempt it on a $300 machine, you might find it unsatisfactory; whereas, if you were to attempt it on a $1,200 machine, you might be thrilled; and if you were to try word processing on a $3,000 machine, you might find yourself unable to write even a shopping list without it.

If you don't process words (or do bookkeeping, or have a passion for electronic games, or one of the other things that personal computers do remarkably well), it's hard to know if the many things that personal computers do marginally well will appeal to you enough to cause a change in habit.

If you are in the habit of calling your broker or waiting for the daily newspaper to see how the stock market is going, you might not find the allure of an updated-only-fifteen-minutes-ago stock price worth turning on your computer. In some areas, personal computers might offer more power than you need—and in other areas, they may offer much less.

I wish I could give the rather pat advice, "Try before you buy." Unfortunately, personal computing is like flying a plane or visiting Europe or sailing a boat—you'll never know till you try it, and trying it is expensive.

If you're uncertain, continue your investigation. If any of the "drawbacks" in this chapter seem like sound, logical, clear-headed arguments for not buying a personal computer, then you probably shouldn't get one—yet. If these drawbacks appear to you as intolerable nitpicking that no reasonable person would consider for more than a few moments at most, then you're ready.

How long that readiness will last is anybody's guess, and if you guess wrong, it could be a costly error.

You can minimize the chances of disappointment by lowering your expectations. Personal computers do many things well, many things not-so-well, and a broad spectrum of things somewhere between "well" and "not-so-well."

Be realistic. Don't expect too much from your computer.

Don't expect a personal computer to change your life, unless you are a professional writer who already knows how to use a typewriter; a small businessperson who has fairly standard small business needs (word processing, accounts receivable, accounts payable, etc.); or someone who devotes a large portion of his or her time doing something personal computers do well (electronic spreadsheeting, stock marketing, cross-index filing, and the like).

If you don't fall into one of those three categories, it might be best if you lower your expectations to a workable minimum. By "workable minimum" I mean, don't lower them so much that you don't get the computer, but lower them enough so that disappointment will not be automatically included in the purchase price.

Another way to help ensure that you'll use your personal computer more often than your Norman Rockwell Thanksgiving turkey platter is to choose carefully. As much as possible, select the computer and programs that meet your current needs and fit comfortably into your lifestyle.

If you want to play computer games, buy the best game-playing computer you can afford—and make sure you like the games that are available for it.

If you are running a small business, there is no need to buy a computer and software designed for a ten-million dollar corporation. (Yes, the salesperson might say you can grow into it. When you're grossing ten million, however, you can *buy* into it.) If you get more program than you need, you'll have to learn about the complexities of a program that you might use only 25 percent of, and those complexities, besides being expensive, might one day cause the computer to be turned off for good.

If you're just curious about computers and want to get your feet wet, a fish pond will do—there's no need to install an Olympic-sized pool.

As pointed out before, however, if you need word processing, plan on spending enough for a decent personal computer, a quality printer, and the best word processing program you can find. The same is true of business: buying too much computer can be a waste; buying too little, disastrous.

Hamlet was obviously giving advice on selecting a computer when he cautioned: "Suit the action to the word, the word to the action; with this special observance, that you not o'erstep the modesty of nature."

2. Computers are powerful and, therefore, capable of powerful mistakes. It is hard to duplicate, using ordinary methods, the efficiency and effectiveness of a computer. It is equally hard to duplicate, using ordinary methods, the degree of devastation and disaster possible on a computer—unless you consider fire, flood, and nuclear fission "ordinary methods."

Let's assume, for example, that you run a company and have all of your accounting information on a single hard disk. A hard disk is a platter of metal, usually aluminum, spinning at something like 1,800 revolutions per minute, which is equal to 30 revolutions per second. Pretty fast. Let's say that one day, the hard disk decided it was tired of being a hard disk and wanted to become a frisbee.

The disk exercises a remarkable amount of free will for a disk, releases itself from its normally secure housing, and flies out the window, landing in the *Guinness Book of World Records* for The Greatest Distance Traveled by a Personal Computer Hard Disk.

Television news crews are dispatched to interview your disk, while Tom Brokaw and Peter Jennings argue over which one of them will handle the story. (Neither one wants to, but they hear that Dan Rather is opening his broadcast with it, so they feel *somebody* has to interview the damn thing—David Letterman not having yet been informed.)

433

Military error without a computer.

Military error with a computer.

The MacNeil-Lehrer NewsHour cancels its planned satellite interview with Fidel Castro and devotes a special, expanded 90-minute version of the show to your disk. William F. Buckley, Jr., objects, saying the disk should be on his show.

"The disk is a news event," defends MacNeil, "It belongs on our show."

"The disk is a projectile," counters Buckley, "And therefore belongs on *Firing Line.*"

In a ceremony on the White House lawn, your former hard disk is made an honorary frisbee. "This is one small step for disk," the hard disk says as you flip off your TV and mutter something about ungrateful hardware. You try to figure out a way to recover months of priceless financial data and decide there is no way.

A company once, in a less colorful way, lost all of its accounts receivable information. The company sent out polite form letters asking how much money, if any, each customer owed. Not surprisingly, the company was soon out of business.

Even a single floppy disk can be a tragic loss. The entire text of this book fits comfortably on one 3 1/2-inch disk. If I were to lose it prior to the publication of the book, and I had failed to make back-up copies (which I almost always fail to do), it would surely go beyond tragedy and deep into soap opera. O, the gnashing of teeth and the pulling of hair. Cecil B. DeMille never directed *angst* on a grander scale than I would emote.

There are two possible causes for such unthinkable, but possible, occurrences: computer error and operator error. As much as I hate to admit it, the latter far exceeds the former. By "computer error," I mean both hardware and software. Once again, the latter is the cause of far more difficulty than the former.

Businessman, upon being informed that his hard disk had been turned into a frisbee.

The causes of costly mistakes, in order, are: (A) Operator error; (B) Software error; (C) Computer error.

Using software that's been around for a while and a computer that's a relative newcomer, the last two categories might trade places. Almost without a doubt, though, operator error will be responsible for more "computer errors" than anything else.

Suggestions for minimizing this drawback are:

First, make sure you know what you're doing. It's fine to experiment with a computer—there is almost nothing you can do from the keyboard of a personal computer that will cause any permanent damage to the machine—but don't experiment while you're working on something important or irreplaceable.

Before trying anything new, try a test first, or *at least* save whatever is in memory to disk. If, for any reason, the computer "crashes," (shuts down, freezes up, or turns off), whatever was in the memory is lost. If it's on a disk, then the chance of retrieving the information is greatly enhanced.

Second, buy quality, time-tested software. This may not always be possible. You may need a program that is one-of-a-kind and newly introduced. In that case, watch for bugs and be very careful. If you are using the program to process information that is important to you, call the software manufacturer periodically and ask if any bugs have been reported that you should be aware of.

On the whole, however, most of the major categories of software—word processing, spell-checking, accounting, electronic spreadsheeting, filing—have products that have been around at least a year, have sold thousands of copies, and have had most of the bugs removed.

Third, take good care of your machine. It doesn't require much. It is estimated that the majority of electronic parts that do not fail within the first twelve months will last for 500 years. How they make such calculations, I shall never know.

It's a comfort, though, to think that, unless life extension science takes the same dramatic leaps as computer science (and soon), our personal computers will be giving pleasure to generations yet unborn. Well, maybe it won't last *that* long, but a computer should hold up until you buy your next computer.

The only parts of the computer that need periodic servicing and attention are the moving parts, and then only the floppy disk drive and the printer. (A good key-

"...and then the hard disk sort of rattled around and went klunk, and then the video screen turned bright orange and started showing old 'Lucy' reruns, and then..."

board seems to go on forever, and a joystick, well, use it for twenty years and buy a new one.)

Floppy disk drives should be cleaned periodically. It takes about two minutes: all you do is put a special head-cleaning disk in the drive and turn on the computer. Most disk errors are caused by dirty heads, which two minutes of cleaning would have prevented.

Even if the computer misbehaves totally and eats a disk, the failure of the operator to make a back-up disk can cause the problem to be much larger than necessary.

Power failures, too, cause the computer to lose its memory. Power failures happen with varying degrees of frequency in various locales. While living in Detroit, I don't recall any except during electrical storms. In New York there were only two, although they each lasted several days. In Los Angeles, the power company named in honor of Mr. Edison seems to fail, on the average, once every other month.

Murphy's Law #253A states, "The power will fail only when you are about to find out 'whodunit' in a television mystery, have a souffle in the electric oven, or put something irreplaceable into the memory of your computer and have been too lazy to save it to disk." Law #253B reads, "This will only happen when you are dangerously behind schedule, exhausted, and in a bad mood."

A good slogan to adopt while working with a computer is that of the compulsive bargain shopper: "Save, save, save." I am very bad at this sort of thing, but I do make it a habit to save whatever I am working on whenever I get up. Considering that I get up at least every fifteen minutes, it's a rather good plan. Other people less antsy than I might want to save at the end of every page, or every ten minutes (set a timer), or at some predetermined interval or place in their work.

Some software can be set to make automatic timed backups.

3. Eyestrain. Some people find that peering into a monitor causes eyestrain, most do not. For those who do, here are some suggestions.

First, try using a monochrome display rather than CGA color. The images on CGA color screens are not as sharp as images on monochrome screens. The fuzziness might be causing the problem. (This suggestion does not apply to using EGA or VGA color screens.)

Second, if you are using a monochrome black and white screen, try a green or amber screen. Green or amber is supposed to be easier on the eyes.

Third, the glare of room lights off the glass of the screen can cause eyestrain. Get a filter that reduces the reflected light.

Fourth, try a "slow phosphor" video display. The image on a screen changes thirty times per second. This rapid changing is what gives the illusion of motion when Lucy hits Ethel in the face with a pie or a pizza or something. Ordinary monitors are designed to display the one-thirtieth-of-a-second image, and then to fade quickly to make way for the next flash. Slow phosphor holds the image for a longer period of time. Before the last image fades, another has already taken its place, and before that one fades, another has taken its place, and so on. This delivers a video display that is rock-steady. The disadvantage of slow phosphor is that, because it holds onto a light image so long, when you change something on the screen, "ghosts" of what were formerly there will momentarily remain. These polter-geists remain for less than a second, but for someone used to quick-fade phosphor, it can be annoying. It is, however, far less annoying than eyestrain.

Fifth, try the screen on a portable computer. The LCD displays on portables don't use electrons bombarding phosphor, and some find them gentler on the eyes. Others find them more difficult to read and the cause of more strain. See which you prefer.

Sixth, read the solutions to disadvantages 4 and 5 below.

Eyestrain does not affect the vast majority of people who use computers. These suggestions were offered for those who do have trouble.

4. Neck and back strain. Most back and neck strain experienced in front of a personal computer comes from poor ergonomics (the fancy word for making machines fit human design and not the other way around).

We have grown accustomed to looking *down* at a page when we type. This is because those who learned typing on a typewriter found that, invariably, that's where the paper was. The paper was where the typing was, and that's what we wanted to see. Monitors can be placed a bit higher—closer to eye-level—and not having to look down for hours at a time can, in terms of neck and back strain, make quite a difference.

Also, the screen need not be as close as the keyboard. As I write this, the monitor is at least four feet away. To read the entire screen, I only have to move my *eyes,* not my head. (The closer I get to the screen, the more my head would have to move—some law of physics at work there, no doubt.) This causes less strain on my neck and back. Further, the field of my vision encompassed by the screen is small compared to the amount that would be involved if I were up close. I don't know if it's true or not, but my mother always told me it was bad for my eyes to sit too near the TV screen.

I will, Mom's advice notwithstanding, move closer to the monitor when I edit this chapter. I will be looking at the text in a critical character-by-character way. Now

441

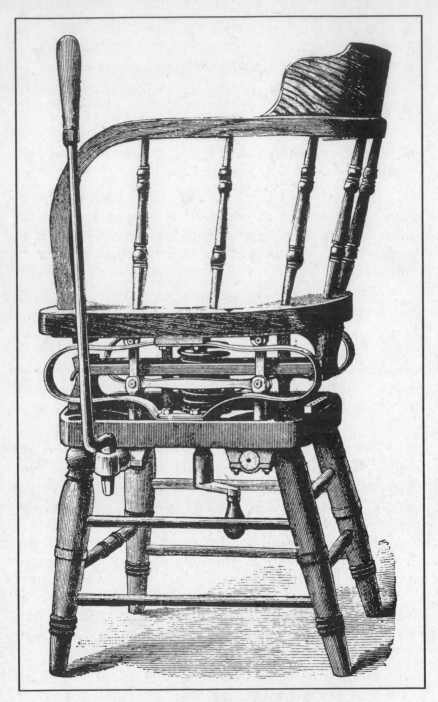

An ergonomically correct chair.

I'm just looking at words, sentences, and ideas. For those, four feet is close enough.

Even when I move up close, I will never be as close as I would have to be if the keyboard were permanently glued to some spot directly under the monitor.

The keyboard should be at a height that allows the forearms, when typing, to be roughly parallel to the floor (or desk or any other horizontal surface you'd care to name). Tilting the keyboard slightly up at the rear helps, too. (Most keyboards have retractable legs built in for this purpose.)

Some people (myself among them) like those chairs you half-sit and half-kneel in. They're called Blans chairs or posture chairs. They look funny, but they're very comfortable. A visit to an office supply or furniture store for a test sit is highly recommended.

And let's not forget about taking breaks, stretching and all those other anti-tension techniques we all know and love.

5. Radiation. All TV screens, including the one in your bedroom and the one in your living room, radiate radiation. The electron gun shoots electrons, "radiating" the phosphor until it glows. Some of this radiation leaks out.

How much leaks out is not known. How much is safe to be exposed to is not known. What the effects of this are over time is not known. A few things are known:

(A) The farther you are from the screen, the less radiation you are exposed to. Radiation levels drop quickly with distance. A few inches from a screen, a measurable amount of radiation is given off; several feet away, the amount is no longer measurable.

(B) Color monitors give off more radiation—as much as five times more—than monochrome.

(C) Radiation is not good for you.

444

I remember looking at a sign in front of a building on my first trip to Los Angeles in the early 1970's. It said, "UCLA CENTER FOR UNCLEAR MEDICINE."

I thought, only in Southern California would a medical center admit that there were any areas of medicine that were unclear; and to put it on a sign, and to devote a whole *Center* to it—well, I was impressed.

A friend had to point out to me that the sign read UCLA CENTER FOR *NUCLEAR* MEDICINE. Since that time, I have been unable to look at the word NUCLEAR without seeing the word UNCLEAR.

The reports that have surfaced over the past twenty years have only made it more unclear. Atomic bombs, meltdowns, nuclear energy, annihilation—did this perplexing subject have to pop out of Pandora's Box *on television,* too? Do we have to face major moral, social, and medical issues every time we turn on the TV or switch on the computer? I mean, can't they leave us *SCTV* reruns and Flight Simulators? Is nothing sacred?

A polling of the scientific community only heightens the confusion. Some say radiation from monitors causes cataracts, miscarriages, leukemia, and arthritis. Other scientists say that the chance a radioactive electron has of passing through the glass of a video screen is about the chance you would have of driving through Nevada with four feet of beach balls on the ground and a gallon of gas in the car. (I did not make that up. A nuclear scientist made that up. A man with credentials.) They say that even the sun gives off radioactivity, and that there is as much danger when exposed to daylight as there is to monitor light.

The more intricate the arguments, the more persuasive each side becomes. The only advice I could offer concerned computer users: use a monochrome monitor, and put it as far away from you as possible.

But then I wondered: should I be giving this advice at all? Maybe there's no danger to begin with. What's the point in scaring people? *The China Syndrome* was bad enough. No point in starting *The Computa Syndrome*. Is it fair to imply that people might be buying a personal Chernobyl? I was in the midst of deepening confusion when, suddenly, a solution appeared.

The I-Protect Company markets lead-impregnated acrylic shields that fit over the computer screen and block, according to I-Protect, 100% of all X rays and most ultraviolet radiation. The acrylic (fancy word for plastic), it turns out, was originally designed for windows in nuclear power plants.

I ordered one. It arrived, a sturdy piece of plastic, transparent, with a slight tint. It attached easily to my monitor with velcro tape. I felt safe from radiation, as Lex Luthor felt safe from Superman while wearing his Kryptonite-impregnated leisure suit. It was the magic shield of Gardol from my youth.

The 12-inch screen costs $99. They have sizes ranging up to 19 inches ($189). (I-Protect, 6151 W. Century, LA 90045; 213-215-1664.)

Anyone who works on a computer long hours and at close range should consider one of these shields a necessity.

"But I can't see any radiation."

"And what about computer viruses?" you ask. What about them? Your personal computer is about as likely to be infected with a computer virus as you are of being infected with bubonic plague. The media loves to sensationalize any disaster that happens to a very small number of people, and we're all supposed to worry about it happening to us. In a book I co-authored with John-Roger, *You Can't Afford the Luxury of a Negative Thought,* we explore this media hysteria in a chapter entitled *Don't Believe Everything You Read in the Papers (Magazines, TV, etc.)* as it relates to disease. Whether human disease or computer "disease" (a silly concept to begin with), the press needs to sell its papers, but we don't need to buy their fear. I'm not going to give the subject any more time or attention than this, and I suggest you do the same.

Well, those are all the drawbacks I've discovered about personal computers, except for unknowledgeable salespeople, lack of product support, and manufacturers' arrogance and incompetence. But I'll discuss those in the chapters ahead. Besides, I never let those things stop me from having something I want. If I did, I wouldn't have a telephone.

"The chapter's over. You can come out now."

"Tina! Bring me the Mac!"

Chapter 41

Why You Should Probably Buy Neither an Apple Nor an IBM

Apple all but invented the personal computer. IBM came along, and gave it a name (the PC) and legitimacy. So, if one wants a personal computer, *surely* one should buy either an Apple or an IBM, right?

Not necessarily. In fact, probably not.

The reason is standards, or lack thereof. The standard in personal computers is "IBM compatible." More computers, software and peripherals are sold in the IBM standard worldwide than all other standards combined.

Apple never cared much about the IBM standard. Apple, Apple thought, invented and popularized the personal computer, and if the world of personal computers wanted a standard, they could jolly well adopt the Apple standard.

The world of computing might have been willing to do that back in the late 1970's, but Apple wanted no part of it. It would not license its design to anyone else, and if some other manufacturer tried to copy the Apple, Apple would sue. What Apple wanted was for Apple to make the computers—*all* the computers—and everyone else would have to be happy making peripherals and software for Apples.

In the early 1980's, IBM pretty much ignored Apple altogether and introduced the IBM PC. Along came the clone makers, and, astonishingly, IBM didn't sue. Everyone was expecting an IBM lawsuit any day. Who were these upstart companies copying IBM? The copies got more and more precise. When would IBM put a stop to it? IBM introduced the AT. The copycats introduced AT clones. IBM hardly sent a threatening letter. One of the great litigious companies of the world became suddenly docile.

By the mid-1980's, IBM lost its opportunity to sue. (If you don't exercise your right to defend a patent within a certain period of time and against a certain number of interlopers, you lose the right forever.) Soon companies that, for fear of litigation, wouldn't dream of copying IBM (Digital, Hewlett Packard, Xerox and others) were making "IBM compatible" machines with impunity (and with varying degrees of success).

The combination of a standard (at last!) and the free market was the best thing to happen to personal computers in the 1980's. Quality and reliability increased, innovation flourished, prices dropped. It was (and still is) a classic example of the free enterprise system at its best.

Apple was not happy. Steven Jobs eased out Steve Wozniak and brought in John Sculley. John Sculley threw out Steven Jobs. Somewhere in all this, the Macintosh was introduced.

The Macintosh, cute and cuddly as it pretends to be, is not "the computer for the rest of us." It's too expensive. Dollar for dollar, part for part (Macintoshes and IBM compatibles use the same basic parts—disk drives, chips and such), specification for specification, Macintoshes are about *twice* as expensive as generic IBM clones.

Why? Behind Apple's cute and cuddly exterior beats a heart of corporate greed as cold as any monolith computer was accused of having back in the computer-hating fifties. Apple runs itself the way defense contractors are run by the Pentagon: whatever it costs to make and market (including all mistakes and hefty executive salaries), add a 15% profit on top, and pass the total price cost along to the consumer.

What if it gets to be too much? Won't the customers go to the competition? Not if they want a Macintosh. There *is* no competition.

Apple holds the patents on the Macintosh with an iron hand. Apple once sued a company for copying the "look and feel" of the *trash can* on the Macintosh screen. Apple won. Apple didn't win in court. They won by slapping the trash-can-stealing company with a lawsuit, and who wants to spend millions of dollars in legal fees to protect the right to use a trash can on a computer screen? Nobody, and Apple knows it. Apple now has proprietary use of all trash cans on all computer screens in computerdom. (The irony is that Apple stole it from Xerox.)

Even were Apple a believer in the free enterprise system, I would not highly recommend the Macintosh as an alternate standard. There is almost nothing the Macintosh can do that an IBM cannot. In every area but one, the IBM has more—and more powerful—programs than the Macintosh. (That one area is music.) And I'm not just talking about twice as many programs, I'm talking about *ten times* as many—probably more.

All the cute and cuddly stuff, by the way, is not the computer; it's the programs. There are any number of cute and cuddly programs for the IBM. The mouse? There are more rodents—in kinds, sizes and price ranges—in IBMland than Appleville.

So, unless your primary use of your personal computer is the composing and recording of music, I'd stick to IBM compatibles.

If I suggest sticking to IBM, why not go all the way and get a "genuine" IBM? Alas, IBM abandoned its own standard.

The installation of expansion boards is one of the great headaches of the IBM standard. There are little switches (called **dip switches** because only a dip would design switches so small that you can hardly see them, and need the point of a pen to turn on and off) to adjust; pins to set; and some boards can go in some expansion slots, but other boards cannot. And after it's all installed, there's no guarantee that one board will work with all the other boards in your system.

IBM to the rescue! In 1987, IBM introduced a new line of computers (the **PS/2** for **Personal System/2**) which included a microchannel. **Microchannel** is a system of handling expansion cards. It automatically adjusts the new card to the computer, and makes sure all the cards work in peace and collective harmony. Great idea. But there were problems.

The first problem was IBM. IBM wanted a percentage of the retail price of every computer using the PS/2 system, which included the microchannel. This time they *would* sue. IBM's request for money was met by the greatest yawn in computerdom since the introduction of the Lisa. The IBM-compatible makers continued making better, faster, cheaper computers that did not include the microchannel or anything else for which they had to pay IBM a royalty.

The second problem was a lack of expansion cards. The microchannel system required all new cards from hundreds of card manufacturers—the thousands of cards made for IBM compatibles simply didn't fit. Another yawn, this time from the card manufacturers. Yes, years later there are some microchannel cards, but nothing approaching what one might call "total support" or even "an alternative standard."

This means IBM is software, but not fully hardware, compatible with the IBM standard. (Most IBM compatible software will run on IBM PS/2 machines, and most printers will connect to it, but expansion cards: No.)

So what does that leave one? Only the rest of the world. Which is what the next chapters are about.

"What do you mean, 'overdressed'? We're going to look at IBM's, aren't we?"

A Periodic Table

No.	Symbol	Name
1	G	GLUE
2	S	SPIDERS
3	Tu	TUBAS
4	R	RAIN
5	L	LUCK
6	Sp	SPRINGS
7	T	TODAY
8	Ci	CIRCLES
9	P	PLAY MONEY
10	C	COTTON
11	E	ELBOWS
12	F	FISH
13	J	JOGGERS
14	D	DIRT
15	W	WRONG
16	H	HONEY
17	M	MONEY
18	F	FACES
19	W	WINKS
20	Mu	MUD
21	Pd	PUDDLES
22	Ju	JUSTICE
23	Ck	CRACKERS
24	Rt	RITA
25	Rc	PHOTOS
26	Jo	JOE
27	Yo	YOU
28	Me	ME
29	Y	YELLOW
30	Da	DACRON
31	Ri	RICE
32	An	ANIMALS
33	Fe	FEAR
34	I	INK
35	Pa	PASTE
36	Cr	CROUTONS
37	Bg	PLUMS
38	Wh	WEALTH
39	Ev	EVIL
40	Cn	CARTONS
41	Li	LIPS
42	Po	POOLS
43	U	UNDERWEAR
44	Cy	CRAYONS
45	Dg	DOGS
46	Mr	MARS
47	N	NATO
48	Ru	RUGS
49	Ic	ICONS
50	Mt	MEAT
51	Tv	TVS
52	St	STOP SIGNS
53	Fb	FLUG BUGS
54	Ca	CARS
55	Ld	LADLES
56	Gu	GNUS
57-		NEAT STUFF
-71		
72	To	TOGAS
73	So	SOAP
74	Le	LEMONS
75	Lv	LOVE
76	Ta	TAPE
77	Tk	TALK
78-	Eg	EGG NOG
79	Co	CONCRETE
80	Go	GOODIES
81	Lf	LIFE
82	Tr	TAR
83	Sc	SCORPIO
84	Ar	ART
85	Ha	HAWAII
86	Sl	STEALTH
87	Us	US
88	Th	THEM
89-		DUMB STUFF
-103		

Lanthanides:

No.	Symbol	Name
57	Lt	LUTES
58	Cc	COCO
59	Im	IMPS
60	Er	ERROR
61	V	VACUUM
62	Bc	BIG CATS
63	Ct	CATS
64	Tu	TRUST
65	Cu	CRUD
66	Se	SEX
67	Lc	THE DOG
68	Sh	SHOES
69	Id	IDEAS
70	Mk	MONKEYS
71	De	DEATH

Actinides:

No.	Symbol	Name
89	Cd	CANADA
90	Fg	FIRST GRADE
91	Wb	WATER BALLOONS
92	Ly	LUCY
93	Sy	STANLEY
94	Hi	HICCUPS
95	Fd	FIDO
96	Cg	CIGARS
97	Lg	LUGNUTS
98	Ff	FOO-FOO
99	Cw	COW
100	Gm	GUM
101	Mn	MOON
102	Su	SUN
103	Fr	FROST

You can use T.K. Atherton's handy Periodic Table in selecting your personal computer.

454

Chapter 42

Selecting a Personal Computer

Whenever I hear the words "selecting" or "choosing," I am reminded of a piece I read in *Daily Variety*. "Johnny Mathis 'coptered to his Irvine Meadows concert, but when the chopper refused to start up after the show, Mathis chose to be driven home by car to L.A."

He *chose* to be driven home by car to L.A.? What, do you suppose, were his other choices? Riding a bicycle? Hitchhiking? Moving to Irvine Meadows?

If you are in the market for a personal computer and you only have $100 to spend, your choices are about as narrow as Mr. Mathis'. If you have $300-$400 to spend, your choices broaden. If you have several thousand to spend—or, rather, invest—the selection, and selecting, can be almost staggering.

My first piece of advice: don't take it all that seriously. If you buy a personal computer now, and you like it, chances are* you'll be buying another one within the next few years. Most gourmet cooks are on their second or third Cuisinart. You may not like hearing this, just as car buyers in the early 1900's on the verge of buying their first car would not like to have been told that they would own ten or fifteen more cars during their lifetimes—but most of them did.

Still, you should choose your first personal computer carefully. Your first experiences with your first computer will invariably color your views of personal computers and computing for some time.

---

*One of my favorite songs, Johnny. Honest.

There are three factors to be considered when buying a personal computer:

1. What you want to use the computer for.

2. How quickly you want to do that on a computer.

3. Your budget.

Let's look at each of these points individually.

1. What do you want to use the computer for? Before you go looking at computers, have a good idea of what you want to use the computer for. If you want to do word processing, for example, your need for graphics will be small. You do not need to buy a machine with top-of-the-line color graphics. Some people go into a computer store, are dazzled by the graphics display of a given computer, buy the machine, and find they never use the graphics capabilities they spent so much for.

The reverse is true as well. If you need a computer primarily for pie charts, architectural renderings, or desktop publishing, you will want to make sure you have the right graphics for the machine.

2. How quickly do you want to do that on a computer? The world of personal computing is changing so rapidly that, every day you wait, the personal computer you eventually buy will do more and/or cost less.

This has always been true of technology. Light bulbs, when they were first introduced, cost a dollar. That was back when people were making about ten cents an hour. Although light bulbs are a dollar again, people make more than ten cents an hour.

It's how badly you want the new technology, and how much it will do for you, that determines if you should buy now or save later.

In 1975, I bought one of the first video recorders offered for the home market, a Betamax. Each tape

Before selecting your own computer, you might want to check out what your friends have.

recorded for an hour. The timer turned the machine on and off, once, in any 24-hour period. It cost about $1,000.

In 1976, I bought a Betamax II. This recorded for two hours, allowing me to tape entire movies while away from home. The timer, still, turned on and off once during any 24-hour cycle. It cost about $1,000.

In 1980, I bought a Betamax III. It recorded for up to five hours. I could set the timer to tape four different programs on four different channels over a fourteen-day period. It had a remote control switch that allowed for fast-forward (no more commercials), rewind (instant replays), slow motion, and freeze-frame. It cost about $1,000.

In 1984, I bought a Beta Hi-Fi. It has all of the above features, plus wireless remote control, the ability to record an unlimited number of programs over a two week period, and the finest sound this side of digital disks. The cost? Oh, about $1,000.

In 1990, the Beta format is dead, but a Super VHS machine with all the Beta Hi-Fi features *and* a picture that's twice as sharp, eight hours of recording per tape and a timer that will record over a year costs not $1,000, but less than $700.

And so it has been and will continue to be with personal computers. If someone were to ask me about my early purchase of a video recorder, "Now don't you wish you waited?" I would reply with an unconditional "No." I feel I got a thousand dollars' worth of use out of the first Betamax, and certainly more than a thousand dollars' worth of use out of the second, third and fourth. If you asked, "Aren't you sorry you spent fifteen years with a dead standard?" I'd reply, "No. I enjoyed every minute of it."

But that's me. I use video a lot and enjoy it a lot, and I do not feel that $4,000 for fifteen years' worth of use is unreasonable. But some people watch just one program a week. It would be hard to justify the expenditure of even $200 for a video machine—unless that one program was very important.

I cannot, just because I happen to love and adore my personal computer, recommend that you run out and buy one of your own. I use mine every day. You might not.

If you have a specific need for a computer, but are waiting for prices to drop, buy the computer now. What you get from the computer as it fills your need will more than balance whatever saving you may gain by waiting. If you don't have a need for a computer, you can get it sooner or later, and it won't make much difference.

"No more of my sweet favors until the computer you promised me arrives."

3. Your budget. Personal computers range from $100 to $5,000. That's quite a range; and there's quite a range of features within that range. Which computer to get—or to get a computer at all—will depend to a certain degree on what you have to spend.

Personal computers, like cars, offer everything from transportation specials to limousines.

Before purchasing a personal computer, many people try to figure out which computer manufacturer will be in business five or ten years from now. These might be the same people who bought a DuMont television back in the early fifties.

I wouldn't spend a great deal of time wondering about that. Nobody knows. Here, for example, are some of the cars that were on the market in 1927: Ajax, Auburn, Buick, Cadillac, Chandler, Chevrolet, Chrysler, Cleveland, Dodge, Durant, Erskine, Essex, Flint, Ford, Gardner, Gray, Hudson, Hupmobile, Jewett, Jordan, La Salle, Locomobile Jr. 8, Maxwell, Moon, Nash, Oakland, Oldsmobile, Overland, Packard, Paige, Peerless, Pontiac, Reo, Rickenbacker, Star, Studebaker, Velie, Willys-Knight, and the ever-popular Whippet-Overland.

Do you think you could have selected one of the eight cars from this list that would still be manufactured 60 years later? And, even if you could have, would it have made any difference?

The gold rush is on, and California is again its focal point; only this time it's not Sutter's Mill but Silicon Valley that draws the prospectors. "Computers or Bust!" More than one company has staked its corporate stick on some aspect or other of the microprocessing world.

There will continue to be an alarming increase of computers and computer companies, and an amazing number of failures. There will be bankruptcies, buyouts, and mergers.

So, don't pick a computer based upon how long you think the company might last. The list of computers changes monthly—certainly yearly—and ten years from now we will all laugh at the funny-sounding computer names, and the old timers among us will tell tales of how they once knew somebody who actually owned one.

How Computers Are Manufactured

To know why name brands are not important, it helps to know how computers are manufactured. Computers are made up of component parts (disk drives, chips, keyboards, monitors, etc.). These parts are manufactured by a handful of companies and sold to the companies that manufacture computers. *No* computer company makes all the parts itself.

Unlike the days when everything on a Ford was made by Ford (Ford even made its own glass from sand and steel from ore), computers are assembled from parts purchased from other vendors. This means that the same disk drive that's in a genuine IBM or a Macintosh can also be in a no-name "generic" computer.

This standardization of suppliers—regardless of final assembler—makes almost all computers equally reliable.

Buy, then, by price, specifications and length of warranty, not by whose name is where. Remember that some awfully big names (AT&T, DEC and Xerox among them) jumped in and *out* of personal computers, while some total unknowns have thrived.

Let's look at the basic component parts of the personal computer from a buyer's point of view.

461

Microprocessors

Processors for IBM compatibles are 8088, 80286, 80386, 80486, etc. The 8088 remains the 8088, and the rest are shortened to 286, 386, 486, etc.

People often brag about how much *faster* one processor is than another. This may be true, but all things are relative. Say processor B is four times faster than processor A. In other words, a function that would take a quarter-second on processor B would take a whole second on processor A.

Let's suppose you perform this function twice a day. At the end of the day, using processor B over processor A would save you one-and-one-half seconds. If, however, you perform this function ten times a minute, processor B would save you not just time, but also your sanity.

All things being equal, why not get processor B? Well, all things are seldom equal, and for processor B you'll pay more. Is it worth it? That depends, of course, on how much you need it and what you can afford to spend.

Faster is not necessarily better. Does it matter if the top speed of your family car is 120 or 240 mph? How well it handles at 40 is far more important than its ultimate speed.

The right price/performance ratio for you might well be an 8088 machine, just as a four-cylinder car might be all you need, or a nineteen-inch television more than sufficient.

Look at the machine and how it does the sort of things you need it to do. Some automobile manufacturers do more with four cylinders than others do with six.

Memory

A full 640K of memory comes standard in most computers, and 640K is recommended. Most programs don't need more than this (desktop publishing does), but you might enjoy having an extra megabyte or two for RAM drives, or for "supercharging" your programs that can use extended or expanded memory. (Please see Chapter 4 for a discussion of expanded and extended memory.)

Operating Systems

"Operating system" is a shortened version of **Disk Operating System**, also known as **DOS.**

A disk operating system simply tells the computer how to store information on the disk, and how to retrieve stored information from the disk. For the most part, the operating system is transparent to the user. The user is involved with running a specific program, and the computer runs the DOS to let the computer know how to interact with the disk drives.

The choice of an operating system for personal computers is not all that complicated nowadays. Most machines come with MS-DOS. Eventually they will come with OS/2, a new, improved MS-DOS, but for now it's MS-DOS.

Disk Drives

Floppy disks come in two sizes: 5-1/4-inch and 3-1/2-inch. 5-1/4-inch drives are the most popular in desktop machines, while 3-1/2-inch drives are standard on laptop machines. I have both for my desktop, so that I can use both sized disks. I recommend at least one floppy drive that holds a lot of information (1.2 megabytes for a 5-1/4 or 1.4 megabytes for a 3-1/2). This

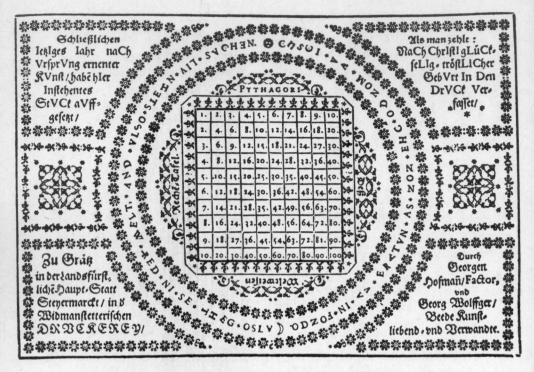

Use this simple chart to help you decide how much disk capacity you'll need.

makes backing up your hard disk much easier (hence you'll do it more often).

Hard disks are fairly standard on most computers these days because they are relatively inexpensive. More and more programs are coming on multiple floppy disks, making it virtually mandatory to have a hard drive. I strongly recommend a hard drive.

How much memory should your hard disk have? 20 megabytes seems to be the minimum. (The original hot-to-trot IBM PC-XT that lit up the computing world only a few years ago had a whopping 10 megabytes.) Getting 30 or 40 megabytes is often not much more expensive than 20 megabytes, and over time you'll probably be glad you made the extra investment.

Keyboards

Keyboards are made by a handful of companies, and are, for the most part, all good. You may have a personal favorite, but the clinker keyboards of the early days of computing seem to have vanished (thanks be to heaven).

Still, there are variations from keyboard to keyboard, and one might have just the feel you prefer. Should you buy a computer just because you like the keyboard? Well, would you buy a car just because you like the way it drives? Other than cosmetic design, the keyboard is the most "personal" part of the personal computer—the one you'll use most often and the one that's most often varies from one computer maker to another.

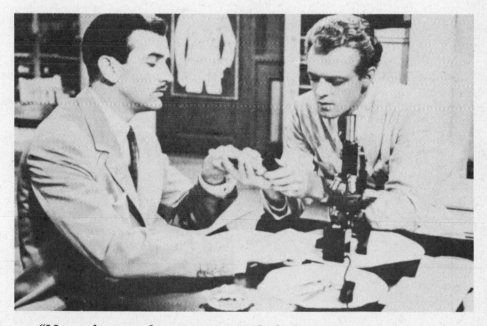

"Now that we have measured the precise curvature of your fingertips, we will select a keyboard especially suited for you."

Mice

The mouse is a little box with a button (or two buttons or three buttons) on it. The mouse is connected to the computer by a thin cord, vaguely resembling a mouse's tail; hence, I suppose, the name mouse.

When you move the mouse around on a desktop, an arrow on the video screen moves, too. The button (or buttons) does (or do) a variety of things, depending upon where the arrow is pointing.

Some people think mice are the greatest thing since canned bananas. I'm not so sure. Personally, I prefer cursor movement keys. With a cursor, the screen is divided into a finite number of squares—a grid, made up of the number of lines on the screen, and the number

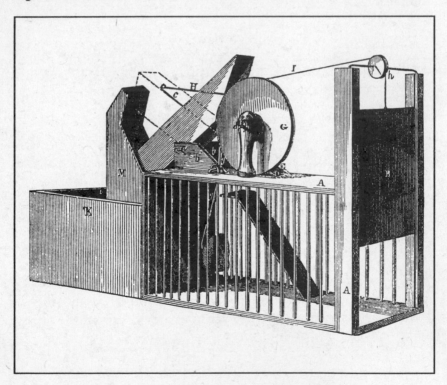

"Of course you don't have to buy a mouse."

of characters on each line. There's a comfort in knowing that the cursor is either in the right square or it's not.

On a mouse-driven screen, the arrow has an almost infinite number of places to point. Infinity is very nice, but mostly in the study of Eastern religions.

I also like cursor movement keys. Hit a key once, and the cursor moves into the next square (either up, down, left or right.) Hold a key down, and the cursor zips along, but always landing on a square. That square is fillable with precisely one letter, number, or punctuation mark. Ah, security.

A mouse requires about a square foot of empty desk space somewhere near the computer. Do you have an empty square foot of space on your desk? I don't. Flat surfaces tend to gather paper, books, and dirty dishes. At least *my* flat surfaces do.

Mice make sense for graphics (it's hard to draw a circle with cursor movement keys). Desktop publishing, too, uses mice to good advantage.

Monitors

A monochrome monitor is all you need for almost all computing tasks. They're remarkably inexpensive and you'll be perfectly happy with one. You might want to compare amber and green monitors to see which you prefer.

Color is nice, however. Most programs use color, and to good effect. If you're going to splurge on color, splurge all the way and get an EGA or VGA monitor. (For letters and numbers, EGA is all you need. For graphics and desktop publishing, go for VGA.) It is far better to use a monochrome monitor than to try to process words and numbers with a CGA ("standard," "basic" color) screen.

Use this handy chart to help you decide which computer to buy.

Here is the same chart, reduced, so you can take it with you on shopping expeditions.

468

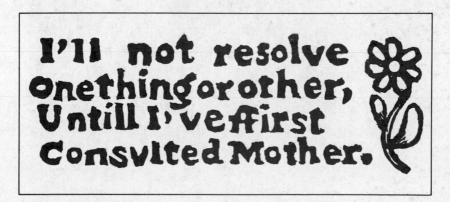

I'll not resolve
one thing or other,
Untill I've first
Consulted Mother.

Chapter 43

Purchasing a Personal Computer

Here are some thoughts on shopping for, select-ing, and purchasing a personal computer.

1. Start by visiting stores. Before you begin looking at computers, look first at computer stores. Make a list of all the computer stores in your area (from the Yellow Pages and newspaper ads) and visit some. You should know within the first few minutes if you'd like to do business there.

2. Don't expect much. When you're considering spending more than $1,000 on a product, you expect from the salesperson a certain attention, kindness, politeness, expertise, or at least civility. Not necessarily.

I once entered a store and a salesman walked up and said, "We have the 1200, 895, in stock." No hello. No may-I-help-you? Just "We have the 1200, 895 in stock."

"I beg your pardon?" I said, affecting a slight British accent and a Clifton Webb tone, which I tend to adopt whenever accosted by security guards, streetwalkers and salesmen.

"We have the 1200. In stock. Only 895." That was his idea of an explanation. I thanked him for the information, and left.

3. Make notes. This will be an important, ongoing part of selecting and purchasing a personal computer. Start by noting the stores you visit and whatever comments you may have about them—anything from "Looks good" to "Never in a million years."

If it's in the "Looks good" category, note which computer and printer lines they carry. And if—miracle of miracles—you should happen upon a polite, well-informed salesperson during your preliminary tour, write down his or her name. In red.

4. Ask friends for suggestions. Any friends or colleagues who own personal computers have already gone through this ordeal which, for you, is just beginning. Humbly implore their aid.

They may know a computer store to visit, or, just as importantly, they may know a computer store to avoid. They may have the name of a good (or bad) salesperson (or consultant). They may confirm your doubts about certain stores, or they may inspire a second look.

Daniel in the computer store.

Like soldiers returning from the war, most personal computer owners enjoy telling their stories of joy and sorrow, of courage and cowardice, of the thrill of victory and the agony of defeat. All they need is a compassionate audience, and maybe a bottle or two of wine.

5. Make an appointment. Call the stores you found acceptable and make an appointment. When you call, ask to speak to the salesperson who knows the most about word processing or accounting or electronic spreadsheeting or whatever your primary computing need is.

Salespeople tend to know more about one area than another—you don't want the games expert selling you a business computer, or vice versa.

The same is true of specific brand names. If you're interested in a specific machine, rather than a specific function, ask for the person who knows the most about that computer.

When you get this person on the phone, chat for a minute and see if you get along. By "get along" I don't mean that you want to get married, or even have dinner together. I mean, if you ask a question, can they give you an answer that you can understand, and are they generally willing to answer the question? If yes, then grapple them to your soul with hoops of steel, to quote (I think) Harriet Beecher Stowe.

With the salespeople who pass your mini-interview, make a specific appointment to come and see them. If they say, "Any day except Tuesday," then say, "Fine, how about Thursday at 3:00?" This will let the salesperson know you mean business.

6. Bring something for the computer to do. If the primary use for your computer will be word processing, bring some words to process. If it will be electronic spreadsheeting, bring some figures to project. If it will be accounting, bring some numbers. The sooner you see a computer and program processing information *you* use every day, the better you'll be able to judge its usefulness.

7. Remember, you're looking at computers *and* programs. When you look at a *computer,* you are looking at the clarity of the screen, the feel of the keyboard, the overall appearance, and the technical specifications (disk capacity, memory, etc.). Everything else that happens is *programs.*

If you like the way a computer processes words or numbers, more often than not what you like is the program, not the computer. Buying a computer because of a good program is like buying a car because you like the countryside in where you took the test drive.

475

Ask the salesperson the name of the program running on the computer. Ask if the program will run on any other computer. (Some programs can, some can't.) If it can, then ask to see the program running on other computers.

An adage in computer buying is, "Find the program first, then buy the computer that runs the program best." In fact, you'll probably be looking at both simultaneously. Learn to separate what a computer is doing (the program) from what a computer is (a screen, keyboard, and list of specifications).

If you do this—and make notes of not only the computers you've seen, but also the programs you've seen—you'll be able later to piece together your own computer and program(s) that best meet your needs and preferences.

8. Be patient. In a computer store, expect delays of all kinds. Your salesperson might get a phone call that will take twenty minutes. The computer you really want to see might be in use, in repair, in the box, or otherwise indisposed.

Use your "free time" to look at software instruction manuals, read computer magazines, eavesdrop on other demonstrations, converse with your fellow exiles, eat a sandwich (bringing a box lunch is highly recommended), play computer games, or just soak up the general ambiance.

9. Look for salespeople as well as computers. If the salesperson with whom you made the appointment turns out to be a dud, but another salesperson in the same store appears to be a winner, it's time for some honest, straightforward deception.

Ask the dud for his or her card, ask his or her day off (ask as though you wanted to make sure not to miss him/her), and make a hasty retreat. On the day off, call ahead and make sure the dud is off, then go to the store and introduce yourself to the winner. ("Winner" is a relative term, especially when applied to computer writers and salespeople.) You will then "belong" to the winner.

10. Try to spend some time alone with the computer. Given the nature of most computer stores, this shouldn't be too difficult. Just say, "Don't those people over there need some help?" There are usually some people "over there" who need some help.

11. Don't be intimidated by jargon. If the salesperson uses a word you don't understand, ask for an explanation. Most Computerese has its English counterpart. If necessary, bring along a translator.

12. Continue keeping notes. As you look at each machine and program, make notes as to its power, speed, ease of use (which is not always the same as ease of learning—in fact, the two are sometimes mutually exclusive), and general reactions. Be sure to list your subjective reactions to the machine. Just as a car is

"Excuse me, please. I seem to be lost. Which way are the printers?"

more than how many MPG it gets, a computer is more than how much RAM it has.

Your thoughts and feelings about a computer might be very clear immediately after leaving the store, but your recollection might be more than a bit hazy eight stores and fourteen computers later.

13. Collect literature. Gather as many of those full-color, glossy sales brochures as you can. Not only do they provide technical information (no point writing something in your notebook that's already printed on the finest paper venture capital can buy), but you can someday publish *The Personal Computer, 1990-1999: A Retrospective.*

14. I can't think of a 14.

15. Hire a consultant. If you stumble on a good consultant somewhere in your journey, hire the person. Computer consultants charge from $10 to $60 per hour. (The average seems to be about $25.) Ten hours with a first-rate consultant might set you back $600, but a good consultant will save you far more than that.

A consultant can, for example, establish your computing needs, suggest machines and programs that will fill those needs, and recommend the best places to buy. After the equipment is purchased, the consultant can assemble and instruct.

I do not recommend, however, giving a consultant *carte blanche.* The selection and installation of a personal computer is far too important to trust to an "outsider," no matter how expert. Be involved in every step of the process.

One word of caution about consultants who sell computers. Some of these people are salespeople who charge for their selling. Others are consultants who become dealers so that they can pass the savings along to their clients. The latter group are fine; the former should be avoided.

A consultant will have his or her favorite computers and programs. This is to be expected. Ideally, however, a consultant has a full range of computers from which you both can choose the one that will be right for you.

16. What happens if it breaks? Personal computers do not break down that often, but what would happen if yours *does?* Does the machine need to go back to California or Florida or Texas or Massachusetts or wherever it came from? Can it be fixed locally? How long will it take? Are loaners available? Are rental units available? Is on-site service available? Will the dealer put in writing any of the broad, soothing promises questions like these tend to elicit from salesfolk?

"Hello! I'm in for accidentally erasing a hard disk. What are you in for?"

You might check to see if any of your credit cards offers "free extended warranty service" on any electronics purchased through said card. These usually double the length of a warranty. If it's free, why not?

17. Is delivery, set-up, training, or anything else included in the price? Computer stores which cannot quote you specific guidelines on such a question are either (A) not being honest, or (B) not going to be around long. A computer dealer cannot afford an open-ended agreement to fully support a personal computer. There may be a mark-up in computers, but not that much.

Most professional (i.e., well-run) computer stores have specific guidelines concerning set-up and support.

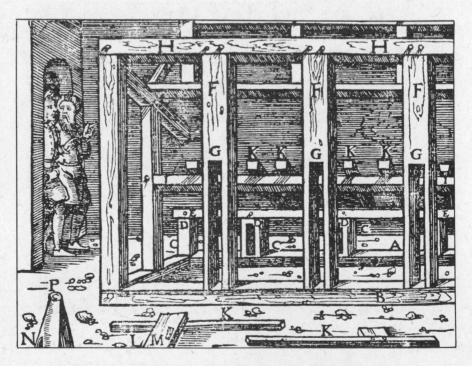

"I tried putting it together myself, but somehow it seems a lot bigger than in the pictures."

"We will install the machine, and provide you with four hours of instruction. After that our rate is $20 per hour." Or: "What you're buying is a computer in a box. We'll guarantee that it works, but set-up and instruction are up to you." Something like that.

The stores that promise eternal hand-holding are either dishonest, or well-intentioned souls who will eventually (A) break their word, (B) go bankrupt or (C) both.

Naturally, computer salespeople are human beings, and if you call and ask an occasional question, they'll answer it. But the salesperson who promises, "Whenever you have a problem or a question, just call me. I'm always here," either sold used cars recently, or will find himself at the bottom of an inverted pyramid that would make the Social Security Administration seem like a solid, fiscally-sound organization.

18. Investigate mail order. Computers and programs are available at significant discounts by mail. If a retail computer store wants you to pay full retail price for a computer or program, it should have to, like Smith-Barney, *earn* it.

What does the computer store offer that should warrant your patronage? Do they have classes? Set-up? Support? What?

Mail-order computer dealers sell hardware about 20% off, and software roughly 40% off, retail. The implied agreement when purchasing from a mail-order discounter is, "I get my money; you get your goods; our relationship ends there." There are some exceptions to this rule, but discounters have even less margin to offer support than the retail stores.

This understood non-support matters little if you have a good consultant, or if you enjoy the adventure of conquering new frontiers alone, or if you have a friend who owns the same computer and owes you a lot of favors.

If you decide that the support from the local dealer is worth it, you can usually get the dealer to lower its price by quoting mail-order figures in the back of the very computer magazines sold in the store. Naturally, retailers will not be able to meet the prices of a mail-order discounter, but they'll probably knock a few points off.

There are also companies that sell *only* by mail. These are often highly respectable companies who manufacture computers, but have no retail dealers. Their "outlets" are ads in magazines and newspapers. Most have a 30-day unconditional full money-back guarantee (and don't dream of buying from one that doesn't—no "full credit"—cash back only). You can try the computer and see what you think. If you don't like it, back in the box it goes.

It's a good idea to use a major credit card when buying anything by mail. If there's a dispute, the credit card company can credit your account and collect from the offending mail-order merchant. Although there's a certain amount of paperwork in this, it's easier than going to Kansas and suing the bastards. Be sure to save all brochures, receipts, service contracts, shipping information, etc.

19. Check with your tax advisor. As with any major purchase, check with your tax person on the relative merits of leasing vs. outright purchase.

20. Have fun. If you relax and give yourself enough time, you can actually enjoy the most intricate and complicated computer game around—buying a computer.

"Hello! I would like to purchase a personal computer."

"Oh, you have come to the right place, sir. We have a wonderful personal computer spinning wheel. On sale."

"But I read this book called The Personal Computer Book and the author never once mentioned spinning wheels."

"Then the author is a fool! Have you ever read The Spinning Wheel Book?"

"No."

"Oh, you have missed so much in life. What do you want a personal computer for?"

"To write with."

"How can you hope to write about life if you've never read The Spinning Wheel Book, which is on sale, too."

"But the author of The Personal Computer Book said…"

"Fool! The man is a fool! I do not care what a fool has to say."

"I don't know what to think."

"Think about spinning wheels. Personal computer spinning wheels."

"But I don't want a spinning wheel!"

"Then how about a puppy dog? A nice personal computer puppy dog…"

Sometimes you meet a computer salesperson you just <u>know</u> you can trust.

While others, somehow, you know you can't.

The Pharaoh's daughter finds a personal computer in the stream.

Chapter 44

Questions and Answers on Selecting and Purchasing a Personal Computer

Should I buy a computer now, or should I wait? The prices keep falling and the computers keep getting better.

No matter when you buy, the prospect of better and cheaper computers will always loom on the horizon. Yes, computers keep getting better and cheaper. The question is not whether you'll get a better deal a year from now (you will), but whether you will get more value from the computer's use during that year.

The answer to that question will depend on what you plan to use the computer for.

If you plan to use the computer in business—anything from accounting to cost projections—you'll, no doubt, save more in one year by owning a computer than you'd save by not owning one.

If you're a writer, secretary, or student, the value gained by word processing will more than pay for itself over and over again.

If you want a game-playing computer, then you might as well buy now. For less than $300 you can get a fine computer and several game cartridges.

If you're curious about computers, are wondering what on earth they are, an inexpensive IBM compatible will provide a fine introduction to computerism for around $500. Don't expect to run your home or business with it. It will satisfy your curiosity, not your need for a business machine. (That will take around $600 more.)

Overall, you'll know when the time is right to buy a computer. It's when you can't think about buying anything else.

Isn't there a danger that the computer I buy now will become obsolete?

That's one of the great myths about computers. Computers never become obsolete. A computer you buy today will do exactly what it does—be it word processing or game playing—twenty years from now. (Providing it's still working, of course.)

Yes, the state-of-the-art will change, but, like a car, if it gets you from point A to point B today, it will make the same journey in the same way as long as you own it (and keep it in good repair).

If you buy a computer today, in a few years you'll probably want another, just as people moved from hi-fi to stereo and from black & white television to color. Did those people get value from their hi-fi's and black & white TV's? Undoubtedly. Will you get value from one of today's computers? Almost certainly.

I want to get a computer for my son's birthday. What should I get him?

A gift certificate. Buying a computer for your son, while a loving and obviously generous thing to do, can be as dangerous as selecting for him a tie or a car or a spouse. Let him know what you'd like to spend, what you're willing to spend, and the most you'll spend (and have a higher figure in your mind that you're *really* willing to spend). Then let him select his personal computer, personally.

***After several months of investigating computers, I
am so confused. What should I do?***

Take a month off. Relax. Don't look at any more
computers. Don't read any more about computers.
When computers come on TV, change the channel. (You
may do a lot of channel changing.)

There is nothing imperative about buying a computer. Computers will be with us for a long, long time
(providing, of course, that we're all here for a long, long
time). There is no rush. Last year's luxury has become
next year's inevitability.

If, after two weeks, you *want* to jump back into
the most frenetic computer game around—buying a
computer—then "Geronimo!" and good luck. If, at the
end of the month, you still dread the thought of returning to Computerville, then take another month off.

If you've been instructed to investigate personal
computers for your company, inform the powers that be

that you are "pausing to evaluate obtained data prior to finalization of the project," or some such important-sounding business phrase.

If you're feeling too confused to make a good decision, don't make one. After a while, personal computer overload should subside, and you'll be glad that you took the pause that refreshes.

Do you recommend buying a used computer?

I used to say that as a rule, no, mainly because with computer technology changing so rapidly, computers lost their value quickly. Someone who paid $3,000 for a computer did not want to sell it for less than $2,500, yet what you could buy new for $2,500 was much better than an old, used machine. Their $3,000 computer might have been worth $700.

In the last few years, a brisk market has arisen in used computers. I'm seeing old CP/M computers—once $1,800—sell for about $100. (Not many people would want one, though—you can't buy new software for them—but the machines can make great word processors.) Better, though, are used IBM compatibles with hard disks selling for under $500. (Realize you can get a new IBM XT compatible for about $700.) Those who know their computers can find great deals.

If you do not know computers well, I still recommend a new computer with a good warranty.

If you are considering a used computer, remember to negotiate from what a comparable system would cost *today,* not from what the person paid for it two or three years ago.

How much time should I take in selecting a personal computer?

As much time as you need. For most people, a personal computer is a major investment and should be selected and purchased with care.

If you decided to buy a new car, you would have several weeks of test drives, reading about current models, talking with friends, asking advice, and examining your budget. The same is true of buying a computer, but, for most people it will be more difficult, as most people have never purchased a computer before. Imagine going out and buying a car, when you didn't know which of the five wheels was used for steering. (Did I tell you about the sixth wheel in the trunk?)

Some general study about personal computers is in order. As one of those silly rules of thumb, I would allow at least two weeks of study, research, and shopping for every $1,000 you plan to spend.

I live in a small town. We have one computer dealer. He charges full retail prices for everything he sells and knows less about computers than my 12-year-old son. I'm ready to buy my computer, but don't think I should have to pay the full retail price for it. What can I do?

It seems as though you have four choices. You can wait for another computer store to open, open your own computer store (with your son as manager), learn the fine art of haggling, or buy your computer by mail.

Mail-order computer buying is a reasonable alternative to buying a computer in a retail store, providing you (A) know precisely which computer, software, and peripherals you want, and (B) are willing to provide your own support after the sale (in the form of a consultant, exhaustive research, or a 12-year-old son).

After you've found the lowest price on the computer you want, you can use the price as a bargaining tool. If, for example, the computer of your dreams retails for $1,000, and the mail order houses sell it for $700, you may be able to use the lower price as a negotiating tool and talk your local dealer down to $850. In this way you'd get a lower price, plus whatever support the local dealer might have to offer.

Buying by mail is especially tempting if you've found a knowledgeable consultant who will work for, say, $30 an hour. If you can save $300 buying by mail, that savings will provide you with 10 hours of your consultant's time.

Will the local computer store give you 10 hours of individualized attention? Some will and some won't. If your local computer store suggests that you not buy by mail because they, the computer store, can offer home town service and support, ask them *how much* service and support? Are they willing to put it in writing?

Local computer stores are a good place to buy your computer if they seem genuinely helpful (observe how they treat customers who have already purchased a computer from them—do they take as much care in supporting as they do in selling?), offer in-house service, have classes or clubs or dances or other social activities, or let you hang out there.

Where can I find a computer consultant?

Good question. I wish I had a good answer. Most Yellow Pages do not yet have a heading, "Personal Computer Consultants," but give Ma Bell a year, and they will. (Ma Bell will give almost anyone with money a heading, from Massage Parlors to Singing Movers.)

Until Personal Computer Consultants are as plentiful and easy to find as H&R Block, I would, while shopping for a computer, also be shopping for a computer consultant.

A salesperson who seems to know more about computers than the average reconditioned car salesman might be led astray by cold cash. Maybe the teacher of a computer class could be tempted to do a little moonlighting. Maybe a local writer about computers could be enticed from his or her word processor. Maybe a notice on a computer store bulletin board stating your needs and what you're willing to pay ($20 to $60 is the going rate) will bring an acceptable respondent.

And don't forget to spread the word among your friends. They may know someone—or know someone who knows someone—who would be a likely candidate. (Suggestion: it is best *not* to learn from or teach a person with whom you are in a romantic relationship. If you know what I mean, you know what I mean. If you don't know what I mean, you'll soon know what I mean.)

If you already have a computer, and would like to find someone to teach you a specific program, you might try one of the temporary employment agencies. (They *do* have a listing in the Yellow Pages.) Some temp agencies now specialize in personnel familiar with personal computer programs. You *might* find someone who knows the program you're trying to learn.

When the temp arrives, rather than having him or her use the program, ask the person to *teach* you the program. (Most temp agencies have a half-day or a full-day minimum, so be prepared to work.)

Finding a good consultant will take creativity, luck, and no small portion of gall.

Harriet Beecher Stowe (I think).

"Relax, Sir. Your computer will be back from the repair shop any month now."

More and more people are discovering the joys of
personal computing every day.

Chapter 45

An Illustrated Guide to Selecting and Purchasing a Personal Computer

Those who have not taken ample time in selecting their computer have had reason to regret it.

Get the advice of those who have trod the path of computer ownership.

Don't overtax your system by getting one too small to meet your needs.

Be sure to read good books on the subject.

And even if you haven't read any good books on the subject, be sure to ask the advice of someone who has.

Be open to good advice from any source.

Even with expert guidance, it's easy to get in over your head.

After visiting a number of computer stores, you might want to go through the collected business cards and see which salesperson you liked best.

If you play your cards right, you'll wind up with a computer you can be proud of.

Prepare yourself.

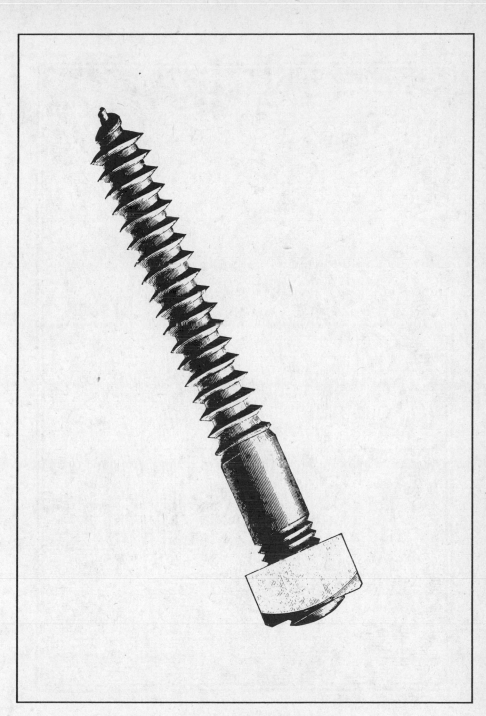

And be careful out there.

Happy computing!

An Introduction to Computer Symbols

The International Association of Computer Reviewers and Publishers of Books and Magazines and Other Materials About Both Computer Hardware and Software Being Manufactured All Over the World at Such a Rapid Rate (I.A.C.R.P.B.M.O.M.A.B.C.H.S.B.M.A.O.W.S.R.R.), in their eternal search for brevity, has created a set of Universal Symbols for Computer Reviewers and Publishers of Books and Magazines and Other Materials About Both Computer Hardware and Software Being Manufactured All Over the World at Such a Rapid Rate (U.S.C.R.P.B.M.O.M.A.B.C.H.S.B.M.A.O.W.S.R.R.).

Computers speak a universal language, and it is only fair that those who must write about computers should have a library of Universal Symbols at their disposal.

Peter McWilliams

De Facto President

I.A.C.R.P.B.M.O.M.A.B.C.H.S.B.M.A.O.W.S.R.R.

Double-sided disk drive

 Computer will perform marriage ceremonies

 Computer plays synthesized dance music

 Suitable for a family

 Suitable for a rather strange family

 Suitable for a large family

 Suitable for a hungry family

Word processing capabilities

 Large file capacity

 Sold door to door by former encyclopedia salespersons

 Sophisticated

 Suitable for a couple

 Suitable for a rather strange couple

 Suitable for a couple who mess around

Suitable for a divorced couple

 Suitable for a male chauvinist

 Large memory

 Small memory

 Conforms to industry standards

 Does not conform to industry standards

 Apple

Pair (Two disk drives)

 Palm (Made in California)

 Peanut (Word processing program approved by Jimmy Carter)

 Lemon

 Turkey

 Fishy

 Multiplies fast

Stinks

 May drive you to drink

 For the birds

 Portable

 Semi-portable

 Normal size video screen

Small video screen

Large video screen

 Very large video screen

 Costs a lot of dough, boy

 If you need to ask, you can't afford it

 Build it yourself

 Not designed for human beings

 Electronic mail

Do whatever is necessary to get this computer

 Confusing

 Gives off a lot of heat

 Save your money

 Hot

 Not so hot

 Not hot at all

Video games available

 Realistic video games

 Trashy

 May put you to sleep

 May make you sick

 Has no idea what times the planes arrive

 Six out of seven people want this computer
but can't afford it.

Chapter 46

Learning to Use Your Personal Computer

Learning a computer *program* is what most people mean when they say they want to learn "how to use a computer." After turning the computer on, anything that you do, from copying a disk to writing a novel to running a business, involves programs (software). They can be simple programs that involve only one instruction (command), or more complex programs that baffle the uninitiated user with hundreds.

Generally speaking, the more commands a program offers, the more powerful and flexible the program is. A word processing program, for example, *requires* only six commands: a way to create a file, a way to insert text, a way to move the cursor around, a way to delete text, a way to save a file, and a way to print your file.

Most sophisticated word processors have a hundred or more commands. These extra commands add extra features, but also add to the amount of time it will take to learn the program.

If you plan to use your computer frequently for a given task—accounting, say—it pays to choose an accounting program with all the features you need, or might reasonably need in the near future, and then invest the time and attention necessary to learn it properly.

On the other hand, occasional and infrequent tasks performed on your computer might require a program that is not as "powerful," but is easier to learn and use. A simple mailing list program, for example, may be a better idea than a full-scale database management system.

First, here are my common-sense school-of-hard-knocks suggestions, and then I'll turn this chapter over to Christopher Meeks, who will give you the benefit-of-years-of-psychological-research approach.

1. Take your time. Learning a program takes time, so set the time aside.

2. Don't plan to do anything with the program until you have mastered it. The time to learn a few basic phrases in German is *before* you arrive in Berlin. Don't try to learn an accounts receivable program on Thursday if you need a computer-generated trial balance on Friday. All it will provide is frustration and anger at everything and everyone connected with computing.

If you can operate a mechanical swan, you can learn to operate a personal computer.

(You should see some of the letters I get from people in the throes of learning a complicated program under pressure. Tokyo Rose didn't get such hate mail.) Use replaceable, unnecessary information until the program is fully learned, *then* begin work on the company books or the great American novel or whatever you bought your computer for in the first place.

3. Read the manual from cover to cover. You would think the instructions for your program would be called the "instruction manual." No. Too simple. In Computerese it's known as **documentation.** ("Never use a simple word if a complex word will do." Rule #2.3a of *The Computerese Manual of Style.)*

Before even turning the computer on, read the documentation from cover to cover, quickly, without attempting to grasp anything. Don't stop to study intricate passages or make sense out of technical data; just read everything, lightly.

Some say this lets all the information seep into your subconscious mind so that at least *some* part of your being has access to all the facts. Others say that a quick reading ("skimming," they call it in academia) gives an overview of the material to be learned. I say it lets you know what you're up against. (See next point.)

4. Don't expect manuals to be clear, simple, easy to understand, or to contain all information necessary to learn the program. The personal computer industry is still in its infancy. In any industry less than twenty years old, there are bound to be some weak links. The weakest link in the world of personal computers is documentation.

Where else can you spend $500 to $1,000 on a program, and find the manual so incomprehensible that you have to spend from $15 to $50 more on a book that will tell you how to use the program? In computerdom, it happens all the time. (And, if you bought the program from Microsoft, the publisher you may be buying the explanatory book from is none other than—ta-da—Microsoft Press.)

Manuals are frequently written by the same people who write the programs. These dear souls, while they can communicate with computers eloquently, have not yet learned the joys of "interfacing" with their fellow human beings using the written word.

Extracting information from some of these dense packs of prose can be difficult at best. The only way to survive some of the passages with your humor intact is to pretend you're playing a computer game.

The game is one of the many variants of *Raiders of the Lost Ark*. You have discovered a box containing some more Dead Sea Scrolls, known as the Not-So-Well Sea Scrolls. A passage has been translated into a form of English. Your task: Figure out what some doomed Egyptian *really meant* by this collection of words.

You have a Rosetta Stone (your computer). You try it this way and that way and another way until, lo, one command suddenly works. You make a notation as to what was really meant, reward yourself with a date, and move on to the next passage.

At certain points, the information will simply not be there. You may need to visit the Scholars (the dealer who sold you the program) or contact the Oracle (manufacturer of the program) directly.

CAN YOU FIGURE OUT WHAT'S GOING ON IN THIS PICTURE? If you can, you'll probably have no trouble figuring out computers from available documentation.

5. Find a friend or colleague who uses the program. The phrase, "A colleague in need is a colleague indeed," could be coined for just this situation.

6. Look for other information. Several popular programs have books written on how to use them. You might want to have a look at these. But remember: Just because they're books doesn't mean they're going to be any clearer or more informative than the documentation.

Computer magazines will often have articles written by users about the pitfalls of learning specific programs. A library with a first-rate periodical section should be able to help.

7. Join a user group. There is no doubt *some kind* of user group in your area. Even though the group may be formed around a specific *machine,* and even if you don't have that machine, you may find someone there who uses the *program* you're trying to learn. Most programs operate almost the same from machine to machine. Some computer stores have bulletin boards. A notice posted there might prove valuable.

8. Make notes. After deciphering the documentation, rewrite difficult passages in your own words. Also, get some highlighting pens, and mark in different colors the sections you think you'll use frequently, often, sometimes, seldom, and never.

9. Don't be afraid to experiment. You can't hurt the computer (unless you throw it out a window in frustration), and the worst you can do to a program is erase it. (At which point you return to your back-up disk—you *did* make a back-up disk, didn't you?) If you wonder as you go along, "What would happen if I did this?", do it and find out. You may discover a use for the program even the programmer didn't consider.

10. Congratulate yourself. Learning a powerful computer program is no easy task. Pat yourself on the back—frequently.

11. Have fun. If you've removed the time and task pressures, learning a program, like exploring any new territory, is an adventure—and adventures, so I'm told, can be fun.

My associate, Christopher Meeks, whom I've worked with for many years, wrote and published an article on learning new software. He said it well, so I give him to you:

Learning New Software

By Christopher Meeks

The camera closes in on a diapered baby roosting on a living room floor. If you know anything about babies, they don't roost anywhere for long.

In moments, the baby zips off on all fours, attacking everything with a gusto of curiosity, from bookshelves to balloons and the family dog.

"This is a film about you," says the narrator. "For you as a baby, and later as a child, had the most marvelous characteristics. Everything in your world was enormously interesting. Everything was worth exploring." The baby tries to stand, and takes a few steps toward a book. "If you wanted something, it was worth going after..." The baby falls down, is about to cry, then tries again. "Oh, sure, you fell down occasionally. But you got up." You persevered.

You, a five-minute movie distributed by the Cally Curtis Company in Los Angeles, could well apply to learning software. In setting off with a new program, you will do wrong things, you will fall, but you also will learn and feel wonderful about it.

Over the years, I've learned dozens of programs, and looked at many, many more as a computer book editor. I've become curious; how does one "learn" a program? Are there shortcuts? Why do some people absorb a program quickly, and others struggle on as if programs were boulders for Sisyphus? And—a question I'll answer here—how does one efficiently and logically learn to use new software?

First, let's take a look at how learning takes place. The basics of learning come down to memory.

Modern psychology divides memory into three types, each with its own peculiarities and powers. Sensory memory affects such things as the remembered scent of strawberries, the silken feel to a fabric, or the sight of a face. All software looks (and smells) much the same in its square, stiff disk jackets, so sensory memory plays little part in learning software.

Motor-skill memory is the remembered feel of doing something physical, such as riding a bicycle. Or typing. This type of memory is an adjunct to learning software. The more you know how to type, the better.

Verbal memory directly concerns software. Verbal memory includes everything a person has thought, heard or read: concepts, ideas, words.

Verbal memory itself can be divided into two types: short-term and long-term. Short-term memory is the type used in remembering a phone number for as long as it takes to dial it. After that, the phone number is thrown out like a filter full of coffee grounds. To use software, you'll want to have the information in long-term memory.

The first step to efficient learning is to overcome your fear of learning, and your fear of what you're learning about.

How you *think* of the computer is a major factor in learning software. Many people fear the machine. And for good reason. For years, computers have brought us bills with mistakes. The mistakes went on and on because "the computer did it." We've secretly known all along there's a computer out there, not as friendly as Santa Claus, who knows not only when we're bad or good, but also when we move, when we get new phone numbers, and when we make dental appointments.

Personal computers, however, are different. *You* control them, much as *The Outer Limits* controlled your TV set. *(You* control the horizontal, *you* control the vertical...)

I remember the exact moment I "manipulated my first text" (as I overheard someone once say). When I bought my first computer, I naively believed I'd plug it in and type away as on a typewriter. I was wrong. I had to learn "commands." After learning a few basic commands, I typed several test sentences; soon I was afraid I'd erase something, or hit the wrong button and see a cloud of smoke shoot up from the back. I pushed ahead. After typing a few paragraphs, the text left the screen and I wasn't sure I'd get it back. But I "scrolled" some pages back and forth, and—Eureka!—everything was there.

Remember: you needn't fear what you can control.

Some of the tricks to learning and remembering for the long term are:

• **Use mnemonic tricks.** Even the great memory experts who perform onstage say they remember trivial and nonsense lists by associating unrelated items to related images. Ever wonder how a waitress can remember all those drinks? (You order a strawberry daiquiri—the waitress sees you're wearing red like a strawberry. Your friend orders a gin gimlet. Your friend is wearing a cotton shirt, and the waitress thinks of cotton gins.)

To illustrate, my first word processing program had a number of oddly keyed commands. Control-X-S (meaning you hit the keys "X" and "S" while holding down the control key) recorded on the disk all that you had written. I thought of that as taking the "excess" (X-S) from the screen and putting it to disk. Another, perhaps more simple, way is to think of the command as "Control-X-Save."

528

Control-Z scrolled one page back. Woody Allen's movie, *Zelig,* took place *back* in the century, so the command could be remembered as "Control-Zelig." Control-V scrolled one page forward. In screen geography, "forward" is down. The letter V points down. Get the idea?

Today's software often has a better selection of keys with mnemonics in mind.

• **Don't bring in static.** An impediment to memorization comes from mental interference or "static." That is, if you're trying to learn a tax program at the same time you are learning a spreadsheeting program, one set of commands tends to get mixed up with the other. It's best to learn similar programs one at a time. Also, if you're pressured to learn the tax program two days before taxes are due, the thoughts of the deadline block your ability to remember.

• **Learn in chunks, and take time between chunks.** People, funny as we are, learn things better in small units, chunks. Too much at once clouds all that came before. Start off with what you can grasp, and then stop, even if just for coffee, before proceeding. A day between chunks can be quite effective. If you don't believe me, ask some bugs. A test with cockroaches proved this. Roaches were placed in an electrified laboratory tray and conditioned with electric shocks not to wander into one corner. Then half the roaches were placed into roach heaven (a dark, damp, cool place) and the others were placed in roach hell (a bright, dry, hot area). After a day, both groups were placed back into the tray. Those who had been to heaven stayed away from the corner; they had retained their lesson. The other group was so confused (or masochistic), they forgot their previous learning and skittered about aimlessly and received shocks.

• **Use self-recitation and quick review.** This means after you learn a chunk, test yourself. If you can't answer one of your questions, go back and find the answer. When starting a new section, briefly review what you've just learned.

• **Scan the whole before learning the specifics.** I've found that if I see the software in action, even if I don't know what's going on, when it comes time to learn it, there are echoes of familiarity. If I can't see the software in action, I might glimpse through the manual to see what's coming.

Another good way to learn is to simply PLAY with the software. If it's menu-driven, try out different options. If the menu says "O – Copy", hit the letter "O" and see what happens. It still may make no sense to you, but later, as you learn the program step by step, some of these experiments will suddenly be familiar and make sense.

The above lessons are designed for learning on your own. No rule, however, says that you must learn in a locked room all by yourself. Often, the manuals are so poorly written, that you *must* get outside help. Here are a few suggestions:

1. Some software companies offer help lines, often toll-free numbers.

2. Perhaps you have a friend who knows the software. Friends like to help out others who have made a similar decision—it's like going to the same church or owning the same car. A corollary to this suggestion is:

2.a. Find and fall in love with a person who has the same kind of software. It's amazing how much you'll learn in no time.

3. Call the store where you bought the software. Chances are the salespeople don't know it any better than you. They're too busy selling the stuff to know how it works. Occasionally, though, you get a salesperson whose specialty happens to be your piece of software.

4. Computer user groups, consultants, and classes in local colleges and computer stores all offer a wealth of easy-to-digest knowledge.

5. A new breed of tutorial software now exists. Computer stores offer programs that work hand-in-hand with the software you are trying to learn. They take you through at your own pace, a tutor without hourly charges and one who never gets frustrated. Some major software programs also come with separate tutorial programs included.

6. Other companies offer audio cassettes with friendly voices. The voices lead and instruct.

7. And, of course, books. Many books. Computer books tie with the number of songs about losing one's honey (maybe the bees took her). If you own a popular program, odds are there's a book that covers it. Most such books are much better than the manuals they replace.

Whatever approach you take to learning, make notes. Notes are great for reinforcing a concept, and allow you to translate the idea into terms that you clearly understand.

And take your time. The machine's best virtue is its patience. Unlike your fifth-grade teacher, it doesn't care how long you take, or how many mistakes you make, in learning a program.

We were all once babies, *tabula rasas*, thirsty for the world. You still have a tremendously abundant capacity to learn. It's you.

PART VIII

Utter Nonsense: The McWilliams II Word Processor Instruction Manual.

INCLUDING:

- McWilliams II Schematic
- Complete Operating Instructions
- Other Uses for The McWilliams II
- History of The McWilliams II
- The McWilliams II in History
- A Tribute to Joan Crawford
- PLUS: An Elusive Interview
  with Peter A McWilliams

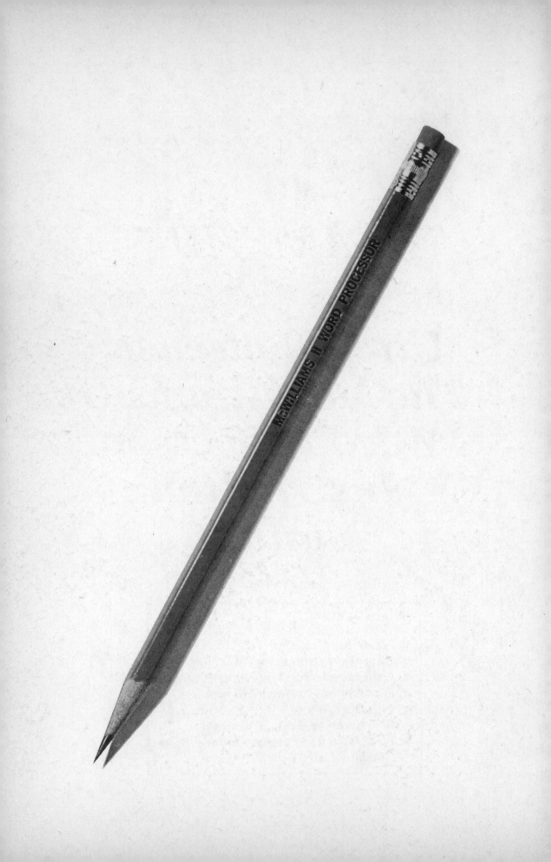

The McWilliams II
Word Processor

Features:

- Portable.
- Prints characters from every known language.
- Graphics are fully supported.
- Gives off no appreciable degree of radiation.
- Uses no energy.
- Memory is not lost during a power failure.
- Infinitely variable margins.
- Type sizes from 1 to 945,257,256,256 points.
- Easy to learn.
- User friendly.
- Not likely to be stolen.
- No moving parts.
- Silent operation.
- Occasional maintenance keeps it in top condition.
- Five-year unconditional warranty.

The McWilliams Computer Corporation

"Combining yesterday's technology
with today's terminology
to make tomorrow's money."

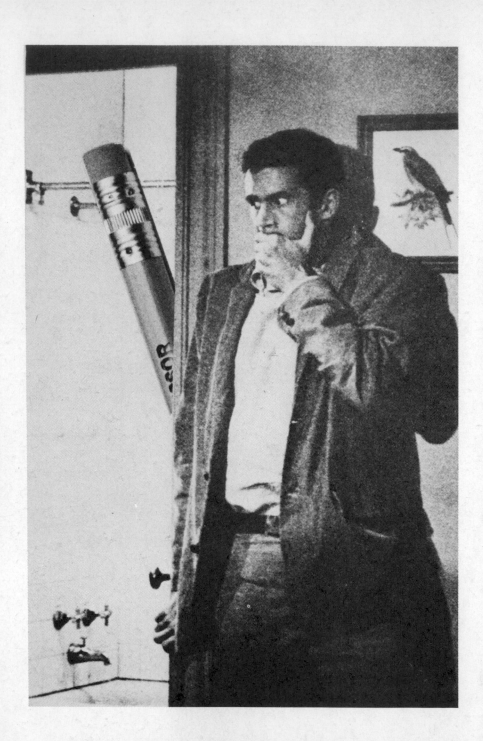

McWilliams II Schematic

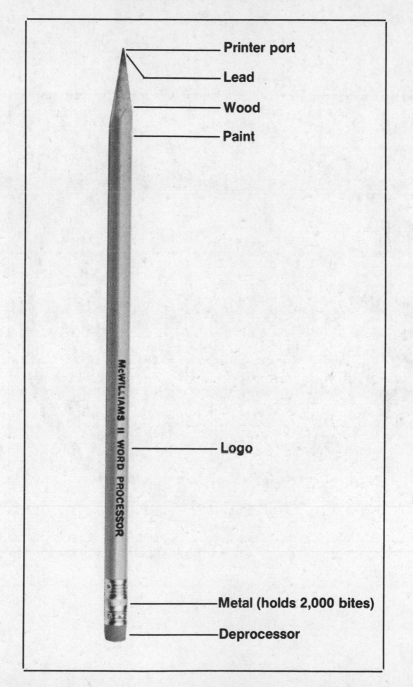

Printer port

Lead

Wood

Paint

Logo

Metal (holds 2,000 bites)

Deprocessor

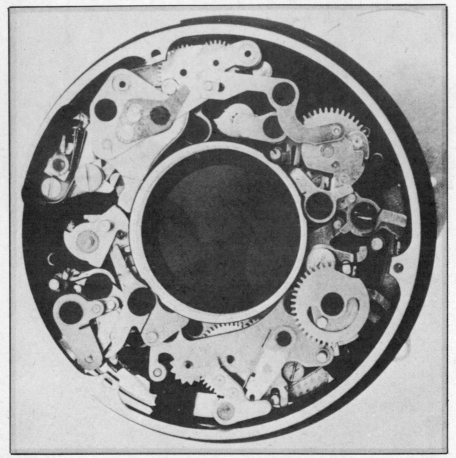

This enlarged cross-section shows how remarkably intricate the McWilliams II really is.

Operating Instructions

Creating a file: Place a **sheet** of **paper** under **point** of the McWilliams II. Create.

Saving a file: Put the piece of paper in a **safe place.**

Deleting a file: Crumple the piece of paper and **toss** in **waste basket.**

Deleting text: Place **eraser** ("deprocessor") side of the McWilliams II over the portion of the file to be deleted. Rub and rub. Portions of text under the eraser will magically disappear.
Brush away magic dust.

Inserting text: Make a **little mark** (ˇ) under the line and between the letters you wish to insert text. Insert text above the line. Use extra **paper** if necessary.

Transferring documents created with the McWilliams II to magnetic media.

Preparing the
McWilliams II for Action

The **point** of the McWilliams II Word Processor is protected during shipping by a sturdy wooden covering. Before you can use the McWilliams II, you must carefully remove this covering.

The George Washington Carver Memorial Sharpener. This precision instrument was named in honor of one of America's greatest botanists, who did remarkable things to peanuts or soybeans or something. Can also be used for chopping vegetables. $25.

The Christopher Columbus Whole World in His Hands Memorial Sharpener. This sharpener honors one of Italy's greatest Americans who, in 1492, sailed the ocean blue to prove that the earth was not flat. He did, and you never need settle for a flat point on your McWilliams II again. $100.

540

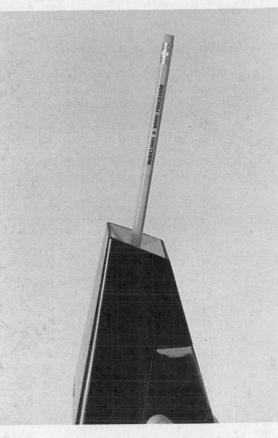

Sharpen your pencils with Pyramid Power!

We've all heard about razor blades being resharpened after a few hours under a pyramid.* Well, now you can use Pyramid Power to sharpen your McWilliams II. Simply insert your McWilliams II, and the Spirits of Ancient Egypt drop by and sharpen your McWilliams II for you. (Motor included in case spirits are out to lunch.)

*See *National Enquirer*, December 17, 1963

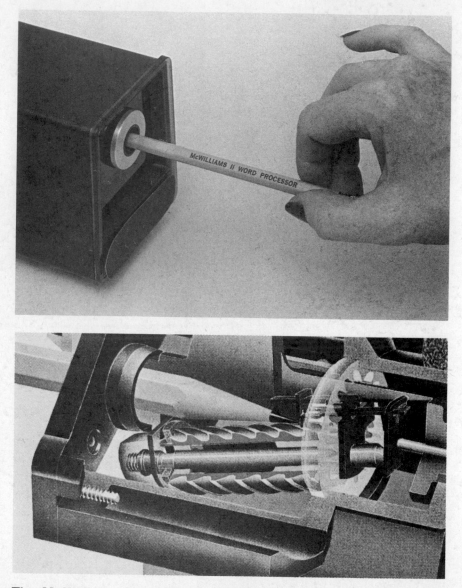

The McWilliams Pro. The ultimate. Electrical energy runs a motor containing ball bearings for the very best point available in word processing today. Fast, precise, exacting. Expensive, but worth it. $500.

Preparing the McWilliams II for Action

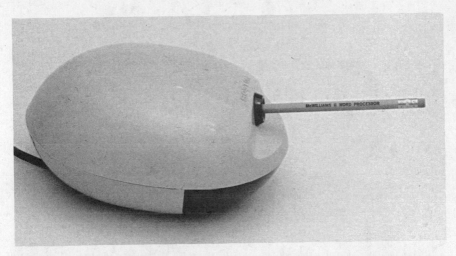

The Museum of Modern Art McWilliams II Word Processor Sharpener.
Stylish. Elegant. Lets the world know you have taste with a capital T.
$650.

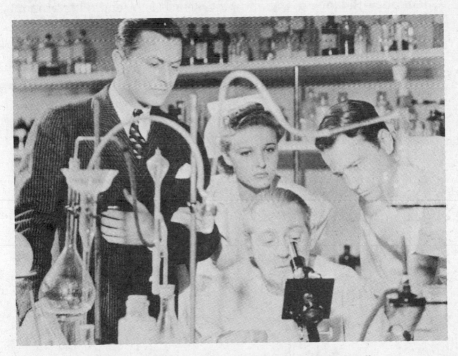

"Yes, I think it's time to resharpen this one."

Applications

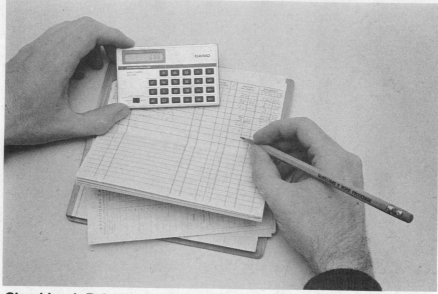

Checkbook Balancing: Use the McWilliams II to record the amount and payee of each check you write, as well as deposits. Add the deposits and subtract the amount of checks written, and in this way the McWilliams II will always keep your checkbook balanced.

Law enforcement agencies use McWilliams IIs.

Electronic mail: Text created with the McWilliams II can be sent over ordinary telephone lines and instantly received in any portion of the world. Follow these simple instructions:

1. Lift receiver off telephone.
2. Dial number of receiving party.
3. Get receiving party on the other end of the line.
4. Read receiving party text written by the McWilliams II.

(Note: If receiving party has a McWilliams II, he or she can make a faithful facsimile of your transmission.)

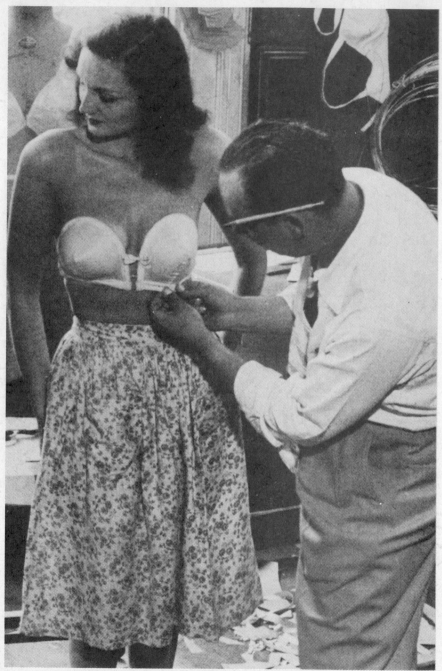

If you're afraid of getting caught at something, put a McWilliams II behind your ear—it will look like you're doing your job.

546

Applications

A McWilliams II could not be found
So the train dispatcher could not write down
The track on which the train should be
(He thought he could trust his memory!)
The dispatcher is now tempest-tossed:
For want of a McWilliams II, a train was lost.

547

The McWilliams II in the Kitchen

In the kitchen: The McWilliams II can be an invaluable kitchen helper. For example, if your recipe was designed to feed four people, but eight are coming to dinner, you will be glad you have the McWilliams II. Simply use your McWilliams II to *double* all amounts listed in your recipe. One cup becomes two cups, one teaspoon becomes two teaspoons, one egg becomes two eggs, and so on. (Helpful hint: Do *not* double cooking times.)

549

The McWilliams II in Education

The McWilliams II will improve your grades and give you a head start in life.

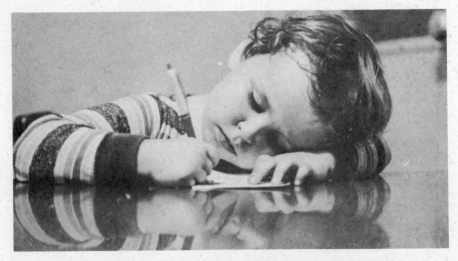

A child using a (ick) ball point pen tends to fall asleep.

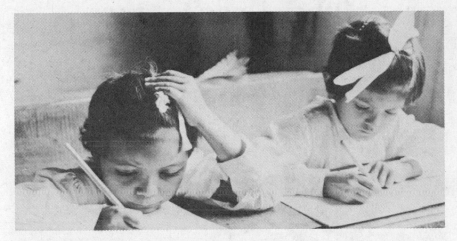

The McWilliams Computer Corporation is presenting (in every state we can get a tax write-off) a free McWilliams II to each and every school.

The McWilliams II makes learning fun!

Other Uses for the McWilliams II

553

It has come to our attention that some Polynesian tribesmen have been using McWilliams IIs to capture and have their way with visiting American film stars. While the McWilliams Computer Corporation does not encourage such use of McWilliams IIs, we appreciate all South Pacific sales, and send our best wishes to the prince or president or prime minister or whatever leader Polynesia has these days.

The Church of Divine Packaging—built entirely of McWilliams IIs. "Prayers are processed faster here than anywhere else on earth," says the pastor, Father McWilliams (no relation).

We have heard that street gangs in New York have been using McWilliams IIs to harass the students of Columbia University. The McWilliams Computer Corporation does not condone such action, but is appreciative of all sales. Thank you.

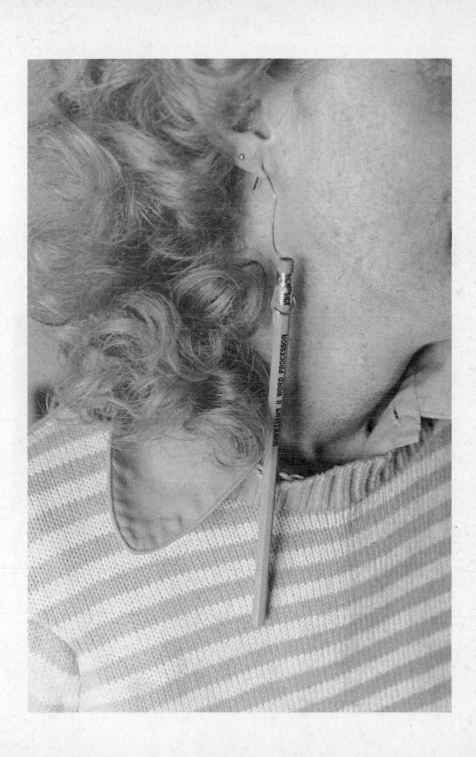

559

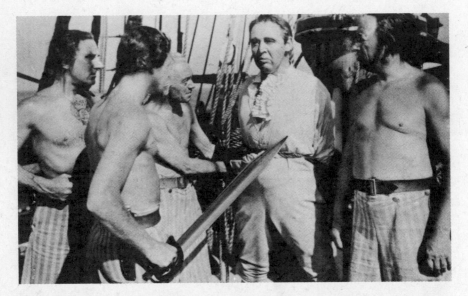

It has come to our attention that some British sailors have been using McWilliams IIs to harass, mutiny and otherwise intimidate sea captains. The McWilliams Computer Corporation frowns upon all acts of violence committed with McWilliams Computer Products, although we appreciate any and all patronage.

Other Uses for the McWilliams II

Other Uses for the McWilliams II

Peripherals

Combination McWilliams II holder and tissue dispenser. Two needs
met in a single product. Innovation is but commonplace at McWilliams
Computers.

$30   (holds 15 McWilliams IIs and 1000 sheets)
$60   (set of two)

The Perrier Jouet McWilliams II holder. $450.

McWilliams II Clip

Holds McWilliams II firmly to outside of notebook or inside of sweat-shirt. Genuine metal! $5 each $10 for 2 $60 per dozen

Global Delete Option: Delete an entire file in only seconds (2,468 seconds, to be exact) with this set of four Mega Deprocessors and three friends. $250. (Friends not included.)

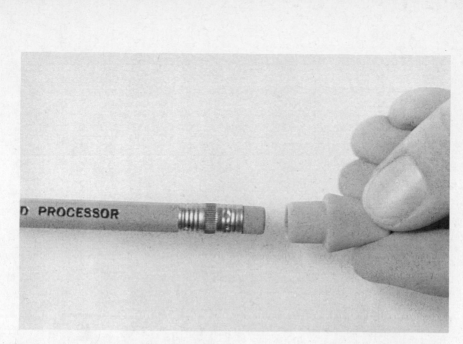

Extra Deprocessing Power is yours with the McWilliams II Mistake-O-Matic® Deprocessor Extender.

McWilliams II Mistake-O-Matic® Deprocessors come in this convenient pack of 144, for those who make gross mistakes.

McWILLIAMS TO-HELL-WITH-XEROX® COPY PAPER

The Xerox Corporation has tried to put the McWilliams Computer Corporation out of business by making word processors. Living up to our motto, "We take everything personally," the McWilliams Computer Corporation responds with a product that will put the copier divison of Xerox out of business.

McWilliams II Replacement Printer Ports. $15.

Peripherals

This book is printed on McWilliams Velvacoat Paper. This paper is scientifically designed to offer the correct roughness/ smoothness ratio for perfect word processing. Made from the wood leftover during McWilliams II production — and we pass that savings on to you!

10	sheets	$10
100	sheets	$100
500	sheets	$500
1000	sheets	$1000

On the rest of this page is a sample of McWilliams Velvacoat Paper. Try it!

Templates turn your McWilliams II into a sign shop! $10 per template.
(Permaplates available at additional cost.)

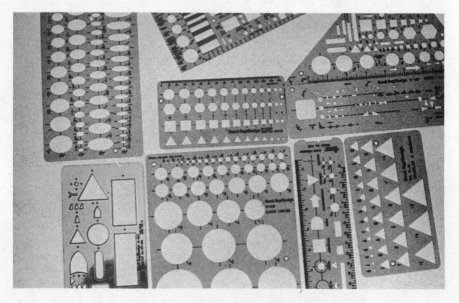

The McWilliams II Graphics Package. $350.

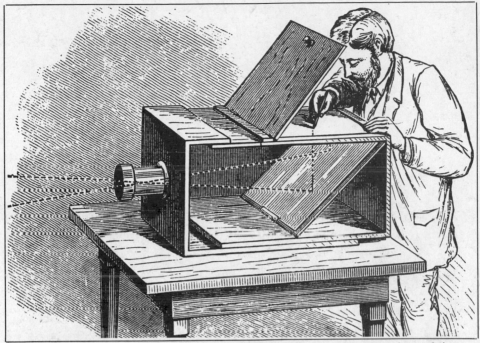

The McWilliams II Land Camera: Instant pictures at a fraction of the cost!

The McWilliams II Letter Quality Printer Attachment. $600.

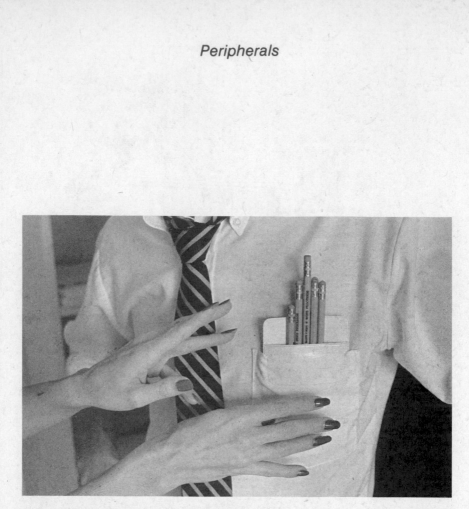

The McWilliams II Pocket Computer Case. Made of genuine vinyl, like the finest car tops. This Computer Case slips into your shirt pocket and provides room for more McWilliams IIs than most people can afford. It's not just impressive: it's ostentatious. $375.

The ultimate McWilliams II Computer Case. Holds not only McWilliams IIs, but also your credit cards and a pair of glasses. People walking around like this in the 1960s used to be called nerds. Now the nerds own computer companies and are all millionaires. Fashion follows money, and so do McWilliams II Computer Cases. $500.

The Western Look is in, and so is this hip-hugging Mr. Ed Memorial McWilliams II Word Processor Holster. A must for quick wits. And artists: when they say "draw," now you can! Specify left or right holster. $150.

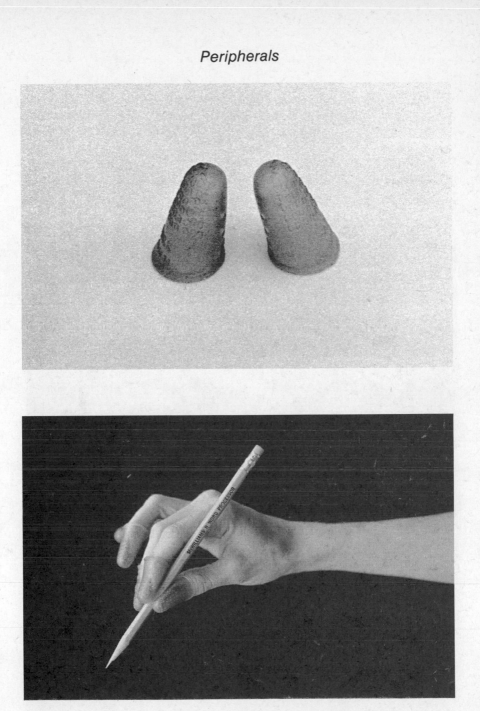

Blisters on your fingers from too much processing? The McWilliams II Prophylactic Finger Protectors put a safety cushion of rubber between your skin and the hard world. $10 each. $120 per dozen.

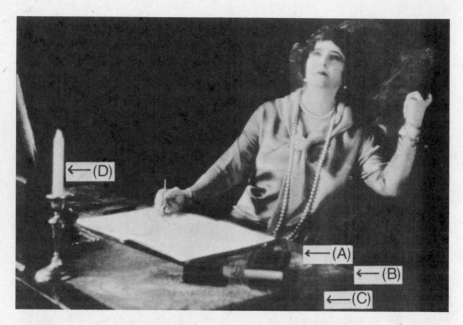

The McWilliams LifeCycle Sharpener

The ultimate in economy and ecology! The McWilliams II is sharpened in hole (A). Wood shavings drop into box (B) and are eaten by termites (C). Methane gas from termite droppings (not pictured, as this is an instruction manual for the whole family) rises and burns in lamp (D).

The more you write, the more you get light, and the more you get light, the more you write. In this way, the McWilliams LifeCycle Sharpener supports two natural cycles: that of composition, and that of decomposition. $375.

LifeCycle Peripherals:

Replacement termites. Genetically engineered for high methane production and lead poisoning resistance. $20 the pair.

McWilliams Matches. Made from the same fine wood as The McWilliams II. Use them to light your lamp or other LifeCycle Peripherals. Then drop them into box (B). An extra treat for your termites: They'll think you're giving them barbecue! $1 each. $12 a dozen. $24 for two dozen. $144 per gross.

Cooktops. Dinnertime? Might as well use the termite's dinner from yesterday to cook your dinner today. Simply plug in the McWilliams LifeCycle Cooktop and *bon apetite!* One burner: $75.
Two-burner: $150. Four-burner: $300. Oven: $250. Crockpot: $175.

Room heaters. Room cold? No problem! The termites have what it takes to keep you warm. 600 BTU: $100. 1,200 BTU: $200.

Termite Home & Family Manual. Are your termites not reproducing fast enough to keep up with your methane needs? Maybe they don't know how. This is a reprinting of the 1948 classic that caused the baby boom in this country. Satisfaction (to whatever degree that term applies to termites) guaranteed. $30.

All termites are carefully tested for sufficient methane production.

Celebrity
Endorsements

McWilliams Computer Corporation's International Goodwill Ambassador, Richard M. Nixon, spreads the good word about McWilliams IIs throughout the world.

"I *believe* in the McWilliams II."

Our Goodwill Ambassador makes his point.

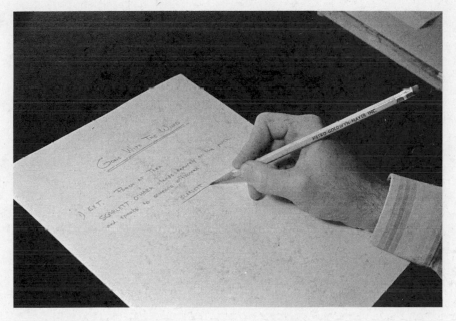

The fabled Metro Goldwyn Mayer Word Processor. (Photo courtesy of McWilliams Computer Museum and Gift Shop, Orlando, Florida.)

Celebrity Endorsements

"Is that a McWilliams II in your pocket, or are you just glad to see me?"

How many more plays could Shakespeare have written if he had used a McWilliams II? Considering that he had to dip his quill every ten words, and each dip took seven seconds, we calculate that over the span of his creative life, he would have written 3 more plays, 12 more sonnets, and had one more child—a great boon to literature and to all mankind.

How many less songs will Barry Manilow write if he uses a McWilliams II instead of a computer? Since each song takes an average of 12 minutes and 14 seconds to write, and since computers roughly double writing speed, if forced to use a McWilliams II, Barry Manilow would write 2,476 less songs this year alone—a great boon to literature and to all mankind.

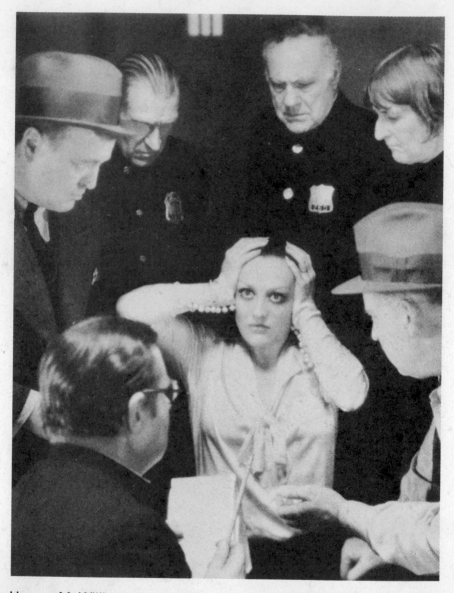

Here a McWilliams II co-stars with Joan Crawford. They were both much younger then.

Crawford, bored with her typewriter, longs for a McWilliams II.

Here Miss Crawford has the McWilliams II in a passionate embrace. (The Hayes office cut one of their more intimate love scenes.)

"Care to dance?" Zachary Scott asks. "No thanks," says Joan, "I've got my McWilliams II to keep me happy."

In "Whatever Happened to McWilliams II?" Bette Davis cooks Miss Crawford's McWilliams II and serves it to her for dinner.

The Dangers of Electronic Computers

This tragedy was caused by a word processor that uses *electricity*. When selecting a word processor, keep safety first. Remember: "No wiring—no worrying."

Little boy, badly burned when the electronic computer he was using exploded, returns to safety and to basics: A McWilliams II.

One of the problems of using an electrical computer: People get their work done too fast and then "hang out," troubling other workers.

Selling it

What company would be complete without a Warranty, a Commitment to Quality, an ad that justifies overcharging just because we happen to have a brand name? Well, here are ours...

Warranty

Every McWilliams II comes with an unconditional five-year guarantee. If anything goes wrong with your McWilliams II, simply return it to us (along with $5 for postage and handling), and we'll be happy to repair it or send you a new one *absolutely free*.

Our Uncompromising Commitment to Quality:

"No cost is too great, no sacrifice too dear, no effort too tremendous, to provide the best word processor we can sell at a competitive price while still maintaining a comfortable profit margin."

THE PRICELESS INGREDIENT

In the city of Bagdad lived Hakeem, the Wise One, and many people went to him for counsel, which he gave freely to all, asking nothing in return.

There came to him a young man, who had spent much but got little, and said: "Tell me, Wise One, what shall I do to receive the most for that which I spend?"

Hakeem answered, "A thing that is bought or sold has no value unless it contain that which cannot be bought or sold. Look for the Priceless Ingredient."

"But, what is this Priceless Ingredient?" asked the young man.

Spoke then the Wise One, "My son, the Priceless Ingredient of every product in the marketplace is the Honor and Integrity of him who makes it. Consider his name before you buy."

The McWilliams II

615

Tennessee McWilliams, chairman of McWilliams Computer Corporation, presents the first of 500 McWilliams IIs ordered by the armed forces. "We're looking for a few good word processors," the Marines wrote. "The McWilliams II: the Brave, the Strong, the Few," wrote back Tennessee.

"AND HE LEFT HER WITHOUT A McWILLIAMS II."

Of course, he didn't *leave* her. He *went*—before the day arrived on which he had planned to buy a McWilliams II. He thought the calendar might wait—he never really *intended* to leave her without a McWilliams II. He simply was so full of living that he couldn't believe he might *stop* living—before he could buy a McWilliams II.

And so, over the teacups, friends, neighbors and acquaintances think of him, discuss him. And, always, there's the same ending: "And he left her without a McWilliams II..."

Don't put off until tomorrow the McWilliams II you should buy today. Send for your free copy of the booklet, "Seven Keys to Contentment with Your McWilliams II," that makes it extremely easy for you to check your McWilliams II needs. It will help you plan ahead.

617

A singing commercial.

"I love my McWilliams II,
A quill and an ink well won't do.
I'm longing to write you a letter
But I require tools that are better."

Old style McWilliams II commercials ("glamor and glitter").

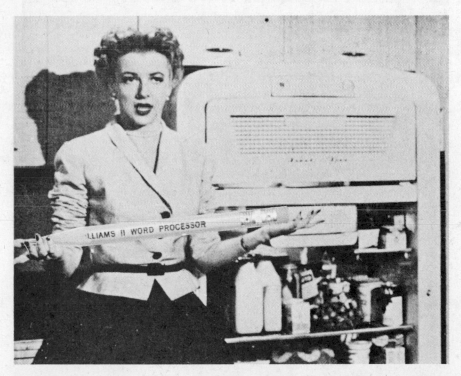

New style McWilliams II commercials feature Betty Furness ("facts and more facts").

"Dora, these pictures are fantastic. No one can do what you do to a McWilliams II."

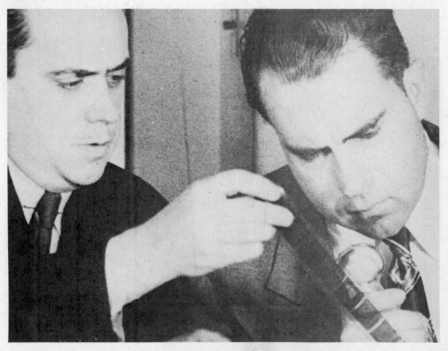

Our Ambassador examines Dora's technique.

Several frames from a film by Dora,
Mistress of Subliminal Advertising.

We hired three famous designers to create a monogram for The McWilliams Computer Corporation (McCC). Which do you think best captures the spirit of the McWilliams II?

Manufacturing the McWilliams II

Waiting for the precise moment to harvest
a branch for a McWilliams II.

As soon as the trees are cut, they are thrown in water. This (A) cleans the logs (forests can be very dirty) and (B) begins the shrinking process.

Wood for the McWilliams II is aged from two weeks to twelve years. "We will sell no pine before its time."

Here the pinkish stuff that makes up the deprocessor end of the McWilliams II is mined.

Pink-stuff miners take a rest.

The "secret sauce"—which forms (when cooled) the deprocessor end of the McWilliams II—bubbles under strict supervision.

Here corn is sorted into...corn? What the hell does corn have to do with word processing? How did this picture get in here?

Mining lead.

Holes are drilled in the wood, making way for...

...the lead which is poured into each McWilliams II.

Juan Valdez comes down from the mountains where he has been mining yellow lacquer (only the finest Columbian lacquer is used on McWilliams IIs). Father McWilliams chats with Juan, blesses the lacquer, and wishes him a safe journey to Silicone Valley.

Here the RAM (Reasonably Amiable Metal) is placed near the deprocessor. It is designed to hold the maximum number of bites without destroying the teeth.

One of the many sub-assembly lines at McCC.

When confronted with the charge that he hires young people to avoid paying minimum wage, McWilliams responds: "Nonsense! I give them a chance—a start in life. If you're fourteen and need a job, you either work for McWilliams or you work for McDonalds—and here you don't have to live a lie. McDonald's says, 'We do it all for you.' At McWilliams at least we are honest: 'We do it all for money.' "

Peter McWilliams shows a new worker "how it's done."

McWilliams Computer Corporation employees enjoy a standard of living never thought possible in America.

These two McCC employees had a choice: buy a table or buy a checkerboard. With the jaunty streak of fun that permeates the entire corporation, they chose the checkerboard.

McWilliams ponders his empire: "If I had it all to do over again, I'd do it—unless I came up with a way that was less work."

An Interview with
Peter A McWilliams

How did you come up with the idea for The McWilliams II?

It happened long, long ago. I was given a typewriter when I was quite young, about seven, and I remember thinking even then: There's got to be a simpler way to process words. But the world didn't seem to go along with my thinking. Word processing machines got more and more complicated: first electric typewriters, then Dictaphones, and finally computers. It got more complex rather than simple.

So you kept your dream alive for many years.

You could say that. It would be more accurate to say I kept my dream alive *despite adversity* for many years.

So you kept your dream alive despite adversity for many years.

Yes.

When did you start work on The McWilliams II?

Well, before the McWilliams II Word Processor there was The McWilliams Word Processor. I started work on that in the fall of 1965.

What were your major obstacles?

Size. I couldn't get it small enough. The prototype McWilliams Word Processor was about twelve feet long and weighed almost fifty pounds. It worked fine, but wasn't practical, unless you only wanted to write billboards. (*Laughs.*)

How did you solve that problem?

Well, I bought a tie-dyed T-shirt, which was very popular then, and washed it in hot water, and it shrunk. At first I was mad, but great inventors must learn how to turn adversity into advantage, so I thought, "Maybe if I washed The Word Processor in hot water it would shrink."

Did it?

We couldn't find a washing machine large enough. (*Laughs hard.*) No, seriously, we sprayed hot water on the Word Processor, and, sure enough, it shrunk. We kept spraying it and letting it dry, and finally got it down to six feet seven inches.

Then what happened?

It stopped shrinking. But I was more than half way to my goal and I wasn't about to give up. I tried everything. Dristan. Preparation H. We even brought in a head shrinker.

From Africa?

No, from the American Psychiatric Association. (*Laughs hysterically.*) Had you going there, didn't I?

Peter McWilliams, watering the first McWilliams Word Processor, in hopes that it would shrink.

Yes. So what finally worked?

I made a radical discovery: Microchips.

You invented microchips?

Yes.

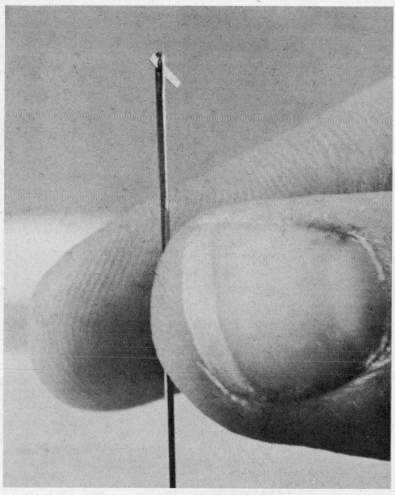

A microchip (birch).

I thought the silicon microchip was invented by...

Who said anything about silicon? I invented *wooden* microchips—small chips of wood, so small you have to use a microscope to see them. You see, I figured that the main part of the processor is made of wood, and wood is made of chips, so if you make the chips smaller, the wood will be smaller and therefore the processor will be smaller.

You discovered that?

Brilliant, huh? I hear the Nobel Committee has been planning to make me a Laureate for years, but they can't decide whether to give me the prize for physics or logic.

The word processor Peter McWilliams was using when he decided to invent the McWilliams II.

They don't give a Nobel Prize for logic.

They don't? Well, that doesn't make any sense. (*Laughs uncontrollably.*) Get it? "Logic—makes sense." Get it?

Yes.

I saw you coming on that one.

How will history remember you?

As a simple, hard-working industrialist who made a fortune in low technology.

What do you think about the Paper Mate ads, in which they call their pens "Pocket Word Processors"?

Absolute rip off!!! As Oscar Wilde said, "Imitation is the sincerest form of plagiarism." They stole my idea, they just stole it. They even stole my initials.

But didn't you get the idea of using a pencil as a word processor from the April, 1982 issue of BYTE magazine?

What? You've done too much research. Who the hell do you think you are, Geraldo Rivera? There's nothing worse than a reporter who's done too much research.

But is it true?

Quit interrupting me while I'm evading the question! Reporters shouldn't do too much research. It isn't polite.

My records indicate that Professor Philip Schrodt of Northwestern University first discovered the connection between pencils and word processing and published his findings in the 1982 April Fools edition of BYTE.

Don't use the word "pencil." We don't use the word pencil around here.

The
PENALTY OF
LEADERSHIP

IN every field of human endeavor, he that is first must perpetually live in the white light of publicity. ¶Whether the leadership be vested in a man or in a manufactured product, emulation and envy are ever at work. ¶In art, in literature, in music, in industry, the reward and the punishment are always the same. ¶The reward is widespread recognition; the punishment, fierce denial and detraction. ¶When a man's work becomes a standard for the whole world, it also becomes a target for the shafts of the envious few. ¶If his work be merely mediocre, he will be left severely alone—if he achieve a masterpiece, it will set a million tongues a-wagging. ¶Jealousy does not protrude its forked tongue at the artist who produces a commonplace painting. ¶Whatsoever you write, or paint, or play, or sing, or build, no one will strive to surpass, or to slander you, unless your work be stamped with the seal of genius. ¶Long, long after a great work or a good work has been done, those who are disappointed or envious continue to cry out that it can not be done. ¶Spiteful little voices in the domain of art were raised against our own Whistler as a mountebank, long after the big world had acclaimed him its greatest artistic genius. ¶Multitudes flocked to Bayreuth to worship at the musical shrine of Wagner, while the little group of those whom he had dethroned and displaced argued angrily that he was no musician at all. ¶The little world continued to protest that Fulton could never build a steamboat, while the big world flocked to the river banks to see his boat steam by. ¶The leader is assailed because he is a leader, and the effort to equal him is merely added proof of that leadership. ¶Failing to equal or to excel, the follower seeks to depreciate and to destroy—but only confirms once more the superiority of that which he strives to supplant. ¶There is nothing new in this. ¶It is as old as the world and as old as the human passions—envy, fear, greed, ambition, and the desire to surpass. ¶And it all avails nothing. ¶If the leader truly leads, he remains—the leader. ¶Master-poet, master-painter, master-workman, each in his turn is assailed, and each holds his laurels through the ages. ¶That which is good or great makes itself known, no matter how loud the clamor of denial. ¶That which deserves to live—lives.

A plaque on the wall of Peter McWilliams' office.

And I have reliable testimony that you first thought of calling a pencil a word processor *after* reading Professor Schrodt's article.

Who put you up to this? IBM? You were hired by my company to come in here and do a nice interview with me so that we could put the interview in my book, just like *Playboy*, and instead you come in here asking embarrassing questions.

I was hired to do an in-depth interview.

In depth, sure. In depth is fine. I love my mother. Why don't you go into that in depth? I'm very kind to my brother. Why don't you in depth about that?

But is the information true?

What does truth have to do with it? You come in here, with your tape recorder and your note pad, and you're not even using a McWilliams II, you're using a goddamn Ticonderoga, and you have the nerve to ask me about *truth*.

That's my job.

Your job is over. Get out of here. And don't think you'll get paid for this, either.

I've already been paid.

By cash or by check?

By check.

Did you deposit it?

Yes.

How long ago?

The History of the McWilliams II

TRADE   MARK   McWILLIAMS

Elder McWilliams counsels Young Peter: "Make cheap, sell high."

Close Encounters of the II Kind: Peter McWilliams finally sees the vision he shaped in his mashed potatoes for weeks on end.

A muse offers Peter McWilliams the secret of the McWilliams II.

The invention of microchips as it really happened.

The invention of microchips, Hollywood-style (from the film, "The Peter McWilliams Story").

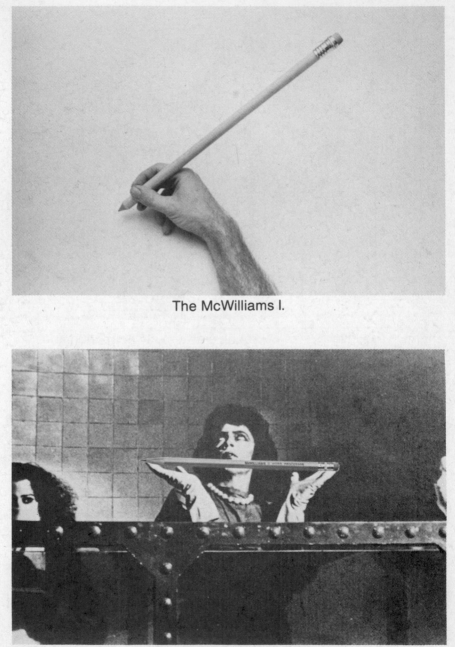

The McWilliams I.

The first McWilliams II.

McWilliams plays a game of chess with his former partner to decide the ownership of McCC. McWilliams lost, and had to keep the company.

The scientists at McWilliams Laboratories work hard, day and night (except religious holidays), bringing new meaning to the terms "state of the art" and "net profit after taxes."

Charles Foster McWilliams addresses the annual McCC stock holders meeting.

Experiments in genetic engineering on a Nevada atomic test site.

McCC, Cairo.

The McWilliams Building.

Life, Liberty and the Pursuit of Profits — New Products from the McWilliams Computer Corporation

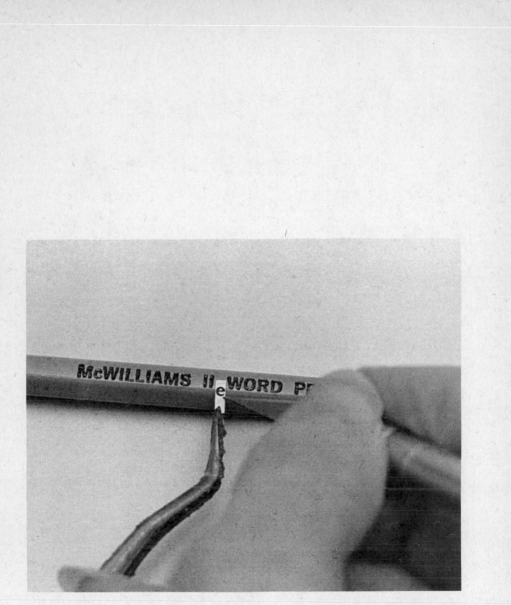

The McWilliams IIe. What does the "e" stand for? Enhanced? Expanded? Expensive? Extra profits? Extortion? Buy one and find out!

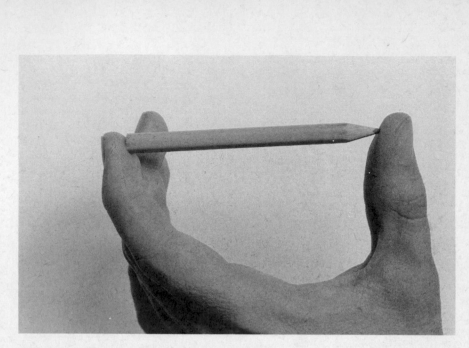

The McWilliams 100: Portability and affordability for those who travel and don't make many mistakes.

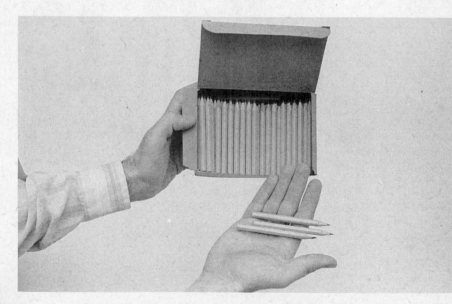

McWilliams 100s come in this handy 100 Pack.

The McWilliams 100 fits in your wallet and tells the world you're ready for business.

T.E. Lawrence (here with Zorba the Greek) said he never could have conquered Arabia without his portable McWilliams 100.

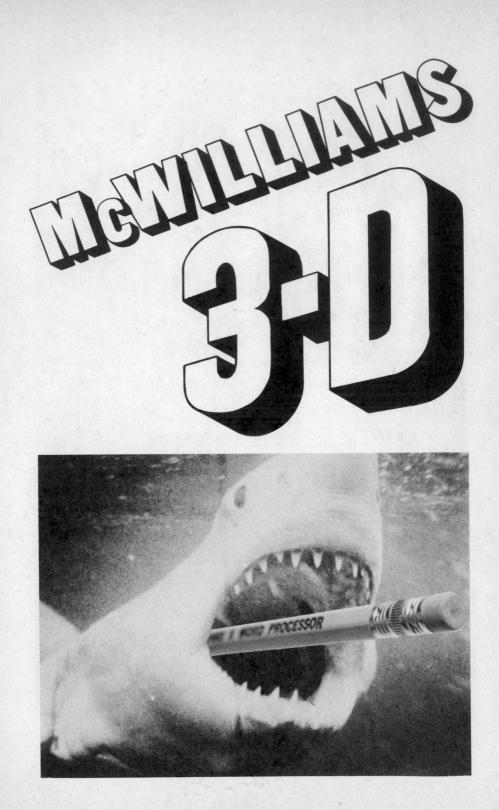

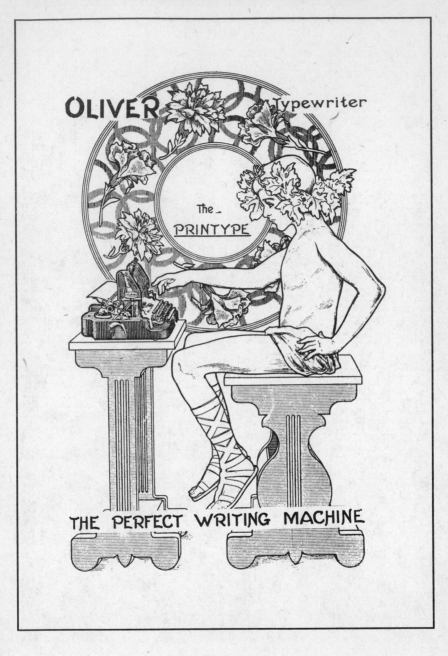

Index